CREATIVITY
IN THE
THEATER

A Psychoanalytic Study

PHILIP WEISSMAN

BASIC BOOKS, INC.
PUBLISHERS
New York / London

TO MY WIFE

Preface

I HAVE BEEN INVOLVED with this book, in one way or another, for the past ten years, during which time I have been in the midst of a full-time analytic practice and had the additional commitment of the writing of clinical papers. Thus, there have been a host of friends and colleagues over this period of time, all of whom cannot be enumerated, who have contributed ideas and criticisms that were helpful to me in this project. One of the early memories in my rather long life with this book goes back to the late Dr. Ernst Kris, who was encouraging and enthusiastic about my initial written work on creativity in the theater. The infancy of this book was also nurtured by Dr. Phyllis Greenacre, who served in the combined role of teacher and friend. Among my colleagues, I am grateful to Drs. Leopold Bellak, Gustav Bychowski, David Beres, Louis Linn, David Rubinfine, Joseph Krimsley, and Victor Rosen for their contributions toward this effort. I wish to thank Eric Bentley, Brooks Atkinson, and Arthur and Barbara Gelb for their generous responses to my needs for a nonpsychoanalytic sounding board for my ideas. I am grateful to both Elaine Cohen and Henrietta Gilden for their enthusiastic and efficient assistance in the task of the manuscript. Finally, to my wife goes my deepest gratitude for her constant encouragement, sympathetic understanding, and invaluable suggestions.

New York City PHILIP WEISSMAN
January 1965

Contents

CREATIVITY IN THE THEATER

Introduction:

A Psychoanalytic Approach
to Problems of Creativity
in the Theater

THE STUDY OF ARTISTIC CREATION and the subsequent investigation of creative imagination and of the creative personality have long been inherent constituents of psychoanalytic growth. Historically, psychoanalysis sought corroboration of its early hypotheses about normal and abnormal mental functioning in the various legacies of culture because sufficient clinical evidence was not yet available. It soon became evident that mythology and literature had a homogeneity of themes similar to the universal fantasies of mankind. This was particularly evident in works of drama.

Aided by the powerful analogy of the Oedipus drama, Freud's discovery of the Oedipus complex was immediately responded to by the entire world as a confrontation with a truth which had to be either vehemently rejected or fervently acclaimed. It is perhaps no accident that Freud turned to a drama such as Sophocles' to confirm his findings concerning the child's universal bipolar tie to his parents, which takes place at the height of infantile sexual development and crucially insinuates itself, by the type of resolution, into a form of normal or pathological adult sexuality. More so than the novel,

1

the drama, restricted in form to dialogue and in time to brevity within a few acts, must of necessity reveal the created character in a more condensed and direct unconscious communication. Like a dream, drama is a vehicle for the royal road, via literature, to man's unconscious.

After psychoanalysis established that historical legends and works of art bore the imprint of man's universal unconscious themes, it then proceeded to explore psychoanalytically the relationship between the artist's life and his work. These psychoanalytic inquiries into the nature of the artist often seem to have been the study of a composite artist, perhaps a more synthetic conception than a realistic or scientific one. Thus, such investigations of the creative artist and his work implied that the findings derived from the study of the life and work of a painter, for example, can be assumed to be similar to the creative life of the dramatist.

Practitioners of the literary arts are a far different lot than those of the musical and visual arts. There are also differences within each art form. Although the playwright, the poet, and the novelist create within the medium of language, each of these artists enlists different defenses and gratifies different psychic needs through his individual creative form.

The aim of this book is to present and clarify the multiple problems of creativity—specifically, in the theater. In the theater arts, there are playwrights, directors, and actors. In many ways, they are psychologically foreign to one another in spite of the common creative language of action. The actor has many psychological features in common with other performing artists such as the dancer and the musician; the director of a play is psychologically more in tune with an orchestral conductor than with a dramatist. The performing arts, such as dance, music, opera, and theater, require creators. There is in each a similar intrafamily psychological constellation. The dramatist and the composer are deified fathers for the directors and performers; their works are safeguarded and re-creatively presented by directors and conductors who parentally guide actors and musicians.

The dramatist, the director, and the actor part company in their search for gratification of their inner individual needs. The actor seeks an expressive outlet and temporary solution for his intensely activated exhibitionistic drives. The artistic director gratifies his special need to relate to people in a highly accentuated paternalistic and maternalistic fashion. The dramatist and composer find outlets for their omnipotent and omniscient feelings via their original creations.

A psychoanalytic exploration of the theater artist should not only consider his specific artistic sphere as a dramatist, director, actor, but should also evaluate his milieu, his endowments, his maturation, and his childhood development. A valid investigation should attempt to estimate whether or not the (ego) functions involved in artistic creation are free of neurotic conflict; then the artist's quantitative patterns for creative output can be explained more clearly. Finally, no such psychoanalytic investigation should ignore the preconscious and unconscious determinants that link a given playwright's life to a given drama. Such predeterminants have their roots in his early childhood. These early phenomena are as vital to the understanding of his life and his work as they would be in the clinical psychoanalytic investigation of a patient's life and accomplishments.

In the course of its investigations of drama, psychoanalysis has gained valuable insights into the nature of the creative process. Does the theater reciprocally find analysis a rich source for its own development? Dramatists, directors, actors, academic and journalistic critics, and particularly biographers have declared their indebtedness to psychoanalysis. Psychoanalytic colleagues who have written on the subject will attest to the wide interest of students of drama in their publications. Literary journals are increasingly publishing the communications of psychoanalysts and psychologists.

While in the main the contributions of psychoanalysis have added to the understanding and appreciation of drama, some aspects of the original relationship persist. The drama continues to be as fertile a source for psychoanalytic validations and discoveries as it was in the early days. The field of drama, more so than any other artistic area, discloses gems of psychoanalytic insights applicable to clinical problems that have remained totally or partially unexplored. In spite of the growing independence of psychoanalysis as a science, occasional intimations from drama continue to be the forerunners of psychoanalytic insights. A few examples that will be elaborated in greater detail in later chapters deserve mention here. Certain aspects of the psychological process of mourning were anticipated in Eugene O'Neill's *Mourning Becomes Electra*. The prostitute heroines of Tennessee Williams' dramas are literary equivalents of recent psychoanalytic studies of the character, development, and psychology of prostitutes and prostitutional fantasies of women. The classical dramas of the Greeks and Shakespeare, the modern dramas of Strindberg and Ibsen and of the contemporary dramatists have and will continue to offer vital insight into psychological character, complexes, and clinical problems.

Nevertheless, the intimacy between analysis and drama also has its dangers. Some dramatists have appropriated psychoanalytic concepts and have created characters and plots solely from this orientation. As a result their aesthetic creations are unfulfilled, and their contribution to psychoanalysis is superfluous, when it is not confusing. Similarly, teachers and directors of drama who are favorably disposed to psychoanalysis have in some cases abused the works of dramatists and the skills of actors by an overconscientious application of psychoanalytic tenets. It is equally true that occasionally some therapists unnecessarily invade the artistic life of their patients with pseudopsychological interpretations of the plays they have written or the roles they have interpreted. However, in total, the liaison between psychoanalysis and drama is a good one. The more learned advocates of both fields have a respect for the others' domain; the ideas of each are utilized when and where they are suitable, rather than indiscriminately incorporated.

A book on psychoanalysis and drama, or for that matter on any other form of art, never fails to provoke in the general reader a curiosity about the author's views on art and neurosis. The author is invariably asked if the artist's neurosis is essential to his art. Can one be an artist and not be neurotic or psychotic? The artist will never fail to ask, "Will psychoanalytic treatment cripple my creative ability and productivity?" The artist's question reflects a fusion of plausible concern and unconscious fears. Psychoanalysts repeatedly point out that psychoanalytic therapy does not harm the artist's talent and more often aids his productivity, especially when it has been affected by a psychological "block." In spite of such reassurances, the obsessive doubts persist. Hopefully, a scientific approach to the psychological development of the artist, the psychology of creativity, and the problems of artistic success and failure will be elaborated and will permit the reader to form a clearer orientation for posing his questions on art and neurosis in a more enlightened spirit.

The artist's primitive fears and concerns about the bad influences of external forces on his creativity are comprehensible, if not altogether justifiable. He is intuitively and experientially aware of the unpredictable ebb and flow of his creative urges in a bewildering disregard of time. Time and creative states show many variations, not only among different artists, but also within the lifetime of any given artist. The creative and productive patterns of each artist must be studied individually and, at the same time, generally related to his specific profession as a painter, composer, poet, novelist, playwright, director, or actor if we choose to understand the ways and means of creative functioning.

Psychoanalysis shares the artist's contention that his creation results from a combination of inspiration and elaboration. During an active creative state one would expect that the time interval between inspiration and elaboration would be reasonably close. We are not surprised to find that a dramatist inspired by an idea sets himself to work immediately, or is bound up for a few months or even some years with his characters and plot. However, we are somewhat bewildered when we find that Shaw, for example, had the inspiration for *Pygmalion* fifteen years earlier while he was writing *Caesar and Cleopatra*. Did Shaw retain the idea for *Pygmalion* and merely shelve it for fifteen years until he had the solution for the play, and the time to write it? A more dynamic explanation is that the inspiration for both plays emerged from a single unconscious fantasy pertinent to Shaw's life. His inspirational flame was at that moment piloting the play *Caesar and Cleopatra* into existence; the unextinguishable unconscious force was to light the fire for a few other creative concoctions before *Pygmalion* was ready to erupt.

The enigma of time lapse between inspiration and elaboration is equally well illustrated in O'Neill's writing. Again, fifteen years elapsed between the time O'Neill expressed his desire to write an autobiographical play and its eventual elaboration. What happened to his intense inspiration for such a conscious autobiographical play? Did it temporarily dissipate itself like a bursting bubble? Was it merely shelved, as O'Neill suggests, until a more suitable time, when all the members of his family were dead and would not be offended by its revelations? The truth is closer to the possibility that O'Neill's urge to write a consciously autobiographical play found its immediate outlet in *Desire under the Elms,* which is actually an unconscious autobiography. Fifteen years later, the inspiration revived itself from its volcanic unconscious sources for the consciously autobiographical drama, *Long Day's Journey into Night.*

The general scheme of time and creativity is strikingly unique in the actor. The actor feels alive during the moment of his performance. When he returns to the wings at the end of a scene, or when the curtain comes down for the act and eventually descends for the final act, he tends to become emptied of the feeling of life that his role had momentarily provided and with which he had unconsciously identified. It is true of course that the serious creative actor is more constantly absorbed in the study of his roles, beyond rehearsal and performance time. Nevertheless, when the preoccupation with and the enactment of his role are left behind, he too feels emptied of an identity.

The understanding of the boundless arrangements between time and creativity in the lives of artists can best be approached if we bear in mind that creative content is ultimately derived from the unconscious part of the mental apparatus, which Freud described as timeless in both its nature and organization. An emergence from the unconscious must find the opportune moment, when the artist's ego can fulfill its elaboration in the proper mental equilibrium of his personal and artistic life.

When we have explored the evanescent vicissitudes of the artist's creative moment, we are still left with an equally chaotic problem regarding his quantitative and qualitative output. Why do some creative careers begin and end early in life? Why do some artists emerge very late in life? Why do others have a lifelong and qualitatively high productivity? Why are some potentially creative artists destined to lifelong failure?

The lives of two actors studied in this volume touch on the extremities—if not the totality—of these problems. Stanislavski's creative life, beginning as an actor and continuing as a director, was one of productive artistic longevity. John Wilkes Booth, considered by many to have been as talented as his renowned brother Edwin, was destined for artistic and per-

sonal catastrophe. The principal answers lie in the early
parental attitudes toward the future artist. Suffice it to say
here that such attitudes can be crucial determinants for the
final outcome of success or failure.

Every artist from time immemorial has been driven to communicate his message to the world, present and future. We,
the audience, can expand our receptivity to a work of art with
a new dimension when we view not only the artist's pure
aesthetic communication, but add to this a knowledge of his
life and psychological development. The studies which follow
are not intended as a substitute for aesthetic appreciation.
Such matters are essentially in the domain of the artist's public
and its leaders—the critics. Nor is it the author's intention to
violate or destroy the aesthetic road by which the artist of
the theater and his audience must travel toward each other.

The goal of this book is to illuminate the routes of aesthetic
communication between the artist of the theater and the
audience with modern incandescence, derived from the dynamic currents of psychoanalysis. Hopefully, the man of the
theater will then be more clearly comprehended and his
creative efforts more thoroughly assimilated.

I

The Psychological Equipment
and Development of the
Artist in Modern Theater

1

The Actor

NOT ONLY THE ACTOR but all creative artists have some need for as well as an ability to exhibit. These qualities are to be found in writers, composers, and painters, who are certainly not considered to be performing artists. Art is a world of creation and communication, and the instinctual vehicle for such communication is the exhibitionistic drive. However, the actor uses his body or its parts as his artistic instrument. Since these are the exclusive instruments of his creativity, the actor's exhibitionism is intensely personal and unique.

Acting will attract those who have excessive inner needs for, and urgent insatiable gratifications from, exhibiting themselves. Psychoanalytic investigation reveals that these are individuals who have failed to develop a normal sense of identity and body image during the early maturational phases of infancy.[1] This is the actor's plight.

The actor's roles give him repeated opportunities to tem-

[1] The newborn is not endowed with an image of his body, but gradually does develop one in a favorable environment. Normally, in the first few months of life he conceives of all the objects in his world as part of himself. Later, within the first year of life he is able to distinguish his mother, as well as other objects, as distinctly apart from his own body. In an unfavorable environment the final separation of the self from the nonself may never be achieved.

11

porarily secure a self-image. During rehearsals and performances he is assured of and committed to a daily opportunity to create and re-create these roles. He is thus in a position to also gratify his need to appear before an audience. Unreliable as some actors might be in their personal lives, the opposite is true of their professional lives. Traditionally, the actor never misses a performance—although he may be ill, drunk, or the victim of a personal or family misfortune. Psychoanalytic observation modifies the actor's slogan, "The show must go on," to "I, the actor, must go on."

Like the actor, the sexual exhibitionist is so constituted that his perversions also have a "show must go on" quality. As we sketch the behavior of the exhibitionist, we note other striking similarities. The actor has some of the characteristics and the *modus operandi* of the sexual exhibitionist. The exhibitionist has the need to show himself (his penis). He constantly struggles to restrict and control his exhibitionistic urges for fear of being caught, incriminated, and punished. The need to allay his anxiety at times is so intense that the perversion must be carried out at any cost, no matter what the social or legal consequences might be. The exhibitionist, like the actor, may also costume himself in either the clothing of the opposite sex, or in the costumes of the same sex, in order to deny the unconscious fear of having been castrated. The exhibitionist and the actor are repetitively compelled to enact another identity which produces a temporary reduction of their anxiety.

The actor differs from the exhibitionist in that the actor suffers from lack of differentiation of self from nonself and faulty body image development—all this beginning in the first year of development. The body image difficulties of the exhibitionist are centered mainly around a faulty image of his genitals. This occurs later—somewhere during the end of the second and third year of life. The exhibitionist's difficulties center around early childhood anxieties, fears, and threats about the danger of losing his penis and coexistent fantasies that the female had—or has—a penis.

The actor's earlier difficulty about his body image may sometimes extend itself into this later (phallic) phase of normal development, when the young child of three or four is attempting to comprehend the whys and wherefores of the presence of a penis in the male and its absence in the female. Because of his earlier struggles about the concepts of his body, the actor-to-be is somewhat predisposed toward developing a faulty concept and image of the current status and future security of his genitals. However, as often happens, the future actor may not develop these extreme disturbances about his sexual organs, because of a normal environment during this later stage of development. If the actor has developed the same difficulties as the exhibitionist, his profession offers him a more socially acceptable solution than is available to the exhibitionist who is not an actor. The actor's legitimate use of costumes and roles then provide him with a satisfactory solution for his anxieties about his fear of losing his penis as well as his search for a body image.

Whereas acting may momentarily fulfill the needs of someone with an undeveloped body image in adult life, there are certain phenomena in early life that affect the infant's undeveloped body image in a similar fashion. In the first stage of life, the mother and the mother's breast are conceived by the infant as parts of himself. The mother's first vocal communication by "billing and cooing" has the standard quality and style of acting a mother's role.[2] In a short time the infant, who as

---

[2] "Billing and cooing," which is instinctively initiated by the mother of a newborn, is of crucial significance in this era of developmental alteration—from mother–child unity to their separation. If the activity continues beyond the realistic affective needs of the infant, it encourages continuance of the symbiotic union of the infant with the mother, and delays development of differentiation between self and nonself.

When the "billing and cooing" in infancy is excessive and predominant, for whatever reason, it also interferes with the subsequent necessary

yet has no sense of his own identity, takes on the role of the mother, amusing her by borrowing her identity. In this sense, the mother is the playwright and director who creates a role for the infant and teaches it to him. Thus "billing and cooing" is the *anlage* of acting a role and performing for an audience.

To illuminate the connections between acting and the psychological vicissitudes of "billing and cooing," body image development, and exhibitionism, the following case material is offered:

A young, successful dramatic actress, in her mid-twenties and married, complained in her analysis that she was unable to enjoy ordinary simple activities unless she imagined she was being observed and admired by someone of significance among her current theatrical associates. Thus if she was smoking a cigarette or looking in a shop window in the city or at scenery in the country she would imagine her dramatic teacher to be watching her. Similarly, she would often perform her household chores in a theatrical manner, ensnared by a fantasy of being watched by a famous director who was hiding in a closet. This type of fantasy and play acting was a "habit" she remembered from early childhood, at which time her father would be the hidden audience. Her happiest memories were of her father wooing her at bedtime as if she were a princess; then he would carry her off to bed. Actually, her father's relationship with her represented a continuance of

---

normal capacity to tolerate the absence of the mother, which leads to an advancing stage of the self separated from the mother (nonself).

Excessive "billing and cooing" is enacted most often when the mother is motivated by her need to receive recognition and response beyond the infant's ability to provide such recognition. Such mothers may be either excessively narcissistic or deeply depressed. In analytic practice, patients reveal the most severe problems of sibling rivalries as much in memories of animated play (particularly in the design of "billing and cooing") between a younger sibling and their mother as they do in memories of the younger sibling at the mother's breast. From the observations of such intense reactions to the phenomenon of "billing and cooing," its crucial significance cannot be overestimated.

her mother's earlier attitude, which had been overprotective and encompassing. When she was a small child, she could rarely express anything troublesome without her mother's empathic reaction overshadowing her own.

Ordinarily, one would not expect to uncover any early memories of the "billing and cooing" era in an analysis. However, the existence of excessive "billing and cooing" may be inferred from the patient's description of her mother and her subsequent attitude toward a newborn kitten acquired in the course of her analysis.

The patient, who as yet had no children, obtained the kitten to satisfy her maternal needs. Her behavior with the kitten imitated her mother's reaction toward herself as a child and reflected her own concept of a mother–infant relationship. She exaggerated the kitten's state of undernourishment; she would "bill and coo" with the kitten and feed her as she sat on the floor and bedded the animal in her skirt. She would constantly try to make the kitten aware of her. Except for this intensive type of play she had little interest in the kitten's needs, but took great pains to pose with the kitten for a photograph to send to her parents. During her somewhat theatrical play of "billing and cooing" with the kitten she never had the fantasy of being secretly watched as a charming actress. The kitten was her audience. It is of further interest that when the patient was on stage she had little conscious awareness of the audience, and her fantasy of being watched by an important theatrical person was rarely activated.

She also had to act out in a compulsive, uncontrollable manner her craving to be looked at with a quality comparable to that of an exhibitionistic perversion. When she was not working in a play she would seek out and answer calls for movie extras and would work in the movie among a group of extras. This was not motivated by financial necessity, although she rationalized that it was. She was uncontrollably motivated to enact the fantasy that some well-known director would dis-

cover her among the extras and she would be elevated to star-
dom. Actually, she was a fairly well-established actress in the
theater and had already had a featured role in a movie. It
is evident that her self-appointed demotion to a movie extra
was a regression to an incomplete self-image. She was thus
compelled to enact in real life her fantasy in which the movie
director represented a potential omnipotent image with which
her incomplete self-image might be fused in her wish to become his star. Thus her acting, like the "billing and cooing,"
offered the solution of a new temporary identity for her undeveloped body image via an exhibitionistic effort.

Accentuated "billing and cooing" is not to be misunderstood
as a *sine qua non* for the development of an actor. All actors
and actresses do not have to have this characteristic as a prerequisite. What is being stressed is that they frequently do
have these characteristics which influence the choice of profession. It may yet be proved that actors with such fixations
and characteristics may well be the "born actors" (independent of the issue of being creative or noncreative) who
become actors in early childhood and are relegated to a lifelong theatrical career.

Many other developmental and environmental determinants
lead to the choice of becoming an actor. In his monumental
study, *Psychoanalytic Explorations in Art*, Ernst Kris noted
that "psychoanalytic material enables us to point to the inter-
action of factors" (Kris, 1952) which leads to a given artistic
outlet for a given individual. Thus he who is—or feels he is—
deprived of the mother's infant play may become fixated at
such a level, in which acting may supplant the infantile frustration and deprivation in the era of early play with the
mother. Needless to say, the unresolved conflicts of childhood
exhibitionism—early (pregenital) and late (genital)—contain forces which strongly shape the direction of an actor. A
father or mother who is or had hoped to be an actor operates
as a motivating force which may direct the child to continue

his parent's occupation or dream of acting.[3] A clinical example in point follows:

Another actress patient recalled that her father loved to read to her from Shakespeare when she was three. Shortly thereafter she would enact scenes from the great bard's plays, with her father and for his pleasure, obviously long before she could comprehend the meaning of the lines. Her learning by enacting a character, which pleased her father, preceded her ability to comprehend. Later, in school, whatever the subject might be, she transformed its contents into a drama to be enacted. Acting a role became her subsequent method, not only of learning but also of living.

The way the actor played as a child reflects itself in the level of creativity he can attain.[4] Play *action* is characterized by the unmodified expression of the instincts of love and hate in the form of play. Play *acting* utilizes a more mature, although rudimentary, process of mental functioning to which the instinctual expression is subservient to the specific play (Ekstein & Friedman, 1957). Normally, as the child grows play action gives way to play acting. Stage acting encompasses both activities. However, the actor who is limited to the play-action level of his art is usually an inferior, exhibitionistic artist and may be emotionally disturbed. The play-acting actor controls and regulates his acting technique and therefore is likely to be a competent professional. Depending on his talent and training, he may give a highly creative performance.

The art of acting involves two essential psychological components: the capacity to transform oneself into a created character and the ability to exhibit this transformation. Psychoanalysis has demonstrated that the character and the career of a given individual are often structured on the defenses of

[3] The psychodynamic origins for such motivations are derived from the child's identification with his parentally derived (ego) ideals.

[4] For detailed examples of the subsequent effects of play action and play acting on stage acting see chapters 6 and 7.

reaction formation and counterphobic denial. Although the actor is measured by his ability to transform himself "physically and spiritually," there is every indication that his defective body image makes such artistic self-transformation more possible and necessary. Fenichel raises the question as to whether "the best actor would be a character who has not yet developed an actual marked personality, but who is ready to play any part given him, who has no ego but is rather a bundle of identification possibilities" (Fenichel, 1946). He suggests that this is more often the case than the exception.

Yet it would be naïve to think that the artistically successful actor who is always sought after and constantly working as an actor has truly solved either his need for exhibitionism or has freed himself from the sufferings of his depersonalization, derived from his undeveloped self-image. Many actors, including creative and successful ones, must act at all times, both off stage and on. When the applause fades and the final curtain falls, there is a depressive return to the empty self. The actor feels incomplete and unloved.

If exhibitionism never fully satisfies the actor's emotional needs, it also fails as the mainstay of his art. The ultimate measure of a creative actor is to be found more in his ability to become a created character than in his ability to exhibit. The more completely an actor becomes the created character, the greater is the unconscious communication between actor and audience. The members of the audience can then lose their own identity and share the experience of the actor in his new identity during the witnessed portrayal.

A discussion of the psychology of the actor should also consider his characteristic neurotic symptoms, when and if they occur. One would expect the typical actor's neurosis to be stage fright. Accordingly, the general cause of stage fright is to be found in the double-edged character of all the psychological mechanisms involved. Stage fright occurs when the unconscious nature of the actor's acting strives to become conscious, in which event the audience becomes the representative of his punishing superego, threatening to turn against him. Stage fright, the specific fright of the neurotically exhibitionistic actor, has in addition a quality of shame which is the equivalent of the unconscious fear of being castrated. Nevertheless, severe stage fright is not confined to actors and actually is more manifest among people who occasionally, rather than frequently, use the stage—such as the child in recitation, the amateur performer, and the publicly honored guest. In view of his defective body image and his exhibitionistic fixations, the actor's problems are more commonly depersonalization, exhibitionism, and related perversions. Severe acting-out neurosis (and even psychosis[5]) may occur, because of the actor's affinity toward regressive play action.

A comprehensive psychological evaluation of the actor must take into consideration certain special features of female psychosexual development that are uniquely reflected in the psychological development of the actress. It is a common observation that the woman's place in the theater is on the stage, rather than in the wings as director or dramatist. Acting in the theater is both more accessible and natural for the female. In childhood girls engage in play acting and play action more universally and with more spontaneous freedom than does the average boy. The boy's greatest interest lies in adventurous physical aggression, experimentation, manual ability, reality testing, and executive expansion (Greenacre, 1960). The universality of penis envy in girls, beginning with the phallic phase between the ages of three and four, finds a natural resolution after the age of five during the latency period in play action and play acting and in seeking instruction in such performing arts as dancing, playing the piano, and dramatics.

Female exhibitionism is displaced from the genital to the body as a whole. Moreover, the female's exhibition of her body

[5] The psychosis of John Wilkes Booth is elaborated on in Chapter 7.

is socially encouraged and is in itself considered a sublimation (Hárnik, 1924). Combined with acting, it becomes an aesthetic sublimation. Since her body exhibitionism is socially acceptable, a woman has the more difficult artistic task of choosing between being a beautiful woman or a beautiful actress. The audience shares this conflict, finding it difficult to decide whether the actress pleases them as a woman or as an artist. Whatever difficulty the actress may have in resolving her personal and artistic conflict, it can readily be seen that the stage is a natural domain for her.

Ultimately, the ability to transform oneself completely into a created character, and thereby achieve true creativity, poses the same artistic problem for the female as it does for the male. Undifferentiated self-images and early mother–infant relationships are as conditioning for actresses as they are for actors. True creativity does not compromise. Frequently, creative actresses who are far from beautiful or young can transform themselves dramatically into young and beautiful heroines.

Whether actor or actress, excessive reliance on exhibitionism assures a communication to the audience which will be artless and superficial. The actor's appeal to the audience is then personal (often sexualized), and the audience's response to the actor is equally personal. Artless theater, like the strip tease, is often intended as a mutual sexual seduction between actor and audience. It is the meeting ground of the voyeur and the exhibitionist.

The serious theater-goer and the creative actor bring to the art of theater the sublimated wishes of their childhood—voyeurism and exhibitionism, respectively. Creative acting implies that the direct gratification of the actor's exhibitionistic instinct be desexualized and deaggressivized (sublimated, if you will) to show a newly creative portrayal of a re-created character. Correspondingly, the audience must aim at a more sublimated gratification of its voyeuristic wishes via a desexualized curiosity to achieve an aesthetic response.

2

The Dramatist

A PSYCHOLOGICAL STUDY of the dramatist cannot avoid comparisons to his performing counterpart, the actor. In spite of some wide differences between them, their creative lives (and often enough their personal lives) are so intertwined and symbiotic that certain aspects of their individual natures can best be delineated in terms of each other.

Both actors and playwrights express themselves in an art of conflict and action. The dramatist originates the plot, the action, and the character. The actor aims to give the play a final form in action and to communicate the intent of the author. The author gives birth to characters and plot; the actor breathes aesthetic life into both and stands the printed character on its "feet."

Ernst Kris suggested that the performing artist, such as the actor or dancer, presents a more typical conflict constellation than does the writer or the poet (Kris, 1952a). Similarly, the dramatist may be expected to have a more complex conflict constellation. Nothing quite as specific as the actor's problems of identity and exhibitionism is found in the study of the dramatist.

Accounts of the childhoods of playwrights do not record the

unusual amount of play action or play acting that characterizes the early years of actors. Nor is it clear what is the stimulus to and the outlet for creativity in the early lives of writers. One would assume that it resides in the area of fantasy life.

M. J. Moses, reflecting on Henrik Ibsen's boyhood, writes (1908),

> Ibsen grew up in the midst of the usual pranks of village boys but he did not play in normal manner. It pleased him far better to brood over the pillory around which a morbid imagination disported itself or to look within the grated openings of the dungeon in search of pale and wasted faces, than to join in the healthy excesses of the village scholars. . . . One sister remembered him as an "uncomfortable boy" whom they would have to prod into action and then he would bungle through the games, unless it happened that they were playing fort, when his ingenuity at building and maneuvering was remarkable . . . foreshadowing the playwright's instinct. . . . Yet notwithstanding all the accounts of his interest in sleight-of-hand performance . . . [and] given public exhibition in one of the spare rooms, Henrik Ibsen was first and last a lad of thought, whose larger and more significant life was spent within himself. . . .

Later in life Ibsen wrote, "I look into myself. There is where I fight my battles."

Although dramatists have strong tendencies toward acting out, this is not the source of their creative talent. Their egos must be so organized that they must have the dissociative capacity to overcome and transform personal enactments from unconscious sources into creative enactments in plays. If the actor's creative success depends on a minimal display of his personal exhibitionism, it can equally be stated that the playwright who enacts his "drama" in life will have difficulties in writing a play.

In Shaw's struggle with his personal feelings for Mrs. Pat Campbell he wrote: "Is this dignified? Is this sensible? At my age—a driveller—a dotard! I will conquer this weakness or trade in it and write plays about it" (Dent, 1952). And so he did. *Pygmalion* represents a redirection of Shaw's personal enactments toward Mrs. Pat Campbell.[1] When comparing his relationship with Ellen Terry to that with Pat Campbell, he wrote,

> Ellen did get down on paper a series of letters which brought her out with flying colors from a correspondence with so artful a practitioner as myself. The whole thing was on paper; it was a correspondence with nothing else; it was literature. But the [Pat Campbell] Stella–GBS idyll was acted not written; it was not on paper and is not literature (Dent, 1952).

The study of Eugene O'Neill's life shows the transformation of a life of enactments into a life of creating drama. This was more forced on him by external circumstances of tuberculosis than by ego control. Prior to this time, his young life was already studded with wild enactments of drunkenness, voyages to sea, an abortive and denied marriage, and fatherhood. He subsequently wrote, "My health broke down, my lung being affected and I spent six months in a sanatorium thinking it over. It was in this enforced period of reflection that the urge to write first came to me. The next fall—I was twenty-four—I began my first play, *The Web*" (Clark, 1947, pp. 10–11).

In such matters it is difficult to disclose the clinical material of dramatists who are in analysis. However, it can be said that they bear out this formulation. There is usually present a strong tendency toward enactments which are curbed by the dissociative capacity of the ego (Glover, 1924) and transformed into dramatic creations. When personal enactments cannot be controlled, they coincide with noncreative phases in the artist's life. Recent studies emphasize the importance in the creative process of self-regulated regression in the service of the ego. Less stressed has been the simultaneous intensifi-

[1] The unconscious determinants for *Pygmalion* were derived from Shaw's childhood and are elaborated on in a later chapter.

cation of ego defenses during the process of creativity. Via suppression, repression, isolation, denial, and other defenses, the creative artist, during his creative periods, suspends direct gratification of his instinctual impulses. In other words, the controlled regression is permissible and possible via the precondition of intensification of defense against direct instinctual gratification. In this setting of intensified ego defenses and controlled ego regression "the most daring intellectual activity (creative activity) can flourish" (Kris, 1952a).

James Joyce's first desire was to be a playwright, at which he failed. His idol was Ibsen (Ellman, 1959). His only play, *The Exiles*, has never been considered significant literature. A cursory examination of his life shows that he had little tendency toward the solution of conflict by action; thus his content lacks the strife of which plays are made.

The dramatist has been described as the creator of action. The psychology of action has to concern itself with a consideration of the hierarchy of ego development and maturation connected with each type of action. Direct action represents the most primitive of impulsive, immediate gratification. Delayed action represents an adaptive solution by the process of thinking to a conflict situation. In contrast, acting out is an unconscious repetitive action of a conflict. Certainly, delayed action represents a higher level of mental functioning than acting out or direct action.

Dramatists may create characters who operate on any one of these levels of action. More often than not, a versatile dramatist creates all levels of action. More accurately, he creates thoughts or verbal representations of actions. What is significant is that the dramatist must contain his personal tendencies toward action—be they impulsive, direct, delayed, or acting out—and must redirect this tendency into his creations. A playwright on political, religious, romantic, or psychological drama cannot be a ruler, a priest, a lover, or a psychiatrist. Hence, whatever his personal traits, habits, and drives may be, in his artistic life the direct expression of his personal actions must be transmuted into his dramatic creations.

Playwrights share with actors the tendency toward neurotic acting out. Whereas the actor's pathological enactments aim at the gratifications of his exhibitionism, the dramatist's acting out is usually more complex and tends toward a major alteration of his life. The personal enactments may parallel the characteristic themes and actions of his dramas. This is understandable, since dramatists are prone to seek solutions in action for unresolved, traumatic childhood experiences. Acting out by dramatists tends to severely and protractedly affect their creativity most directly, since their entire creative energies and resources are drained off by such actions. Thus, dramatists are often given to severe inhibitions in creativity (writer's "block") and concomitant depressive states.

What is there in the psychological make-up of the dramatist that impels him to either personally enact or to artistically create dramas of given actions? His enactments, which may be diverted into plays, have characteristic conscious qualities and purposes which are derived from specially arranged unconscious sources and motivations.

The dramatist aims to communicate something newly created; not unlike the audience, he is involved with curiosity and voyeurism. He is the reporter, the viewer of the self-created world. Consciously, he is involved with a statement and resolution of the world as it matters to him.[2] Consciously, he designs his characters as he fantasies them to be. Unconsciously, he is often involved with unremembered aspects of

[2] This was as true of the ancient Greek dramatists as it is of our current playwrights. Sophocles and Euripides, in their plays, reflected on the moral, social, and political atmosphere of their times. The *au courant* dramas of the theater of the absurd and the existentialist theater are written by today's playwrights who are preoccupied with the world of tomorrow.

his childhood. In this sense, the playwright is quite often involved in a literary re-creation of forgotten childhood experiences. With some dramatists, such as Shaw or Ibsen, the created enactments derived predominantly from childhood events and were transformed and substituted for enacted creation, i.e., plays.

Shaw's created *ménage à trois* of Eliza, Higgins, her vocal teacher, and Pickering in *Pygmalion* is unconsciously rooted in Shaw's forgotten experiences in early childhood when he lived in a comparable parental triangle consisting of his mother, Vanderleur Lee, her voice teacher, and his father. M. J. Moses (1908), in his book on Henrik Ibsen, *The Man and His Plays*, states of Ibsen's *Peer Gynt:* "Thus does [his] art [playwrighting] entwine itself upon past incidents disguised however they may be; in subtle manner does imagination grapple with well-nigh forgotten happenings."[3]

During any given creative task the dramatist *consciously* attempts to portray his special views, sensitive evaluations, and to devise original solutions for various aspects of his created world—aspects which may be psychological, philosophical, political, or religious. Through this same creative effort, he is *unconsciously* driven by revived, forgotten, unresolved, traumatic, and unpleasant childhood experiences to re-create new solutions that aspire to restore an integrated equilibrium to the disturbing effects of these long, lingering incidents and fantasies.

As all children are passive witnesses to the lives of their parents, which are often traumatic to them, it is possible that the playwright's fantasies aesthetically re-create such traumatic experiences as a kind of repetitive compulsion to undo painful

[3] It is of interest that Moses' book was written in 1908, antedating by many years the psychoanalytic insight of an inevitable correlation between a dramatist's given play and repressed childhood experiences. Not only do original works of art often anticipate psychoanalytic insights, but creative criticism and biography may similarly turn out to be forerunners of psychoanalytic findings.

past experiences.[4] The traumatic experience produces a lasting need to repeat actively what was originally experienced passively. Lowenfeld suggests that early traumatic experiences are preconditions to artistic creativity.[5] Kris suggested that creativity utilizes traumatic experiences in the direction of the increasing distance from direct reaction to them (Kris, 1952a). It is not uncommon for playwrights to repeat various designs of oedipal conflict. A particular playwright may repetitively stress the father–son conflict; another, the incestuous mother–son or father–daughter relationship, and so on.

Playwrights are centrally concerned with creating a family world that they may view historically, biographically, religiously, socially, or psychologically. It is not surprising that the central theme of dramas throughout the centuries rarely deviates from the contents of the oedipal conflict. Freud's discovery of the universality of the oedipal conflict has been attested to by daily confirmations since the beginning of psychoanalysis. The affirmation of this historical universality is found by examining the subject matter of dramas from the times of the ancient Greeks to today. No other theme has so occupied the dramatist's imagination as the subject of the conflict within the family. While it is true that the *Oedipus Rex* drama reigns as the most exact example of man's unconscious Oedipus complex, there are other Greek legendary dramas

---

[4] In Greenacre's opinion, the presence of the repetition compulsion in a child's creative play reflects a lesser state of creativity than does its absence (1959).

[5] Since dramatists' plays almost always deal unconsciously with personal traumatic experiences, one might falsely conclude that all dramatists are therefore neurotic. To forestall such a conclusion, the following explanations are in order. Traumatic experiences do not in themselves lead to neurosis. An experience is referred to as traumatic when the child's ego is unable to cope with an unpleasant episode at a given moment. It is quite possible to undo the ill effects on the child's ego of such a traumatic event, without neurotic symptom formation. With the aid of recurrent dreams and repetitive play, the overwhelming anxiety arising from the traumatic experience may be gradually removed.

which are more oriented toward the more consciously elaborated versions of the Oedipus complex. Dramatists and their
audiences are usually more attracted to the Electra–Orestes
legend than to the Oedipus legend; the Electra–Orestes theme
and plot are related to situations which occur more frequently
in life. Such a tale offers the opportunity for a more facile
identification by all concerned, including the dramatist, the
actors, and the audience.

The House of Agamemnon is a Greek oedipal legend which
has been utilized by dramatists throughout the centuries. An
Athenean citizen of the fifth century B.C. during his lifetime
could have seen original productions of the plays of Aeschylus,
Euripides, and Sophocles based on this legend. A citizen of the
twentieth century A.D. could have seen a number of original
contemporary dramas based on the same legend. In France, we
have had plays by Sartre (*The Flies*) and by Giraudoux
(*Electra*). In the United States the legend has been dramatized by Eugene O'Neill (*Mourning Becomes Electra*) and in
1959 by Jack Richardson (*The Prodigal*).

Man's basic drives are love and aggression. King Agamemnon's inner conflicts lie between his drive for power and his
love of war and family. His wife, Clytemnestra, struggles with
her need to love and be loved, with her conflicted loyalty to a
long-absent husband, and her murderous hatred of him for
inflicting such deprivations on her. Their children, Orestes and
Electra, already damaged by their parents' problems, have still
more complex conflicts. Should a child kill the mother who
bore him, no matter what her crime? Can such a child live in
any sort of peace after the avenging murder is consummated?
Muddled by the passions of love and hate for the parents,
natural to childhood, their dilemma seems insoluble.

These are the problems that Aeschylus, Euripides, and
Sophocles attempted to resolve two thousand years ago. Shakespeare's Prince Hal and Hamlet bear the stamp of the same
theme. One would venture the guess that literally hundreds of

plays can be traced to the same source. In our time, four highly creative dramatists have utilized this legend to offer a modern solution to man's timeless and universal conflicts. Kris (1952a) raises this question: "Under specific cultural and socioeconomic conditions during any given period of history—how have the traditional themes been varied?" Both in the past and present, depending on changes within the culture, various dramatists have utilized the House of Agamemnon legend in widely different ways (Weissman, 1960).

Why does the playwright create for a medium which is basically animated, exhibitionistic, voyeuristic, and auditory? Are his heroes and heroines autobiographical participants of the primal scene? Has the dramatist been actual witness to such a scene or has his imagination forced him to an inescapable confrontation with the contents of it? Does Hamlet know if his mother loved his father, his uncle, or himself? Is man's oedipal conflict no more than the child's universal drama of the primal scene, which dramatists have endlessly brought to light and portrayed?

Eugene O'Neill has recorded the fact that he dreamed entire scenes of some of his plays and directly incorporated their content (Gelb & Gelb, 1962). The playwright's medium, the stage, approximates the medium of the dream screen. Unique to the dramatist is writing pure dialogue and creating scenes as a special aspect of his imagination. The dramatist's script is much like the manifest dream. The produced play can be compared to latent content and secondary elaboration of the dream. The dramatist then is the spinner and spectator of aesthetic creations, and, as in dreams, he may appear in them directly or disguised. Thus, the dramatist originally occupies the same position to his own process of creation as his eventual audience—a passive recipient. In a discussion of the psychology of creative processes, Kris writes, "The maturing of thought, the entry into awareness from preconsciousness to consciousness, tend to be experienced as derived from outside,

as passively received, not actively produced" (Kris, 1952b).
With the exception of the movies, which is a derivative of
dramatic art, no other art form so closely shares the shape and
style of a dream.

Communication in every form of art brings the exhibitionistic drives into the fore. What about the dramatist? How do
his exhibitionistic fears and wishes compare to the actor's?

Authors' exhibitionistic sufferings and gratifications are not
identical with those of actors'. The playwright is creatively
represented by his ideas of action rather than by a personal
display of his actions. Spared the actor's personal public appearance in a play, the failure of the writer's drama does not
unconsciously represent a rejection on the castration level. The
actor's shame is unconsciously the anxiety of being castrated
and is related to the problem of stage fright. However, the
intensity of the feeling of failure is as pronounced for the
dramatist as for the actor. The dramatist's failure is more in
the area of loss of self-esteem and derives from failure to
satisfy the ego-ideal. In a successful creative effort, the audience represents to both actor and dramatist an encouragement
of self-approval. The fear of the superego is abated. As Kris
puts it, "the illicit becomes licit" (Kris, 1952a).

The playwright, like the novelist and the poet, is in the
position of a solo flyer who charts the unknown. Via his failure
and even his successes, he is concerned with anxieties of self-
esteem. He is totally dependent on himself for mothering his
creations, whereas the actor finds parts already created or
which have to be created to cloak his artistic needs. So com-
paratively narrow is the actor's need that his own role is sufficient to gratify his aesthetic and unconscious needs. The playwright must successfully create in a single communication a
varying number of characters that in their integrated construction represent a single aesthetic communication.

Since the dramatist, in his earliest development, readily at-
tains the primary object (the mother's breast), he can easily

give it up and remain free to seek gratification from hallucinatory wishes, concretized in his special art form of writing plays.

In contrast, the actor seeks for a primary object in his audience which, when found, reinforces his self-image, but does not establish an object relationship.

What is the playwright's relationship to the audience in contrast to that of the actor? In any given performance of a play, the actor has a more direct and intense relationship to the audience than the author. Customarily, at the first performance, the author may be called on to share the applause with the actors. On such occasions the author is often quite reluctant to appear and may not even be present in the theater. This clearly indicates a more distant relationship to the theater audience. The playwright's relations with the audience are in the design of the artist's "love affair with the world."[6] In contrast, the actor has a "love affair" with a specific audience of people. He anthropomorphizes the audience into a single person. Actors often refer to audiences as dull, responsive, sitting on their hands, intelligent, or being in a good or bad mood.[7]

The implication is that the dramatist advances to a higher level of differentiation in his early development than does the actor. The objects of the writer's world are clearly delineated as objects apart from himself. After the dramatist gives birth to his creation, both he and his creation live independently of

[6] Greenacre, in a study of the childhood of the artist (1957), suggests that the creative artist's "love affair with the world" is rooted in his capacity from early infancy for greater than average sensitivity to sensory stimulation to the primary object (his mother's breast) and to all related peripheral objects which arouse similar sensory responses. Subsequently, the intensified responsiveness to the related peripheral objects is developed into an affinity for attachments to "collective alternate" objects at the expense of the personal object. It is the artist's attachments to "collective alternate" objects that is expressed in terms of a "love affair with the world."

[7] The reference to the audience as if it were an actual individual unconsciously relates back to the actor's mother–infant "billing and cooing" relationship.

each other. Aesthetically viewed, the actor breathes life into the created character; psychoanalytically viewed, the role that he enacts breathes shape and form into the actor's undeveloped body image.

It is increasingly clear that playwrights are creative parents who feed and nurture the needs of the actor. Some playwrights are so thorough-going in the creation of certain characters that they almost assure the actor's success in the given role. The actor usually remains the dependent child. Exceptions to this are, of course, frequent. Such an actor usually extends his career to the level of director and has the capacity to identify with all the characters in a play as an actor, and with the author as interpreter of his artistic intentions.[8]

The theater artist who becomes both a creative actor and author is not common although the combination does occur.[9] From what has been said as to the needed psychological qualifications, it would seem that the likelihood of being creatively successful in both media would not be expected. Shakespeare's genius transcended these boundaries. Not only was he poet and playwright; he was actor and director. Even as dramatist, he was the rare exception who could transcend his personal life in his plays. The differences in character and ego development between actor and author, here elaborated, account for the rarity of the combination of these two art forms in one individual.

[8] Stanislavski is a good example of such an actor-director.

[9] Chekhov was an actor during his youth for a short time. It grew out of the need to enact dramatic sketches of his own adolescent inventions (Magarshack, 1952).

3

The Director

HAVING EXPLORED the psychological development both of the actor and the playwright, we might complete our understanding of the creative personalities in the theater if we investigate the psychological make-up of their liaison man, the director. What is the nature of his creative contribution in the theater? What are his specific artistic endowments? What is there in his psychological environment and development which leads him toward and aids him in his chosen work of directing? What are the ties between the artistic director and his creative sources, such as the dramatist and the composer? And what are the bonds between the artistic director and his creative outlet—the performer, such as actors and musicians?

The artistic directors to be considered will be those who stage works requiring the coordinated use of a group of performers. Thus, the orchestral conductor, the director of opera, and choral conductor fit as readily into this group as does the director of dramas. The psychology of the nonartistic director does not differ too widely from the psychology of his aesthetic counterpart. In addition to histories of various types of artistic directors, examples will be given of a business and a scientific director. These clinical and biographical studies reveal that artistic directors are most often motivated and aided in their work by their particular breed of unconscious oedipal wishes and unconscious inculcations (identifications) of a special combination of parental attitudes and interests.

In normal childhood development, the general content of the oedipal wishes for the male child is to possess his mother and remove his father. It is well known that the specific content of these wishes may be present in multiple variations and will depend on the actualities in the child's life. These variables include the presence or absence of siblings, the child's endowments, and the parents' qualities and attitudes, among still other factors. In one child the emphasis might be on the wish to have sexual relations with his mother; another child might emphasize the wish to become the father of his pregnant mother's unborn baby and of the children already born, which implies a positive oedipal resolution via an identification with the father; conversely, the male child who retains the wish to be the mother to his parents' children has a negative oedipal solution via an identification with the mother. The absence of the father may promote the fantasy of taking a paternal and/or maternal role as head of the family.

Generally, the resolution of the Oedipus complex is accompanied by unconsciously developing the attributes of (identifying with) either or both parents. The identifications derived from the oedipal resolution may be as varied as the wishes.

The variations of wish content and the resultant identifications of the oedipal phase are more than mere reflections of the presence and passing of the oedipal conflict. The specific content of the oedipal period becomes the ferment for the subsequent maturation and development of the child. In cases of partial or total successful resolution of the Oedipus complex, analysts often find that the original oedipal wishes and resulting identifications with the parents have been sublimated into activities that permit the continuation and gratification of the oedipal wishes.[1] Such an arrangement of continuity extending from childhood oedipal wishes to organized sublimated activities in adult life is borne out in psychoanalytic reconstructions of the childhood development of artistic directors.

Our investigation will illustrate that the child's oedipal constellations—which emphasizes the wish to become the parent (usually the mother and occasionally the father) of the unborn and born children and the further wish to bring up these children—approximates most closely the sublimated oedipal wishes of the artistic director. Whereas the negative oedipal wish in the male child to be a mother may have pathological significance in his personal pursuits, it does not have the same significance in the sublimated activity as a director. His wish to be a mother is as useful as the wish to be a father in the artistic function of directing and guiding performers. Maternal or paternal in origin, the identification is transformed and expressed in the sublimated wish to be an artistic parent to his artistic children, the performers. Indispensable to these conditions, as we shall see, is the presence of a high degree of special aesthetic environment and endowment.

What follows will be clinical and psychobiographical evidence from various sources that validate such formulations, including the direct observations from an historically famous child analysis.

CLINICAL EVIDENCE

A thirty-two-year-old man came into analysis with a history of periods of depression and an ulcer. The past two years had been spent as director and then owner and producer of a summer stock theater in the mid-West. He came to New York

[1] The analyst more often deals with the unsuccessfully resolved specific oedipal contents and pathological identifications in the neurotic symptom or character. Clinically speaking, the sublimated activity, the neurotic symptom, the normal and pathological identifications coexist in individual combinations.

to further his theatrical career as a director and producer and to seek help for the recurrent depressions that rendered him inactive. During the analysis he often attempted to discuss his difficulties with his girl friend, who had been a member of his theatrical company. At such times he rarely spoke about his own difficulties, but constantly about hers. His girl friend wanted to marry him but he never said yes or no because of his own overt homosexual problems. He sanctioned her living with another man and became her advisor in the other relationship. Each session found him telling his girl friend's difficulties, never his own. The same obtained for his relationships with men who were his friends or theatrical associates. He was keenly curious, analytic, and advisory about their personal relationships but avoided any reference to his personal relationships with them. In fact, he remained aloof and behaved like an observing parent.

When he was three years old his parents were separated, ostensibly because his father went to the mid-West to start a new business venture. He did not see his father again until he was nine, when his mother and the children went to join the father. In all probability the separation of his parents was intended as a marital separation but this was not disclosed to the children. My patient was thus temporarily fatherless during his oedipal period. He reacted to the situation as if he were permanently fatherless and repressed all memories of his father's existence. Until he was in analysis, he was unable to remember any communication from his father or any reference to him by other members of the family. Thus he made a complete identification with his mother and her interests. His mother was a devotee of theater and music. Just prior to her marriage she had studied to become an opera singer with a famous director of the Metropolitan who had high hopes for her. Her marriage interrupted her studies and a respiratory illness affected her voice sufficiently to terminate her efforts. From the age of five he became his mother's constant companion during the father's absence, since his teen-aged brother and sister were actively involved in their young social lives. He was rarely mischievous as a growing child, whereas his brother was in constant difficulties with his mother over his undisciplined and unruly behavior. Via his early identification with his mother, he suppressed his own aggressive impulses and looked on his brother's activities with the eye of a disapproving parent, like his mother. During his adolescence he alone accompanied his mother to concerts and theaters. In his more recent relationship with his mother, who had been widowed for the past ten years, he felt duty bound to fill the gap in her life created by the death of his father and by the marriages of his ten-years-older brother and six-years-older sister. Currently, whenever his mother visits him in New York, they spend the fortnight going to theater, opera, and concerts.

His first directorial tendencies became manifest after high school. During his college career he organized and led a performing dramatic group. His theatrical productions were highly successful, and he became renowned on the campus as its active dramatic leader. However, he had scholastic troubles and was censored for overcutting classes and failing to submit papers when due. After graduating, he worked for a major broadcasting network and felt due for a raise in salary. When this was not forthcoming spontaneously, he organized his fellow workers and pleaded their cause for higher salaries and improved working conditions. All these directorial, maternalistic activities were extensions of his oedipal conflicts in which he unconsciously identified with his mother since his father was absent.

His girl friend, with whom he had abortive sexual relations, had been formerly an actress in his summer stock company. His boy friend, with whom he had overt homosexual relations, was also an actor in his stock company. His attitude toward both was a parental and guiding one in the personal and artistic aspects of his relationships with them, as it had been in childhood with his older brother and sister.

During his periods of depression he became inactive and lost interest in the theater; when the depression was alleviated, he became extremely active and his interests were revived in new theatrical projects. The depression unconsciously represented the child's wish to be taken care of by the mother. The active phase represented the identification with the mother in which he actively took care of others as children—especially actors—in his directorial work. Thus he transformed the original relationship with his mother (in which he was constantly taken to the theater and concerts) into an ego-ideal of doing the same for others through his theatrical activities as a director and producer. He also identified with paternal figures, such as the operatic director who held high hopes for his mother's voice career. Since his father was completely away during his oedipal and postoedipal development, his mother had to fill the role of father as well as mother during this time. Whatever paternal identification he made in this fatherless era was via his identification with his mother in her combined role of mother and father. When he was reunited with his father at the age of nine, he began to take on specifically new identifications. At first, they were with his father's scholastic interests and achievements; subsequently, with his business and executive interests which helped to shape the son's later development as a director and more particularly to his final interest as a producer in the theater.

A thirty-five-year-old man was a highly trained instrumentalist who became a successful conductor of an amateur musical organization, in spite of severe emotional difficulties in executing his work. As a child he had been of delicate constitution and appearance. His hair was unusually light and fine. His appearance was outstanding, and therefore he had special privileges at home and at school. At home he was released from some of the household chores that were expected of his brothers and sisters. At school he was permitted to walk to the front of the class, without permission, and examine the blackboard at close range, since his vision was extremely poor. Unconsciously he reacted to his handicap as if it were an advantage. He received further special consideration from his musical mother who identified with her handicapped son, tended to deny his handicaps, and extolled his virtues. As she taught him to play the piano and hovered over him, she told him that he would make a fine conductor with his light hair and sensitive hands. He saw himself as an aesthetic-looking conductor, like Stokowski, and imagined that all conductors had white hair that made them godlike figures, deified by performers and audience.

During puberty, he revived oedipal masturbatory fantasies in which he was a "godlike" figure who would plant the seeds in his mother, whom he endowed with the qualities of an angel. This fantasy frequently occurred while practicing the piano, when his mother characteristically would stand behind him with her body occasionally pressed against his back, intensely and intimately involved in guiding him musically.

He was his mother's special child. He identified with her in their shared musical interests and activities. His fantasies were derived from her wishes for him. In the subsequent sublimation of these fantasies into his conducting career, he replaced his mother as teacher and substituted the members of his orchestra for himself in the child's role.

He received an advanced musical education at a leading university which was staffed with the best teachers in performance, theory, and composition. His career as conductor was frustrated as well as fostered by his oedipal wishes. When he was to conduct, he would often fantasy that some attractive but unattainable woman would be present, would worship at his feet, and would fall in love with him as a deified figure.

Since he saw himself as a unique, deified being, he experienced psychological difficulty in looking at his musicians while directing them. He also had difficulty in being spontaneous, improvising, and experimenting since he was both godlike and childlike, as in his oedipal fantasies.

PSYCHOBIOGRAPHICAL EVIDENCE

Writers on the psychology of creativity more often than not turn to the biographies and autobiographies of famed men for confirmation of their findings. The justification for this direction lies in the fact that the creative talents of such men are unquestionably attested to by the whole world, by the survival of their works, in contrast to analysands who usually have more earthbound talents. (Whenever the analyst has the good fortune to deal with a renowned talent, the ethical problem of public disclosure of the intimate details of his life becomes a barrier.)

Edward Gordon Craig, the son of Ellen Terry, the famous actress, and Edward William Godwin, a famed London architect, has been for the past half-century, along with Konstantin Stanislavski, one of the outstanding influences of stage production and design in Europe, Russia, and the United States. They share in common not only their unique influence on production in the modern theater but also the unique distinction of having written down their ideas for posterity[2] (Craig, 1957; Stanislavski, 1924). Both men have fortunately written autobiographies late in life with the wise awareness that famed people tend to give the public a false idealized image. It is the awareness of this pitfall that makes their autobiographical studies more useful for a psychobiographical investigation than is the case with most autobiographies. Since Stanislavski's life

---

[2] Craig spent a year with Stanislavski at the Moscow Art Theater, where they worked together with special emphasis on revolutionizing Shakespearean productions.

was involved with acting as well as directing, we shall with-hold an evaluation of him for a subsequent chapter in which both his genius and his prolonged productivity will be considered. At the moment, we shall confine our attention to the case of Gordon Craig.

His mother, Ellen Terry, began as a child actress (Craig, 1957). Both her parents were actors. She was married at sixteen to the painter, Watts, from whom she quickly separated. Shortly thereafter and undivorced, she fell in love with Craig's father, and they lived together out of wedlock. Three years prior to Craig's birth, Ellen Terry left the theater to live with Godwin and then gave birth to Craig's sister, Edy. She remained out of the theater until Craig was four, although one year before that his parents had separated and the boy did not see his father thereafter.

Ellen Terry returned to the theater for financial reasons, worried about the bailiff. In his autobiography, Craig bemoans his mother's financial situation as an actress at that time, since her engagements immediately after her return to the theater were short-lived and she worried about money. He also felt that his mother should have attempted to return to the theater in cooperation with his father, who subsequently made a reputation for himself in the theater as well as as an architect. Not until she worked with Henry Irving did she feel secure. Their theatrical association lasted for twenty-four years. During his childhood Craig was aware of his mother's uncertain conditions and vowed that some day he would establish a theater with permanence. While he worshiped Henry Irving for rescuing his mother, his oedipal fantasies were such that he wanted to do the same. He subsequently became an ardent disciple of Henry Irving.[3]

[3] Henry Irving was a true paternalistic figure. It is said of him that he had numerous pensioners on his list. This consisted of many actors who had worked with him and were unemployed or unemployable. He always held their hopes high by saying that something might turn up for them and gave them a weekly stipend.

Craig's long ambition, which was a sublimated elaboration of his oedipal wishes, was to have his own permanent theater where security for actors and experimentation with acting could be achieved. His concern for actors was a displacement of his wish to provide for and protect his mother's children. These wishes were derived from an identification with his mother and her theatrical interests and was reinforced by a positive oedipal wish to be the father who could guide and provide for his mother and her offspring. His memories of his early years are expressed in embittered statements as to why his mother had to leave him as a child, his resultant fear of the dark, and his longings for a father who would be there to guide him. All these mortifications were resolved by his reversing the roles and becoming the parent to his mother and then to actors in adult life. The addition of a strong paternal identification along with the necessary maternal identification seems to have enhanced Craig's directorial qualities so that the achievements in these areas were of permanent and monumental proportions.[4]

A VALIDATION FROM A HISTORICAL CHILD ANALYSIS

Earlier it was mentioned that the material from a historically famous child analysis would be reviewed and re-examined for the purposes of the current investigation of the psychology of

[4] Both Stanislavski and Craig discuss their obstinacy during childhood. Elsewhere it will be shown how Stanislavski utilized his aggression in the service of his artistic personality. The famous conductor, Bruno Walter, in his autobiography (1946), also discusses his obstinacy and describes the subsequent development of his aggression and obstinacy: "I have been able to muster up sufficient strength . . . expressing itself in obstinacy. . . . I frequently assumed a yielding attitude . . . in order to save all my fighting spirits for the uncompromising assertion of my artistic convictions." Obstinacy during childhood was a clear characteristic in the clinical cases that have been described. In all cases, the obstinacy seemed to be continued in their directorial activities and represented the neutralization and utilization of aggression in subsequent functioning as artistic leaders.

the director. It is the analysis of little Hans which was supervised, assayed, and described by Freud (1959). It is a well-known fact to many that little Hans became a prominent opera director.

Freud stated that little Hans had "two concluding phantasies, with which his recovery was rounded off. One of them, that of the plumber giving him a new and, as his father guessed, a bigger widdler" (p. 272); his other fantasy was the wish to be married to his mother and have many children by her. As for his father, "instead of killing his father, it made him innocuous by promoting him to a marriage with Hans's grandmother" (p. 273). Freud concludes, "With this phantasy both the illness and the analysis came to an appropriate end" (p. 273).

Not only did these fantasies end the analysis; they also represented the final resolution of Hans's oedipal conflict. The fantasies as quoted are so described in Freud's discussion. However, if we refer back to the case history and analysis, we can learn from the notes recorded by Hans's father more minute details that might be useful to our inquiry about the psychology of the director. These fantasies represent as detailed a description of oedipal wishes and identification as one ever gets in an adult analysis.

The father interpreted to little Hans his fantasy in which the plumber had given him the bigger widdler with the following comment: " 'Like Daddy's, because you'd like to be Daddy' " (p. 240). Hans replied, " 'Yes, and I'd like to have a moustache like yours and hairs like yours.' (He pointed to the hairs on my chest.)" (p. 240). This is a clear illustration of the boy's identification with his father as he emerges from his oedipal conflict.

The actual words of Hans's second fantasy are worthy of reexamination. "This morning I was in the W.C. with all my children. First I did lumf and widdled, and they looked on. Then I put them on the seat and they widdled and did lumf, and I wiped their behinds with paper. D'you know why? Because I'd so much like to have children; then I'd do everything for them—take them to the W.C., clean their behinds, and do everything one does with children" (p. 239). Here little Hans identifies with his mother's maternal role, which eventually became useful in his artistic work as a director.

Hans's father addressed an interesting postscript to Freud on the boy's case history. "'An unresolved residue remains behind; for Hans keeps cudgelling his brains to discover what a father has to do with his child, since it is the mother who brings it into the world'" (p. 242). To which Freud comments, "For the rest, our young investigator has merely come somewhat early upon the discovery that all knowledge is patchwork, and that each step forward leaves an unsolved residue behind" (p. 242). Freud, in his discussion of little Hans, does some knowledgeable patchwork. He points out that when Hans was overtaken by a wave of repression against his masturbation and by disgust toward excrement and of looking on at other people performing natural functions, "a certain amount of sublimation set in. From the time of the beginning of his anxiety Hans began to show an increased interest in music and to develop his inherited musical gift" (p. 279 n.). Freud has blended little Hans's oedipal fantasy of taking care of the excretory functions of his children with the sublimation into musical interest.

From the details of these fantasies and their subsequent sublimation, one can visualize that such a child could become an operatic director, with a bigger "widdler," moustache, and hair on his chest, like his father, who teaches, demonstrates, and integrates the vocal and dramatic and musical activities (via a displacement upward of the discharges of the excretory organs) of his performers (children), like a mother. Little Hans began with a negative oedipal wish in which he is identified with his mother. With his sublimation of the wishes to rear these children and via the successful resolution via his analysis of his oedipal conflict in which he finally identified with his father, he was subsequently able to fuse these two identifications in his lifework as an artistic director.

One factor that appears in little Hans also seems prevalent in most other examples of the artistic director. The director-to-be usually has a set of parents with a special arrangement of interests. The mother is usually intensely interested or endowed in an artistic area and the father is a man who integrates or directs the activities of others, either in artistic, intellectual, or business endeavors.

Gordon Craig's mother was Ellen Terry; his father was a famous architect. Stanislavski's maternal grandparents were the famous French actress, Vardy, and a well-known architect. His mother was highly interested in the arts; his father was a successful textile industrialist. Bruno Walter's father became a successful executive in a large silk concern. His mother was musically trained in piano and voice. His father was enamored of the mother's musical talent and encouraged Walter's career. The father of the director-producer patient was an industrial engineer, who had been a brilliant scholar; his mother has already been described as a devotee of the theater and a former operatic student. The orchestra conductor's mother was herself a highly gifted pianist and his father, a leading intellectual, religious writer, and scholar.

THE NONARTISTIC DIRECTOR

Two brief clinical examples of nonartistic directors are offered for purposes of comparison to the artistic directors. The first was a successful man whose interest was to take over the directorial management of existing businesses and who supplied jobs for all his older brothers. His unconscious wishes in these undertakings were to be submissive to older men and then annihilate them. This was based on his unresolved oedipal conflict with his father. This man, who married an actress, began to study acting with an eye to future possibilities of being able some day to buy a play which he himself might direct. Since his marriage, he occasionally ventured into producing plays and succeeded in arranging for some highly acclaimed artistic productions. Had he had an artistically oriented mother, in addition to the late-in-life exposure to the theater through his wife, one could justifiably surmise that he could readily have become a theatrical director and producer as a first and final choice.

The second was the director of the dental department of a large teaching hospital. He was the first born of three sons and the favorite of both his parents. In his oedipal fantasies he was the son of God, a priest, who was served by his younger brother. His father's attitude toward him was that the son was superior to himself. The mother always served him first and gave him the choicest and largest servings at mealtimes. Throughout his life he evidenced dictatorial attitudes, first toward his father and younger brothers, subsequently toward his fellow students and professional colleagues. His considerable directorial ability was impaired by his overaggressive dictatorial qualities which often led him into difficulties with his superior, his peers, and his subordinates. Neither the scientific nor the business director had a mother who displayed interests in any of the arts; both their fathers were successful in their communities in politics and business.

From the examples cited, the following formulations are suggested. The artistic director-to-be, as a child, designs his oedipal structure as one in which he takes the mother's place as heir to her children and their management; the final identification is often related to the idealization of the parents' interests in each other. Most often, as has been illustrated, the mother has an artistic interest or profession and the father's work involves integrating the functions or ideas of a group. More often than not, the father's love for the mother encompasses her appreciation or endowment in the arts. It is likely that the oedipal child subsequently displaces his interest in and envy of the sexual life between his parents onto the aesthetic interest and activities of the parents. This is increased during the postoedipal phase when the parental ego ideals become firmly established in the child's psychic structure. The identification with the ego-ideals derived from the parents' interests and ideals, as well as the sublimation of the child's sexual wishes and rivalry with the father, reinforce the child's own artistic endowment and drives toward a paternally influenced directorial career in a maternally influenced artistic world.

Biographical studies suggest that, when the father has been an actor or performing artist and the mother may or may not have been an actress, the male child more often will have the oedipal roots and resolution toward becoming an actor. It is understood that a child with extraordinary talent for original creating or directing will not be deterred from such a course because his father was a performer or his parents had little artistic endowment. The road might be more difficult because of incompatibility with ego-ideals and the obstructive attitude of the parents.[5] Much of what has been said applies to the male artistic director. The truth is that females rarely become conductors or directors. The female child who identifies with her mother has a more direct outlet in eventually rearing her own children and has less need to redirect such wishes to a directorial substitute.[6]

The oedipal development of the future director, which motivates him toward the role of directing and coordinating the

[5] Neither of Leonard Bernstein's parents had any musical or artistic endowment. His father bitterly opposed his plan for a musical career (Ewen, 1961). This was accomplished in spite of the unfavorable parental attitude and the absence of a stimulus toward music in the home.

[6] Greenacre has accounted for the absence of original creations by women and the emphasis on the performing arts (1960). The same psychological characteristic of the female castration complex and their capacity for biological creation contributes to the infrequency of female directors, artistic or otherwise.

artistic activities of others in a parent–child continuum, enhances and advances his artistic endowment. From the same oedipal ferment, the director is unconsciously motivated to take over the work of a dramatist or composer and bring it out in performance as if it were his own child whom he completely understood and thus may rear as he sees fit. A director, like a teacher, is aided in his work if he has maternal qualities. To transform these psychological ambitions and characteristics into an artistic achievement, the director must have special inherent endowments as well.

A drama director or musical conductor brings the written work of the dramatist or composer into an interpreted existence. Every drama and musical score that is original and artistic must be expressed in terms of aesthetic ambiguity which will permit for a varied and multiple cluster of aesthetic communication to the audience. Hence, no performance of a written work of art can be more than a single interpretation. The greatness of a director depends on his capacities to identify with the creator and to create in performance an optimal and original communication which enhances the author's creation without distorting it.

A director identifies with the contents of the created work and interests himself in communicating its contents. He is more identified with the dramatist or composer than with the audience. He re-creates the orginator's creative expression. If the director succeeds artistically in his interpretation, he must be endowed with "an intactness of sensorimotor equipment, allowing the building up of projective motor discharge for expressive function"[7] (Greenacre, 1957). In fact, he is required to have all the additional characteristics that are considered prerequisite for the creative artist. Thus, he must be endowed with greater than usual sensitivity to sensory stimuli; unusual capacity for awareness of relations between various stimuli;

[7] Greenacre, in her study on the childhood of the artist, elaborates the four essential basic endowments of the artist.

basic predisposition to an extraordinary empathy for external animate and inanimate objects. What he need not have is the capacity to create original works of art. In lieu of this, he utilizes his capacity for complete identification with the originator (similar to his identification with his mother) from whence he makes his own artistic contribution as a creator.[8]

Should the director or conductor have the additional good fortune to be endowed with the talent to create his own original works, he will have the advantage of being able to direct the performance of his own works, as well as those of others. Beginning with Shakespeare, the combination of playwright-director in a single person is not an uncommon phenomenon. The combination of composer-conductor is even more frequent, as exemplified by Mendelssohn, Berlioz, Liszt, Wagner, with Bernstein a current example.

The composer or dramatist who lacks the capacity to identify with his creation may well fail when conducting or directing his own works as well as those of others. He fails as director of his own work because once he has created the work it is no longer part of himself and he would need the ability to identify with the creator to perform his own works as well as those of others. Directors often succeed as performers when they have the additional endowment and training in the performing art.[9]

It has already been pointed out that actors often suffer from an undeveloped self-image and intensified conflicts around exhibitionism, whereas the dramatist has the tendency toward enactment (inclusive of acting out), from which he dissociates himself in his capacity as an artist and utilizes its content for

[8] Bruno Walter says of his contribution to music: "I have made only the music of others sound forth. I have been but a re-creator" (1946).

[9] Toscanini began as a cellist in an opera orchestra. When the conductor became ill and was unavailable, Toscanini was asked to conduct the orchestra; this incident marked the beginning of his career as conductor.

his dramas. The director's maternalistic oedipal wishes and parental characteristics have been described. Theoretically, a given individual may have an inadequate self-image—an exhibitionistic orientation and/or tendencies toward enactment, and/or the typical director's oedipal designs. Such an individual would be expected to be interested in all three aspects of the theater, i.e., actor, director, and dramatist. It would be of interest to determine whether psychobiographical studies of such men as Shakespeare and Molière, who had these three talents, would validate these formulations.

During the creation of a production the director, like the playwright, is regarded by the actors with the same emotional attitudes as children show toward a parent. If the dramatist is deceased or disconnected with the production, he may be regarded by the actors as an unseen immortal god who is consciously or unconsciously represented by the director toward whom these feelings of reverence and respect are transferred.[10] The dramatist–director relationship has many variations. Actual experience and reputation of either the director or the dramatist are often the crucial determinants of the working relationship between them. Thus the young dramatist who is acceptable to the established director, feeling overwhelmed and honored by the opportunity, takes a passive, submissive role in their mutual undertaking. Conversely,

[10] The paternalism of directors toward a theatrical group extends to the personal lives of the actors. Directors are wont to give parental advice and the most common abuse of this role occurs when directors take on the role of psychoanalyst for the actor. An anecdote illustrating the director's paternalism is told of Tomashevsky, who traveled far and wide throughout the United States with his Jewish group of actors. On the night of a great snowstorm in a small Midwest city, he peered through the curtain to estimate the size of the audience, which was no more than a handful. He turned to the actors gathered about him and said: "Children, America is a wonderful democracy and tonight we are in the majority!"

The extravagant paternalism of Henry Irving has already been described.

the young director who is acceptable to the established playwright approaches his assignment like a dutiful, submissive child. Yet, if he is to succeed as a director or conductor in his own right, it is essential that at the last moment he have his own sense of conviction and capacity for self-assertion to produce the drama or score from his own aesthetic orientation. His aggression must be in the service of his artistic functions.[11]

The psychological interplay among the dramatist (creator), director, and actor (performer) may be expressed in a simplified summation. The actor is the child in whom the parentally identified director has instilled the re-created essence of the work of the dramatist—the true parent.

These formulations on the development of the artistic director are offered as hypotheses which require additional validation by future clinical psychoanalytic investigations. The main disadvantage in dealing with the psychology and endowment of the drama director and the musical conductor, as if they were one and the same, is that beyond the features they have in common, the ultimate differences between their art media are not taken into consideration. Music is a nonverbal, auditory means of communication, most often performed on external instruments, with the exception of singers. Drama is verbal and written and, when performed, is spoken and acted. One would expect to find significant differences between the psychology of musicians and theatrical people, determined by the

[11] A current example in the field of conducting relates to the occasion when Leonard Bernstein, then an unknown assistant conductor, had to replace, on very short notice, the veteran guest conductor, Bruno Walter, at the New York Philharmonic Symphony Orchestra. Bernstein rushed to the bedside of the ailing master, who instructed him as thoroughly as he could in the short time left, how he had intended to interpret the various selections on the program. Bernstein, unnerved, listened as attentively as he could. However, when he stepped on the podium and tapped his baton, he was unable to remember what he had been told and began to conduct as he understood the music. This launched him on a new and brilliant career as an orchestral conductor.

differences in the two art forms, that are beyond the scope of this preliminary investigation.

One vital distinction between the drama director and conductor does belong within the scope of our explorations. The conductor is not only an integral part of the performance but is also most prominently on display. In this sense, he is always functioning in the dual role of performer and director. His body and his mind are his musical instruments. From the vantage of psychology, his exhibitionism and body image are additionally involved, in contrast to the dramatic director, who is not seen.

The justification for the combined investigation of artistic (and nonartistic) directors is that it offers sufficient common findings in early psychological development, particularly in the area of their oedipal design and parental identification, which could be useful in a general understanding of such personalities. It is of some value to have available a pattern of over-all development as one proceeds to the psychoanalytic investigation of the single individual.

4

The Critic

CREATIVE IMAGINATION IN THE THEATER is not confined to only those who originate, direct, and perform. Perhaps the most neglected member of the creative world has been the audience for whose consumption the work of art has always been intended. Understandably, the audience must be endowed with some form of creative capacities which lead to aesthetic responses to an artistic communication. The members of any given audience are so numerous and therefore so varied in their individual make-up that the aesthetic endowments of any single member selected at random would not adequately describe the remainder of the group.

Although the critic may not be typical of the audience, he may well be considered its representative. The exploration of the psychology of the critic may tell us much specifically about the creative nature of the critic as well as provide us with some indirect psychological insights into ourselves as members of an aesthetic audience.

Whatever else a critic may or should be, he is minimally expected to be a connoisseur. In any field of human activity, some are designated as critic or connoisseur by society. In preliterate society, the leader or the master was the connoisseur. The step from connoisseur to critic implies progression from knowledge to judgment. Connoisseurship is related to scholarship, and criticism superimposes the factor of judgmental values. Many fields of man's endeavor call on the critical connoisseur to play the role of historian, evaluator, judge, arbitrator, attributor, and interpreter.

When confined to the fields of artistic creativity, the critic must have a sound knowledge of man's art treasures, past and present. He must have the ability to identify the artist and his works, the skill and the knowledge to attribute unidentified treasures of art to the proper era and the proper artist. Ideally speaking, he should have insight into the nature of the artist and the creative process and how they are integrated. For these functions, it is apparent that psychological intuition or orientation would be desirable.

It is not uncommon for a critic to be devoid of creative powers in the given field of art he is serving. Critics are rarely creative as painters, and creative painters are rarely important as critics. Psychologically speaking, particular requirements are necessary for the function of the critic, since every creative artist would otherwise be the best candidate for the role of art critic. This is not the case. It is as uncommon to find in a single individual the combination of critic and creator as it is to find someone who is both critic and director. This is due to the critic's capacity to identify mainly with the creator's final communication and to his more restricted capacity to share in or identify with the artist's creative capacities which a director must do when he stages a re-creation of the artist's work. Shaw is a rare example of both artist and critic; he was considered a major dramatist but a mediocre drama critic (Bentley, 1957). He was an excellent music critic, and it is not surprising that he was not creative in the field of music. Shakespeare's genius enabled him to transcend the usual limitations of an artist. Only someone of Shakespeare's stature could be both playwright and actor, to say nothing of poet and director. However, even Shakespeare never functioned as critic. These data substantiate the validity of the concept that the critic's capacity to completely experience the artist's work does not extend itself into an equal capacity to be creative in the same art form. As we shall soon see, there are distinctive differences between the artist and the critic in their basic endowments.

There is no question that creative artists have much to tell us about the nature of art and the creative process. Their comments reflect their self-observed creative processes, which are valuable sources of information for other developing artists and their education. However, their criticism excludes consideration of aesthetic communication to the audience, which should be a field of interest to the critic. Arthur Miller, the renowned American playwright, recently remarked (1965), "I never learned anything from critics. They are for the public and not for artists." T. S. Eliot (1942) points out that a poem may have meanings to the reader which differ from those of the author.

The creative artist need not be a connoisseur in his field to be creative. The artist's knowledge of his field may be confined to his awareness of its constituents, but need not be organized into scholarships. The works of his contemporaries or predecessors do not communicate to the artist the usual responses evoked in critics and expert audiences. Along with other experiences in life, the works of other artists stimulate activity in the direction of new creation in a creative person. The artist's subsequent response to his own creation is unique. It does not stir him to a re-creation as it does the critic and the responsive audience. Rather it occupies the position of a past experience subject to all the psychological laws of memories, inclusive of residual instinctual elements, the distortions of screen memories, and typical defenses. When confronted by his own creations, an artist may be able to revive the original creative experience, particularly the inspirational phase, rather than re-create in the manner of the audience. The artist's successive reactions to his creations may be compared to the change from parents' enthusiasm for the newborn to the later feeling for an offspring who has learned to go its own way. Central to the artist's nature is the process of original creation, so that his responses to his creations as well as those of others are quickly redirected to a new creative possibility and do not achieve a full elaboration as in the case of the audience.

Both artist and audience have often expressed the view that they could well do without the critic, who, they feel, frequently functions as an obstructive middleman in matters that are strictly between them. The organized scholarship of the critic, which is or should be greater than that of the artist or audience, is perhaps the crucial factor justifying his existence. A critic, unhampered by the urge to be creative in the given artistic medium in which he functions as critic, is in a better position than the artist to receive the full impact of another person's creative communications. Thus he is better able to evaluate and pass judgment on them. It is not remarkable to find that connoisseurs and critics contribute little to the creative commonwealth of their given art form. They rarely give birth to artistic creation in the same field. Coincidental and unevaluated is the fact that many renowned critics have also been biologically childless.

Samuel Johnson, Pope, Sainte-Beuve, Macaulay, Pater, Ruskin, Lamb, Berenson, Beerbohm, Shaw, Mencken, George Jean Nathan are some examples. These twelve childless critics emerge from a random sampling of fourteen famous critics. Of the remainder, Emerson had two wives and four children; Addison had one child who appears to have been mentally defective.[1] The biological childlessness of critics is not vital to the present thesis. It merely accentuates the possibility that the childless state of the critic may extend from his personal to his artistic self. It might be fruitful to study the childhood

[1] I am indebted to Miss Barbara Braun for researching this information.

of the childless critic to see if this state was psychologically overdetermined and how it could be correlated with the subsequent choice of becoming a critic. Biographies of critics should be studied to reveal the nature of their oedipal conflicts. One solution which might be predicted is the surrender of their own procreative wishes, which would then permit them to be both curious about and aggressively critical of their creative parents.

According to Kris, it is estimated that the critic's response to an artist's work is a re-creation of a semblance of the artist's original experience (Kris, 1952). He also suggests that the critic's attitude toward a creator's work may extend in its possibilities from an identification with the creator to rival of the creator, to father and prophet of the creator. These formulations are still deductive suppositions concerning the psychology of the critic; they are derived not from psychoanalytic studies of the lives of critics but rather from clinical hunches which are woven into a theoretical reconstruction of the psychological process in the idealized critic. Critics often behave as if they have incorporated rather than experienced a creative work and subsequently respond as if the engulfed creation is their own and the original work is neither identifiable nor attributable to its original creators. All these reactions on the part of the critic may have their counterpart in the primitive psychological phenomenon of the couvade, in which the male develops the state and feelings of the pregnant female and behaves as if the creative process, biologically impossible for him, is going on within rather than outside himself. In such cases, the sensations, signs, and symptoms of pregnancy are points of departure from the procreative phenomenon with which they are associated; the male has incorporated into himself the female's state of pregnancy at the expense of an empathic reaction to her newly created transformation.

Other psychoanalytic writers have also suggested that the expert spectator and the critic re-create a semblance of the artist's original experience. Another view is that the artist forces his view on his recipient by identifying with him (Schneider, 1954). There is little doubt that the artist–critic relationship calls for mutual identifications of one with the other. However, to account for all the factors involved in the critic's response to a creative work as an exclusive interchange between artist and critic remains a facile and broad account of more complex phenomena that must be involved. The critic's response to a work of art also partakes of an interchange between the audience and himself.

The connoisseur or critic first makes a preconscious or unconscious identification with the artist, to whom he makes an aesthetic response. His identification with the artist then reaches consciousness. It is my impression that the ultimate function of the critic is his ability to make conscious to the spectator what the latter has experienced preconsciously or unconsciously. To achieve this end, the critic must have an identification with the audience, so that he may actively communicate to them what they have passively experienced.[2] We should bear in mind that, in his historical origin, the critic was a leader of the people rather than of the artists. Professional critics are attuned to a given audience's interests and mode of enjoyment. They make their evaluations in accordance with a specific image of the audience they represent.[3] They attempt to minimize (with varying degrees of success) their very personal responses to a creative work and to serve the collective image of their audiences. The reviewer, such as a music or drama critic of a newspaper, serves the collective

[2] The role of the critic, according to Kris, is to explain the process within the artist by means of his interest in the artist's actual experience and biography; such explanation deepens the understanding of the artist's work.

[3] It has been suggested that art is consciously or unconsciously addressed to an expert audience. In urbanized civilization, art lovers are a small, elite group, distinct in social status, mores, and language.

image of the audience consciously; the scholarly critic identifies himself unconsciously with his audience.

An estimate of the conscious and unconscious processes of artist, audience, and critic at best can be only roughly achieved. The artist may deliberately permit himself to regress to a lessened state of consciousness in which unconscious derivatives reach his awareness. He then utilizes and elaborates the unconscious content in his creative work.[4] In reverse, the audience proceeds from a conscious perception of the work of art to a preconscious elaboration, which subsequently reverberates in its unconscious. Similarly, the critic proceeds from a conscious perception to a preconscious infiltration and unconscious responses. At this point, the ideal critic goes beyond the reaction of the audience. He assimilates and synthesizes his unconscious responses and experiences to the given artistic communication. Viewed from the field of aesthetics, he measures the total communication from standards of correspondence, interest, and coherence for subsequent appraisal of the aesthetic experience. He must also evaluate the degree of completeness and integration of the aesthetic product. A critic approximates the state of optimal functioning when his aesthetic evaluation encompasses and communicates an integrated account of both the artist's and audience's conscious, preconscious, and unconscious participation in a creative experience.

What is the essential equipment for an ideal critic? To detail this may present great difficulties in view of the multiple functions of a critic and the changing emphasis on the major functions of art and criticism. In the latter days of the era of classical art, the function of attribution was emphasized. It was deemed necessary that rediscovered art treasures of earlier centuries be properly identified as to their period and, whenever possible, assigned to the authoritative artists. Psy-

---

[4] Kris has termed this process regression in the service of the ego.

choanalysis has stressed the similarity between the artist's creative powers and woman's creative powers in childbirth. In this sense, one might acknowledge that the prototype art critic was King Solomon, who, like the art critic, had to solve a problem of attribution of the infant who was biologically claimed by two women. With intuitive insight into the psychology of the creative process of motherhood, his plan to divide and thus destroy the infant evoked the protest of the true mother, who was willing to give up her creation rather than see it destroyed. Like the art critic who is able to identify himself with the creative person without being one, King Solomon was able to identify himself with the feelings of a mother and thus devise a solution in which true criteria for ownership could be established and accurately attributed.

Problems of plagiarism and falsification still confront classical connoisseurs of art. In the current romantic era of art, both artist and critic promulgate the view that art shall gratify and express an individual's inner life. Here the critic as well as the artist must be attuned to man's capacity for unconscious communication. For the critic of classical art, attribution is the problem of identifying the proper artist of the past with a remaining work of art. For the critic of romantic art, attribution is the problem of finding the inner part of the artist's life that belongs to the given work under consideration; such criticism can deepen our understanding of the artist and his work.[5]

The critic and the audience must have aesthetic capacities and endowments which enable them to respond to works of art. In the preceding chapters, the basic characteristics of various types of creative artists have been detailed. To understand better the differences between artist and critic, it may be useful to specify the line of demarcation between their respective endowments and equipments. For the creative

[5] In the change from classicism to romanticism, psychoanalysis has played an increasingly influential role in the fields of art and art criticism.

artist, Greenacre (1957) has postulated four general characteristics: (1) greater sensitivity to sensory stimuli; (2) unusual capacity for awareness of relations between various
stimuli; (3) basic predisposition to an empathy of wider
range than average—the empathy to extend from one's own
body to external objects and a peculiar empathic animation of
inanimate objects; (4) an intactness of sensorimotor equipment, permitting the building up of projective motor discharge
for expressive function.

The first part of the third prerequisite is an unusual empathy
which extends from one's own body to an external object. This
would be a prerequisite for functioning in the romantic concept of art, in which the individual is emphasized. The second
part of the third prerequisite calls for a capacity for a "peculiar empathic animation of inanimate objects," which seems
to be close to the nature of classical art, in which the external
world, as distinguished from man's inner world, is emphasized.
Whether empathic for one's own body or for inanimate objects,
these traits seem to be prerequisites equally for artist, critic,
and audience in both classical and romantic art.

Certainly the fourth prerequisite, projective motor discharge
for expressive function, is not essential for the critic, since
this represents the specific equipment of the artist's capacity
to create original works. Greenacre's first two requirements,
which relate to high sensitivity to stimuli and to the relationship between stimuli, are to be found in the expert audience
and the critic. The expert critic must have a higher sensitivity
than the artist to the interrelatedness of stimuli. The artist
must have the ability to create works expressed in aesthetic
ambiguities, but often enough only the critic will have the
capacity to elaborate the given ambiguities into more variations than the artist could conceive.

Therefore, the critic does not require the highest capacity
for projective motor discharge for expression function, but he
does require a high degree of sensitivity to sensory stimuli

and to the relationships among such stimuli. This capacity must be so developed that he can absorb an artist's communication and disperse its contents into the depths of his own unconscious. Then he must reintegrate the unconscious communication into an expert statement of the effects of the artist's communication on the audience. The artist's task is confined to communication to his recipient. He is not responsible for an accounting of what transpires in the audience. With such a status of sensitivity to sensory stimuli, we may well understand that such faculties might be organized in the critic by means of various autonomous functions which promote his curiosity, knowledgeability, and scholarship in a given area of artistic interest.

The manner in which a critic identifies himself with the artist is important, for the effects of such identifications are crucial when the critic is dealing with the biography of an artist. Freud warned of the pitfalls of unconsciously determined idealization of the artist by the critic, which results in an artificial reconstruction of the artist. He writes that

> [B]iographers are fixated on their heroes in quite a special way. In many cases they have chosen their heroes as the subjects of their study because—for reasons of their own personal life—they have felt a special affection for him from the first. . . . They thus present us with what is in fact a cold, strange, ideal figure instead of a human being to whom we might feel ourselves distantly related. That they should do this is regrettable; for they thereby sacrifice truth to illusion, and for the sake of their infantile phantasies abandon the opportunity of penetrating the most fascinating secrets of human nature (Freud, 1957, p. 130).

A danger opposite to that of excessive idealization occurs when "the biographer displaces his unconscious hostile feelings on to the subject of his biography—ironically evident in some popular biographies of Freud" (Beres, 1959). Not only are such excessive identifications ("overhostile" and "overloving") pitfalls for the critic, but they are equally hazardous for the artist who may be creating a drama, a novel, an epic poem, a painting, or a sculpture based on the life of a great man.

An inspirational response can reside in the critic for some time and may subsequently be elaborated by him with the aid of his connoisseurship of the given art, the particular artist, his collected works, and the specific work under consideration. Criticism may be as original as art itself. The critic fulfills a creative function when he can transform the audience's immediate implicit responses into a more permanent explicit appreciation and understanding.

Our psychological exploration of the critic views him as unhampered by creative urges in his critical field. While the critic may be limited in his endowments to originate in the areas of his connoisseurship, he may have a greater capacity than the artist for awareness of relatedness among sensory stimuli which reside in and emanate from works of art. Psychoanalytically uninvestigated but phenomenologically suggestive is the speculation that the critic's noncreativity may be rooted in psychological childhood determinants, since critics are often childless in their adult lives. If a critic is blessed with keen psychological intuition, he can enrich us with deeper creative insights into the aesthetic response of the audience of which he is ultimately a member.

5

The Psychobiographical
Approach to Creativity
in the Theater

UNTIL NOW OUR AIM in the investigation of creative imagination in the theater has been to go beyond generalizations regarding the artistic personality. By confining our interest to the theater we have been forced to focus exclusively on the theater artist rather than the artist in general. By separating the artist of the theater into actor, director, and dramatist we were further pressed to confine our generalizations to the specific common denominators applicable in each category. To achieve these formulations a mixture of clinical and biographical examples of each variation of theater artist has been compared. Needless to say, no two actors or playwrights are psychologically identical.

Classical psychoanalytic methodology is one in which the single individual is investigated for the purpose of reconstructing specific infantile and later experiences and interpreting the complex and the pathogenic reactions to them. Traditional analysis focuses on the patient beyond his general type of neurosis, oedipal conflict, or sublimation. It emphasizes his individual breed of neurosis and the personal stamp of his oedipal conflict. Individuality rather than generality, whenever possible, is the goal of psychoanalytic work and insight. No two fathers or mothers are exactly alike, nor does a given combination of parents ever repeat itself. It is well established that the mother or father is a different parent to each of their various children. The firstborn has different meanings to different parents; their attitudes are derived from their own position among their siblings and their relationship to their own parents. Every psychoanalytic therapy acknowledges and accounts for these individual idiosyncrasies. Eventually every clinical entity, be it neurosis, psychosis, delinquency, or psychopathy, must be analyzed finally in terms of a given patient within whom such an entity is found. Similarly, any study of mental processes, such as a study of creative imagination, must be understood finally from the individual life of a genuine artist in whom these creative capacities are found.

We shall next be exploring the lives of four personalities involved in the theater. Since we shall deal with their personal lives, the approach approximates biography. Because we shall also be estimating the personality structure, the conflicts (which need not be neurotic), and the unconscious determinants in their creative works, the orientation stimulates a psychoanalytic study. Thus the fusion of the two methods may be considered as psychobiographical studies.

Psychobiographical studies differ from ordinary biographical studies in their apparent disregard for correlating the personal events at any given time in the artist's life and the creative works of the same era. Whereas biographies stress such a correlation, psychoanalytically oriented biographies attempt to go beyond these immediate connections. As in psychoanalysis itself we are in constant search for unconscious determinants. Although matters of the present also contain unconscious determinants, we extend our interest to earlier periods of the artist's life, particularly his childhood. Here we often find repressed material which forms the dynamic nucleus of the origins of many of the artist's works and which may even cover the span from the beginning to the end of his artistic career.

Psychobiographical studies may seem to lack the slavishness to chronological orderliness and the organization of separation between the personal and artistic life. The psychobiographical approach may lack the voluminous completeness of representational biographical portraiture, since it aims for a more dynamic and economic statement of essential portrayal of the fusion between the personal and the artistic life. A psychobiographical investigator does not overlook the totality of biographical data. He preferentially states only that which appears to be vital and pertinent to the area of his specific investigation. He does not exclude biographical facts because they contradict his formulation; apparent contradictions must be accounted for in plausible psychological explanations.

Psychobiographers are also careful to assess the accuracy of biographical facts associated with an outstanding personality. Awaiting the biographer is the pitfall that a personal myth has been elaborated about or by the outstanding figure which distorts his realistic image. The most common distortion of the artist concerns his ascent from humble origins and the dramatic discovery of his artistic gifts in childhood. There is the true story of the literary figure who was shown the manuscript of his biography, about to be published. He commented that all the facts were accurate, but it did not seem to him that it had ever happened this way.

Finally, the psychobiographer has accepted the clue proposed by Freud that historians, biographers, and critics, in order to gratify a revived infantile concept of the father, may unconsciously overidealize their subject and thus distort their portrait, evaluation, or appraisal of him. These warnings were uttered by Freud in his psychobiographical study, *Leonardo da Vinci and a Memory of His Childhood,* published in 1910. Freud's study of Leonardo was a pioneering effort in psychobiography and posed many new unsuspected questions about the artist's personality. According to Meyer Schapiro (1956), the art historian, no better answers than Freud's of fifty years ago have as yet been given to these questions.

Psychoanalytic biography, therefore, was an early and natural outgrowth of psychoanalysis. It has been said that "biographical reconstruction is an inherent aim of the psychoanalytic process, and psychoanalysis as a genetic psychology is in essence a science of biography" (Beres, 1959). Psychobiographies of artists are concerned with reconstructions of aspects of their lives that would be either not available or not stressed in the conventional biography.

Some authors have minimized the significance of psychoanalytic formulations on the creative personality and creative imagination which are derived from psychobiographical sources of deceased artists. They argue that the free associations and the dreams of the artist would be required, as they are in analytic therapy, to authenticate any psychoanalytic interpretations.

There is little to be hoped for in these areas if we must rely solely on the knowledge that would emerge from the clinical psychoanalysis of artists who are patients. Artists do not undergo analytic treatment in order to learn the nature of their creativity or the unconscious determinants of their created work. Since they are patients, the analyst is mainly involved with their pathological conflicts. Only if such conflicts touch on the artist's creativity does the analysis deal with the artist's creativity. In actual practice the analysis may or may not involve the artist's creative process. Hence the findings from clinical practice tend to be sporadic and incomplete. The psychobiographical study of the deceased artist permits the analyst to consider primarily and more freely the artist's creativity.

In the four ensuing chapters, we shall attempt to advance our understanding of the actor, the dramatist, and the director by the added evidence of individual psychobiographical

studies. In addition, we shall aspire to understand from these
individual studies what developmental factors led to success
in one and failure in another. We shall also attempt to understand the unconscious biographical determinants in the lives
of two dramatists that influenced the creations of a few specific
dramas.

II

The Actor's Psychobiography: Some Predeterminants of Creative Success and Failure

6

Stanislavski:

Fame and Success

THE NAME STANISLAVSKI is to the art of acting what Shakespeare is to the art of playwriting.[1] In the broadest outline, from the beginning of this century, Stanislavski was the guiding genius of the Moscow Art Theatre until the 1930's when he was forced into semiretirement by a heart ailment. He died in 1938 at the age of seventy-five. The Moscow Art Theatre has been described as "perhaps the greatest acting unit the world has ever known." For forty years Stanislavski was, not only its codirector and guiding force, but also one of its chief actors. Stanislavski's most celebrated achievement is the development of a theory and system of dramatic acting and teaching referred to as the "Stanislavski Method."[2]

[1] John Gielgud, in an introduction to one of Stanislavski's three books, *An Actor Prepares* (1936, p. x) has aptly stated, "He is Olympian, a specialist in every department of the theatre, who cares so passionately for his art that he wishes to bequeath something from his great store of experience and knowledge to anyone who cares to read what he has set down."

[2] This theory, briefly stated, emphasizes that it is essential for the actor to enter the lives of the characters he portrays, as thoroughly as possible in order to understand their emotions and personalities.

The psychoanalyst, interested in creative imagination, turns to psychobiography and, in Stanislavski's case, finds that many positive factors contributed to the development of his great talent and lifelong productivity. Stanislavski's life suggests that the notion an artist must suffer to create is wrong. One should rather say that an artist will suffer only if creativity is hindered by environmental or developmental factors. Art and neuroses are not synonymous; a study of the artist's life need not be a study of pathography; favorable developmental and environmental factors may further the fuller discharge of creative capacity. While his conflicts need not be pathological, there is no implication that the artist's life evolves without conflict. Frequently his personal conflicts are intimately interwoven in his creations.[3]

There is every indication that in our attempt to advance in the study of creative imagination and artistic talent, we must leave the safety and security of the exclusive preoccupation with an individual's pathological conflicts. We must investigate how the artist functions in spite of his conflicts, reactive to his conflicts, and utilizing his conflicts. We must therefore turn to the period when conflicts begin to develop: to the artist's early childhood.

Konstantin Stanislavski was born in 1863. From his autobiography (1924), I quote the following description of his parents and family life.

They were home-loving people. My mother spent all her time in the nursery, devoting herself completely to her children—and there were ten of us. My father, until his marriage, slept in the same bed with his father, who was famous for his old-fashioned patriarchal method of life. After his marriage, my father passed

---

[3] But it is also possible for the artist to adopt (and adapt), by identification, another's tragedy which he need not have experienced himself. Kris pointed that out, e.g., Prince Hal's conflict went far beyond any personal experience of Shakespeare's.

to his [own] conjugal couch, where he slept to the end of his days, and where he died. My parents loved each other when they were young and when they were old. They loved their children and tried to keep them as near themselves as they could (p. 23).

This description of Stanislavski's family life certainly portrays a background of reasonably sound maternal care and parental accord. Perhaps most fundamental and crucial in all these factors was the nature of the early maternal relationship. Greenacre is of the opinion that the infancy of the gifted person or genius is characterized by an early and marked sensitivity to sensory stimulation from the primary object (the mother's breast). She states, "We might conceive that the potentially gifted infant would react to the mother's breast with an intensity of the impression of warmth, smell, moisture, the feel of the texture of the skin and the vision of the roundness of the form, according to the time and nature of the experience" (Greenacre, 1957, p. 57). We would then suppose that it is most fortunate when an optimally endowed infant has in addition the loving and nurturing care of the mother. This particular combination may produce one type of genius who as a child is readily recognized as a prodigy, then shows subsequent fulfillment (young genius), and a final maturing, developing, uninterrupted creative expression throughout his life. This would certainly be true of Stanislavski's life.

This is not to be understood as a belief that a good nurturing mother, or being a favorite child, creates a talent or genius. Nor is it intended to indicate that a poor mother can destroy a potential talent. Perhaps we are saying no more than this: the early and full functioning of a creative talent can be enhanced by such an optimal relationship. Greenacre makes the point that fortunate is the potentially gifted person who has a suitable father with whom to identify. I would again add that it might even be the ultimate of good fortune for the gifted

one to have not only such a father but also a mother with
whom the earliest object relationship is optimal. Stanislavski
was thus doubly blessed.

His mother had been deserted by her own mother and left
with her father whose second wife became a good stepmother
to her. Perhaps her own early experience motivated her to become a good mother. The fact that Stanislavski's father slept
with his own father until he married suggests that Stanislavski's
father may also have experienced the loss of a mother through
death, divorce, or illness and that such a deprivation may have
accentuated his development as a home-loving, family-devoted
man and father.

Having a wealthy father is frequently a disadvantage to a
son. The father's wealth and success, by representing paternal
potency to the son, often threaten the maintenance of the resolution of the Oedipus conflict in adult life. Moreover, parental
wealth often robs both the child and the parent of realistic
preparations for the child's independent future. Stanislavski's
father was a rich man, the owner of a mercantile firm that was
a hundred years old. The generation of his parents was in the
first stage of a cultural revolution—the creation of the Russian
intelligentsia, which was completed in Stanislavski's generation. His parents had already crossed the threshold of culture.
In spite of the lack of higher education in the tradition of the
aristocracy, they were privately educated and "made much of
culture their own. In the transition, the educated, cultured but
impoverished aristocracy hesitatingly mixed with wealthy merchants who became the conscious creators of the new life.
Numberless schools, hospitals, asylums, nurseries, learned so-
cieties, museums and art institutions were founded by their
money, their initiative and even their creative effort. They
made money in order to spend it on social and artistic institutions" (Stanislavski, 1924, p. 12).

In his autobiography (1924), Stanislavski then tells about

the ideals that his parents' generation of merchants created for his own generation.

> We, the children of the great fathers and creators of Russian life, tried to inherit from them the difficult art of being able to be rich. To know how to spend money is a very great art. . . . The majority of our generation of rich people received a good education and were acquainted with world literature. We were taught many languages. We traveled very extensively and, in a word, we were plunged into the very heart of the maelstrom of culture. Having become equal in education to the nobles and aristocrats, class distinctions disappear as if of themselves (p. 23).

In this state of cultural flux, to be the artistically gifted son of a culturally-minded merchant has the aura of a blessed event. To have a son who not only might perpetuate the cultural heritage as a filial duty, but who also could enrich the entrusted culture, must have been the rare fulfillment of a father's own unfulfilled aspirations and fantasies. Such a father will supply all available resources and energies at his command to stimulate a child's first expression of talent. Conversely, for the gifted child, the awareness that one's natural inclinations are rewarded by parental love reinforces one's innate powerful energies.

Stanislavski's talents contributed to the happy solution of his oedipal conflicts. His dramatic play in childhood won his father's approval. Thus his early exploits did not make him his father's rival in these areas. Rather, he felt subservient to his father's wishes. In addition, he had his mother's admiration; she also loved the theater. In an earlier chapter it has been suggested that an artistically oriented mother and an executively oriented father seem to be the characteristic parental combination for the artistic director. Stanislavski gave evidence of his directorial leanings quite early in life.

In his teens, Stanislavski produced amateur theatricals in his

home which he both directed and acted in. His father, older
brothers, and older sisters usually were members of his cast.[4]
In the dramatic world of his home, he was the precocious
patriarch from an early age. In Stanislavski's home, as in the
homes of rich Russians, the custom of the domestic theater
flourished. The domestic theater was often part of a wealthy
man's estate. Here dramatic productions were given by a cast
consisting of the members of the family and the servants.[5]

Stanislavski's home had such a theater wing, and his earliest
memories concern his first stage performance between the ages
of two and three.[6] He recalls that the production consisted of
executing tableaus of the four seasons of the year. In the first
scene, the stage floor was covered with cotton representing
snow. He was dressed in a fur hat and coat and wore a beard
and was told to sit motionless on the floor. During the scene
he felt embarrassed, bashful, and frightened. His performance
was greeted by a round of applause which he liked. After this
he was again put on the stage in a different pose. A lit candle
was placed in a small bundle of branches to produce the effect
of fire. He was given a piece of wood and told to pretend that

[4] Magarshack (1951) states that Stanislavski was the second oldest of
the ten children. He was two years younger than his brother Vladimir.
His sister Zina was two years younger than himself; Anna the next sister
was born a year later.

[5] This too was part of the cultural revolution. Prior to this period these
domestic theaters were found only on the estates of the nobility. This
institution originated at the time of Tsar Alexander, in the latter half of
the nineteenth century. He assigned an alien pastor, Gregori by name, to
organize a dramatic group of young people. Performances had the character of church mysteries and were given in the palace for the nobility.

[6] Magarshack (1951) places the stage incident between the age of five
and six years. His source of information is the untranslated memoirs of
Stanislavski's sister Anna. The latter states that the family had no domestic theater until Stanislavski was of the above-mentioned age. She
states that she also acted in this "production" and was then two years old.
It is quite possible that this is a screen memory of Stanislavski's (as well
as his sister's). However, the memory would have different implications
for each of them.

he was putting it into the fire. He was warned that it was only make-believe and not real and that he was not to bring the wood close to the candle. He writes: "Why should I only make believe when I could really put the wood in the fire? And perhaps that was what I had to do, just because I was forbidden to do it?" (1924, p. 24).

As the curtain rose, he put the wood toward the candle. He explains that it felt easy and pleasant to do this, for there was meaning to the motion. Subsequently the cotton caught fire and in the midst of great excitement he was "unceremoniously lifted from the stage and carried into the big house where I was severely scolded. In short, I had failed cruelly, and the failure was not to my taste" (p. 24).

There is every indication in this memory that Stanislavski already felt himself to be more the bad actor than the bad child. The impression is that he was little concerned with his misbehavior and with having started a fire that brought on his head the admonition of his elders. He writes: "These four impressions of the pleasure of success, of the bitterness of failure, of the discomfort of unreasonable presence on the stage, and the inner truth of reasoned presence and action on it, control me on the stage even at the present day" (p. 24).

It becomes quite evident that an "artistic ego" was already in operation and seemed to relegate the "personal ego" of the child to a secondary significance. In what follows I shall show that this pattern persists throughout Stanislavski's life. His personal life was completely subjugated to his artistic life. For the moment, it is to be noted that the nucleus of a total psychic structure was being laid down in relation to the "artistic ego." His feelings of pleasure in success (self-esteem) and bitterness over failure (superego disapproval) as an actor illustrate the early formation of an artist's superego and ego-ideals. His impressions of "discomfort of unreasonable presence on stage and the inner truth of reasoned presence and actions on it" bespeak an ego which discriminatingly rejected and approved of the various artistic emanations of his instinctual drives. Other instances will be cited which illustrate that Stanislavski's acting served the role of sanctioning his aggressive drives throughout his life.

We have already mentioned that via acting he dominated his father and older brother in addition to the rest of his family. Thus, through acting and directing, Stanislavski in later life was able to express his obstinate revolt against old methods of acting, as in earlier life he expressed his superiority over his older siblings and father without feelings of guilt. The stage incident at the age of two or three years appears in his memoirs in a chapter entitled, "Struggle with Obstinacy." He then recounts two other incidents of obstinacy[7] directed against his father which occurred off stage. In these battles he surrendered in obedience to his father. The life of the stage became the area in which his ego constantly accepted revolutionary departures from orthodox acting. However, these innovations had to meet the high requirements of his own standards and ideals. A nonconformist in his personal life, he was a rebel in his life of art.[8]

Throughout Stanislavski's childhood, most of his play had the quality of stage acting. During his mid-latency period, he spent Sundays organizing a circus. He had an orchestra, a ballet master, and actors—his friends, brothers, and sisters. Yet his play acting also permitted the expression of a personal fantasy, as ordinary play of children would. This is clearly illustrated in the following description: "The ballet was called 'The Naiad and the Fisherman' and I did not like it. It called for the representation of love, it was necessary to kiss someone and I was ashamed. What I wanted was to kill, to save, to

[7] Obstinacy is a common characteristic of various artistic directors (see Chapter 3).

[8] Beres (1959) refers to the dissociation of the ego in the creative person. That part which deals with drives directed toward the creative function operates less restrictedly than the personal part of the ego.

sentence, to pardon" (Stanislavski, 1924, p. 49). But he was even more dissatisfied that this was not theater in the absence of costumes and scenery, and so he switched to a marionette theater with "scenery effects and a full line of theatrical necessities." The artistic need for real theater was greater than the personal need of an outlet for aggressive fantasies. In describing his games of war with his friends, he shows great appreciation of the beautiful costumes of the enemy Persian armies, the blowing of the hunters' horn, the imitated Persian headdress.[9]

One of the most amusing illustrations of the precedence of art over personal life is set forth in Stanislavski's autobiography in a chapter entitled "Marriage." This is a ten-page affair in which Stanislavski discusses his theatrical undertakings in the Society of Art and Literature, elaborating on the different plays that he did that season. He continues to discuss the technical acting problem of body restraint. As yet he has mentioned nothing in relation to a personal romance and the chapter is almost completed. Four paragraphs before the end he still ardently discusses his struggle with the problem of body restraint in the roles of Don Juan and Don Carlos when we come on the following:

> It is a pity that the next role I attempted that season was, if not Spanish in verses, still so long in boots, sword, love speeches and high style. I played the part of Ferdinand in the tragedy of Schiller, *Villainy and Love*. Louisa was played by M. P. Perevozchikova whose stage name was Lilina, the same amateur actress who, in spite of society's opinion, came to act with us. It seems that we were in love with each other, but did not know it, but we were told of it by the public. We kissed each other too

[9] Again we note that play acting and stage acting serve as an outlet for his aggressive drives. In an earlier clinical study, I attempted to differentiate normal repetitive (autonomous) play in early childhood from pregenital compulsive (nonautonomous) behavior and compulsive symptoms. The conclusions of this study have relevance to the current issues, i.e., the creative part of the ego ("artistic ego") is related to more autonomous activities.

naturally and our secret was an open one to the public. In this performance I played less with technique than with intuition, but it is not hard to guess who inspired us, Apollo or Hymen. Right after the performance, there appeared willing matchmakers. In the spring at the end of the first season of the Society of Art and Literature, I was declared a bridegroom and on July 5 was married. Then we went on a honeymoon and returned in the autumn to the theatre with the news that my wife could not fulfill her duties in the theatre during all of next year. Everybody will understand why (Stanislavski, 1924, p. 177).

The last three paragraphs of the chapter on marriage refer to the technical problem of acting and the problems of the Society of Art and Literature. Only one more reference to his personal life appears in a single sentence. Referring back to the play *Villainy and Love*, he writes, "Could we, after the marriage, as man and wife, still possess the same artistic technique and inspiration that we possessed until our engagement?" (Stanislavski, 1924, pp. 177–178).

We might measure the ratio of artistic life to personal life in the proportions of the two paragraphs of personal life in the ten-page chapter called "Marriage." Stanislavski had a gigantic romance with the world and a rather stable, affectionate, unheralded personal romance. This often seems to be the pattern in genius and highly creative talent of the more mature and stable type. His romance with the world may have played a role in his integration in the new political regime. In his autobiography, he viewed the revolution from the viewpoint that it produced a new kind of audience—the working man. His new audience interested and intrigued him, and he delighted in their numbers, their characteristics, and their enthusiasm. The domestic theater of his childhood staffed with actors from both rich landowners and servants had early made them equal citizens in his world of art.

Viewing this from a developmental rather than a biographical angle, we are dealing with the problem of the capacity of the potentially highly creative infant to shift and readily extend his relationship from the primary object (the mother's breast) onto the "alternate objects" in the world about that are similar to the original object. This arrangement becomes the prototype for the subsequent love affair that the creative person has with the world. Following Greenacre's hypothesis, an inordinate amount of sensitivity is required in the equipment of such a special person. The following examples and illustrations of Stanislavski's childhood experiences meet the above-stated criteria.

I have already mentioned the episode of Stanislavski's first stage experience. He had exquisite, elaborate emotional responses to the acting situation, which were retained intact and integrated and connected with his work throughout his life. He writes of early memories: "If I am not to reckon my memories of my own christening, which I created after the stories of my nurse in my mind that even until now I consider myself a conscious witness to that ceremony" (Stanislavski, 1924, p. 23). High sensitivity, universal awareness of interrelation of stimuli, wide empathic capacity to the nurse and his own body reactions and sensations, and the subsequent functional expressive discharge are coordinately contained in these reminiscences. He adds, "What I remember best are the emotions which I lived through in the period of my struggle with obstinacy and not so much the facts that caused them" (p. 23). His autobiography is studded with examples of sensitive sensory stimulation in his personal life.

Similar extraordinary responses are to be seen in his early childhood to experiences of artistic nature that he witnessed—the circus, theater, opera, ballet, etc. I quote the first paragraph of the chapter "Value of Childhood Impressions," which illustrates the above and needs no explanatory comments.

My brother and I were taken to the Italian opera in our earliest childhood, when we were six or at most eight years old. And I am very thankful to my parents, for I have no doubt that it acted beneficially on my musical hearing, on the development of my taste and eye which grew used to the beautiful. We had season tickets which entitled us to be present at forty or fifty performances, and we sat in the orchestra very near the stage. But as we often said at the time, the opera was merely a sideline for us, and we begged our parents not to count it as part of our regular theatrical fare, especially the circus. Music made us tired. Nevertheless the impressions I received at the opera are still alive in me and are much clearer, sharper, and greater than the impressions left by the circus. I think that this is so because the strength of the impression was tremendous but was not felt consciously, being received organically and not only spiritually but physically also. I began to understand and value these impressions at their true worth only much later, in my memory. But the circus amused me in childhood, although memories of it were of no interest to me in my maturer years (Stanislavski, 1924, p. 32).

Modestly enough, Stanislavski extends his gratitude to his parents for the opportunities they provided. He remains unaware of the unusual sensory integrative and expressive equipment with which he was endowed and which he brought to these experiences. He approximates this when he speaks of his organic impressions. I think that the study of Stanislavski's creative imagination may add a striking feature to the prerequisites already postulated for the characteristics of creative genius or highly creative talent; that is, the lifelong durability of sensory experiences, perhaps even from infancy, and their lifelong potential transformability into creative expression.[10]

One incident illustrates the striking quality of Stanislavski's long-sustained sensitivity to sensory responsiveness. In 1910, he was traveling in Italy. While walking in the streets of Rome with a friend, they heard someone sing in a nearby house.

[10] Recently a biographical sketch of Picasso showed the same quality in Picasso—the lifelong retention of early sensory impressions and their creative expression.

Stanislavski expressed the opinion that it was the voice of the baritone Cotogni. Further inquiry established that he was correct. He had heard Cotogni sing only once when he was seven years old—forty years earlier.

This and similar incidents bear testimony to his extraordinary sensitivity to all forms of sensory stimuli—sound, spoken, or musical; colors, design, movement, and texture. All this was evident in childhood in his theatrical productions. He was director, stage manager, scenic and costume designer, and musical director. In his mature years all the various theatrical specialties were under his direct supervision. He was considered a master in every department.

Stanislavski left us an account of his theory and technique in his three books, *My Life in Art* (1924), *An Actor Prepares* (1936), and *Building a Character* (1949). Perhaps the most significant and vital part of his legacy is a large international group of disciples and followers—creators in their own right— who perpetuate Stanislavski's system in the theater, dramatic schools, and experimental workshops. In England, the United States, and Israel, there are the most enthusiastic students and practitioners of his system. The Moscow Art Theatre of today still preserves and perpetuates the teachings and traditions of Stanislavski. In addition, a number of significant playwrights accept the Stanislavski Method as the exclusive route to the true interpretation of their own creations.

Stanislavski's artistic standards and demands on himself were responsible for his ability to develop a theory and technique for his art. This was an extraordinary achievement since great actors are too often readily seduced by adoration from their audiences and by self-admiration but are disinclined to self-scrutiny. From his earliest childhood performance he was sensitive to his own embarrassment and disapproval of his initial motionless performance in spite of his enjoyment of the applause. Subjugation of the person to the created character,

minimal awareness of the audience, and increased awareness
of inner feelings became important principles in Stanislavski's
theories and techniques of acting.

Stanislavski's insight into the legendary cloak of celebrated
people, including his own self, is well illustrated in the book
Stanislavski Directs written by a famous disciple, Gorchakov.
When Gorchakov was twenty-six years old he began to work
with Stanislavski as an apprentice in the renowned Third
Studio in 1924. Since 1939, the year after Stanislavski's death,
Gorchakov has been in charge of stage direction at the State
Institute of Theatrical Art in Moscow. As a young man, Gorchakov asked Stanislavski the question, "What is a director?"
Stanislavski correctly understood this oft-asked question to
mean that the young man wanted to know whether he had the
qualities to become a director. A short while before, the young
man had accompanied Stanislavski to the house of Isadora
Duncan, the famous dancer, to bid her farewell as she was
about to depart for France. Stanislavski then asked Gorchakov
what impressions he had had of the meeting between Duncan
and himself. In response to the brief answer that he had only
been aware of being in the presence of two famous people,
Stanislavski commented, "You noticed the most essential element—we were playing at being two world celebrities—but
you did not understand for whom we were acting. You didn't
notice a short man who was sitting in the corner of the room?
This man is Duncan's secretary who was taking notes on all he
saw and heard. He is going to write a book on her life. She was
playing a role and so was I. Do you remember that we spoke
French? How did you think our French was?" In response to
Gorchakov's comment that he thought it was good French,
Stanislavski continued, "We spoke very poor French, pretend-
ing it was exceptionally good. When we were in the hall she
shook my hand so hard I still feel it. Did you notice this? I
think she likes me and I like her very much. You could have
observed this too. You saw only the result of our acting but

you did not see what we were acting and why" (Gorchakov, 1954).

This incident, reported by an outsider, is of considerable value in determining the authenticity of the autobiographical data. A famous person who in a sense can self-analyze or make conscious the tendency of his own and other famous people to alter their true image into a legendary one is more likely to present us with biographical data which are less distorted than is usual. It is a further tribute to Stanislavski's inborn sensitivity that he was constantly aware of everything he was experiencing, both from within and without.

Inherent in Stanislavski's nature was a strong sense of paternalism. Gorchakov writes that Stanislavski paid the members of the Third Studio (a part of the Moscow Art Theatre) a surprise visit when its famous director, Vakhtangov, became gravely ill and Stanislavski felt that this group would be seriously upset by this event. In the same book (*Stanislavski Directs*), an incident is related in which Gorchakov had to seek help from Stanislavski to meet the financial crisis of the Third Studio. He quotes Stanislavski as follows:

> You did not write me for advice or permission for your tour either. Now you are asking for our help like spoiled children. We all have children. I have a son and a daughter (he looked at us sternly, but suddenly softened, we looked so desperate) and they too are the children of the Moscow Art Theatre. I am very excited now and might say unnecessary things but it is because I love the theatre and I am very uneasy about the fate of our new art. The theatre is not only a director and an acting company with well-produced plays; it is the entire ensemble of the theatre—director, administrator, and wardrobe mistress included. Only in this way can the new theatre develop and bring its culture to the audience (Gorchakov, 1954).

To comprehend the nature and scope of Stanislavski's legacy to the world of theater, we must appreciate the origins of his paternalism and the origins of his generous nature. There is

every indication that the optimal opportunities of his early
life became the bequeathing character of his maturity. A re-
capitulation and re-examination of his childhood shapes the
key to the vault of his legacy. In the forefront stands the fortunate infantile foundation of sound ego development springing from the optimal nurturing relationship with his mother.
To be well taken care of, nurtured, and loved in infancy is the
precursor and prelude to the future return of these gifts to the
outer world from which these bounties originated.

As the roots of a "giving to" and "loving of the world" nature
lie in the quality of the relationship to the mother, so equally
does the paternalism lie in the nature of the relationship with
the father. Stanislavski's father felt his son's boundless artistic
expression to be a fulfillment to the father. In his childhood
life of theater (which seemed to encompass almost all of life),
Stanislavski was more often than not director to his father and
older siblings. The intensity of his childhood sensitivity to
theater, merged with the intense love of theater in the Stanislavski household, were the forerunners of a life in which his
personal love, his art, his children, and his disciples were fused
into an inseparable oneness over which he reigned and admin-
istered with the qualities of a loving mother and a mature
father.

In "the love affair with the world" that every creative person
or genius may have, his personal life and development are
crucial to the final outcome. If the creative person has the
capacity and conditions to develop emotionally to the stature
of a parent in his romance with the world, we are assured that
a more permanent and sizable legacy will be left. This legacy
is often missing when the creative talent is embodied in an
artist who is but a child in love with the (parental) world,
rather than an artist who, like Stanislavski, could grow to be a
parent loving his world.

7

John Wilkes Booth:

Failure and Fame

FROM THE PROLOGUE OF SCHILLER'S *Wallenstein**

For quickly from the mind the actor's art
Art marvellous, wears off and leaves no trace
Whereas the poet's song, the sculptor's figures
Still live when many thousand years have passed,
Here dies away the glamour with the actor,
And, as the sound expires within the ear,
The moment's swift creation passes off,
Nor any lasting work preserves his fame.
Severe this art, and fleeting its reward:
The future weaves no garland for the actor
So of the present must he make the most,
Fill to the full the moment that is his,
Secure with might and main the age he lives in
And rear himself a living monument
Within the hearts of men the best and greatest.
Thus he forestalls his immortality
For he that wins approval of the best
Men of his time has lived for evermore.

THE OUTSTANDING DEED in the life of the unsuccessful actor,
John Wilkes Booth, was his final pathological theatrical act—

* English translation by Alexander Falconer Murison (New York:
Longmans, Green, 1931).

the assassination of Abraham Lincoln at the Ford Theatre. We
shall explore, from a psychobiographical vantage point, the
crucial developmental and environmental factors during adolescence, childhood, and infancy that were responsible for the
faltering direction of his brief stage career, which came to an
end in his last infamous and murderous performance. It is the
tale of a disinherited and deluded actor born into a family of
famous actors.

The mood of a melodrama must have been on the twenty-
six-year-old John Wilkes Booth as he scheduled the shooting of
Abraham Lincoln in the Ford Theatre. The assassin planned to
use the customary dramatic cue to indicate the moment for
murder. It was to be synchronized with a line in the second
scene of the third act of Tom Taylor's *Our American Cousin*.
A humorous soliloquy with a note of ridiculous violence, intended to provoke laughter, was to be the distracting signal
to squeeze the trigger.

He rode up on his horse at 9:30 P.M., half an hour before the
selected fateful scene began. He dismounted, entered the
theater, "removing gauntlet gloves, bowing and smiling to
fellow actors and whispered to an actor in the wings. The actor
shook his head and pointed to the tunnel. Booth could not cross
backstage at this time" (Bishop, 1955). After surveying the
audience from the other wing, he stepped out of the theater
with the knowledge that he had ample time before his act. At
the adjoining tavern of Peter Taltavul, where he ordered a
bottle of whisky and some water, he got into a discussion with
an unidentified, intoxicated man who needled him, "You'll
never be the actor your father was" (Bishop, 1955). In this
moment of frightened excitement John's unconscious became
vulnerable, yet he replied pleasantly and calmly, "When I
leave the stage, I will be the most famous man in America."
What multiple unconscious meanings are hinted at in this
brief, ambiguous retort!

The assassin was the younger brother of the famous American Shakespearean actor, Edwin Booth, and both were the sons of an English-born but famous American actor, Junius Brutus Booth. The student of history will recall that a month or so before, Lincoln had been inaugurated as President of the United States for a second term following his re-election the previous November. Booth shot Lincoln on April 14, 1865, a few days after Lee had surrendered to Grant and the Civil War was over. Lewis Paine, an underling in Booth's conspiracy, attempted a synchronized, unsuccessful assassination of William Seward, the Secretary of State.

After Booth shot Lincoln, he leaped on the stage, landing off balance because the spur of his riding boot had caught in the bow tie flag decorating the Presidential box. He sustained a fractured left ankle but felt no immediate pain; his only thought was to escape through the wing of the theater to his waiting horse on the street. Nevertheless, Booth found time to declaim from the stage the Latin phrase, "Sic semper tyrannus!"

On three previous occasions during the three preceding months, Booth had planned to kidnap, no, to capture—as he preferred to think of it—Lincoln, always during a performance at the same Ford Theatre. Booth's melodramatic kidnaping plots involved the cumbersome procedure of dropping Lincoln from his box on to the stage, carrying him off through the wings, and following the same escape route which he actually used on April 14.

To those given to imaginative speculation, a number of questions, doubts, inquiries, and better ways of having carried out this deed may occur. Why did the actor's plan for either kidnaping or killing have to be carried out exclusively on the stage? Why did he have to use a plan which necessitated carrying the President on and off the stage? John Wilkes wanted to be seen, identified, and eventually caught and killed. This was not the escape of the usual criminal. He was a well-known figure in the theater. Furthermore, he had written an undelivered letter to the newspaper *The National Intelligencer* and a sealed letter to his sister Asia, to make sure that no other hand would be mistaken for this act.

The verdict of the period in which this tragedy occurred was that John Wilkes Booth was deranged. His loyalty to the South originated from a psychotic delusion that Lincoln would become a "king" and reign over a dynasty, following his re-election. Credit our grandfathers with the evaluation that the "mad" Booth wanted primarily to become famous. They knew nothing of a possible unconscious hatred of a father, let alone the possibility that will be developed here—that John Wilkes's delusion in which he perceived and hated Lincoln as a reigning king was derived from the denial of rage against his brother Edwin.

In the final terrible days in hiding after John Wilkes had shot the President and learned that he was dead, John Wilkes scrawled a frantic and soul-searching note in his diary. Its contents reveal a direct expression of the unconscious aim of his murderous act. "I do not repent the blow I struck. . . . I think I have done well. Though I am abandoned, with the curse of Cain upon me, when if the world knew my heart, that one blow would have made me great, though I did desire no greatness" (Ruggles, 1953). In this desperate, defiant utterance, Booth labels his own act as the act of Cain, in which the good brother Abel was slain. This was not, as so many had thought, the act of a Brutus who killed a ruler, but the act of a brother who unconsciously kills a brother.

Psychoanalysis has shown that in paranoid delusions the deepest feeling involves an inordinate hatred of a loved person which is too frightening to be recognized.[1] John Wilkes was a man who hated so deeply and rivaled so intensely his family's elders that he was too frightened to know or show the slightest

[1] Nunberg (1938) noted the gratification of aggression as well as libido in the case of a paranoid patient. See Knight (1940) for full discussion and formulations, also Stärcke (1920) and Van Ophuijsen (1920).

emanation of his feelings toward those involved. He had to remove these feelings to a vastly remote representative.

THE CONCURRENCE OF LINCOLN'S
RE-ELECTION, EDWIN'S REIGN,
AND JOHN WILKES'S PLOT FOR FAME

At the time of Lincoln's re-election, Edwin Booth came into
the full bloom of his "reigning" career; within a few months—
before April 14, 1865—he had established himself as the head
of the tribe of Booth actors. At this particular moment, Edwin
was heralded as the "Prince of Players," the greatest Hamlet
who ever lived. In these few crucial months—from the time of
Lincoln's re-election to his inauguration—events in Edwin's
career cast him as the unrivaled actor who was destined to rule
over the American theater until his death.

Edwin had rented the Winter Garden for the current season
of 1864–1865, and for several seasons to come. This was the
beginning of a new adventure in Edwin's expanding career.
Until then, like his father, he had been limited to the necessity
of making arrangements with managers. Now he could select
his own vehicles, cast, repertoire—and in New York! He had
come of age as no Booth ever had.

On November 25, 1863, shortly after Lincoln's re-election, a
benefit performance of *Julius Caesar* was given at the Winter
Garden, under Edwin Booth's leadership. The proceeds were
for the purpose of erecting a statue of Shakespeare in Central
Park. For this occasion, Edwin gathered his talented brothers,
Junius, Jr., and John Wilkes, to contribute their efforts. Edwin
played Brutus, Junius, Jr., played Cassius, and John Wilkes
played Marc Antony.

The following morning the entire family was gathered at
Edwin's house for breakfast. The theater reviews in the news-
papers extolled the virtuosity of both John Wilkes and Junius,
Jr., which prompted Edwin to remark, "I must brush up or lose

my laurels." Then they discussed the recent election. Edwin
commented that he had voted for the first time in his life and
had voted for Lincoln. This infuriated John Wilkes, who dero-
gated the President with the term "Old Abe" and cursed him
viciously. In spite of John Wilkes's feelings for the South, this
outburst was provocative since he was familiar with Edwin's
pro-Lincoln sympathies.

Was this then a provident opportunity for John Wilkes
to displace his inadmissible and unrecognized hatred of the
reigning Edwin onto the issue of Lincoln's imaginary rule?[2] A
year before, Lincoln had paid a surprise and unguarded visit
to the Ford Theatre where he witnessed Edwin's Shylock and
then commented, "A good performance, but I'd a thousand
times read it at home if it was not for Booth's playing." That
same night Edwin was entertained at dinner by Secretary of
State, William Seward. These were the first signs of Edwin's
rise to national fame. To dine with the Secretary of State and
lure the President to an unplanned visit to his performance
would be any actor's dream. What feelings would this stir in
a rival actor brother from a family of notable thespians? John
Wilkes had a pathological need for fame and had openly
stated, "I want fame, fame, fame!"

Historians have been puzzled why Seward was John
Wilkes's covictim. Had this been exclusively a political plot,
Secretary of War Stanton would have been a much more suitable target. His capture or death would have augmented the
disruption of the executive and military functions of the
North. The choice of Seward as victim exposes the emotional
origin of the crime. He was hated because, like Lincoln, he
admired Edwin.

However, John Wilkes did not formulate his first plot to
capture Lincoln until a year later, when Lincoln was re-

[2] Lehrman (1939) notes that in homicide "by means of unconscious
elaboration, the victim . . . becomes a composite personage—a fusion of
rival sibling, parent and self."

elected. He developed his grandiose plans from November 1864 to April 14, 1865. This period coincided with the time during which his brother Edwin achieved outstanding theatrical success.

On the evening after the benefit performance of *Julius Caesar,* Edwin Booth began his career as his own producer, *sans frères,* playing Hamlet. His acclaim grew with each performance. "Booth never lost the name he made that season." "The fashion and the passion, especially among women," was how the New York critic who signed himself "Nyn Crinkle" described Booth's Hamlet. *The New York Times* pronounced it "a part in which he had no living equal." "What Garrick was in Richard III, or Edward Kean in Shylock, we are sure Edwin Booth is in Hamlet," suggested the editor of "The Easy Chair" of *Harper's* for April 1865. "Booth is altogether princely. . . . His playing throughout has an exquisite tone like an old picture. . . . The cumulative sadness of the play was never so palpable as in his acting." "Edwin Booth," writes William Winter, "was the simple absolute realization of Shakespeare's haunted prince, and raised no question and left no room for inquiry whether the Danes in the Middle Ages wore velvet robes or had long flaxen hair. It was dark, mysterious, afflicted, melancholy" (Ruggles, 1953).

His success was accompanied by absolute acclamation from his brothers. The transformation in Junius Brutus, Jr., is the first to be noted. He had commented earlier, "Ted has the public. Yet, let him act a thousand years and he will never be able to approach father." However, after a few months of Edwin's Hamlet, we find Junius saying, "that, while father could make the cold shivers crawl down my back, he couldn't possibly have played Hamlet as Edwin has done for one hundred performances and done it as well" (Ruggles, 1953).

Finally, the silent, young rival, John Wilkes, with a tinge of psychotic unreality and extraordinary keenness, says, "No, no, no! There's but one Hamlet to my mind; that's my brother

Edwin. You see, between ourselves, he is Hamlet—melancholy and all" (Ruggles, 1953). We must remember that Lincoln too had a "melancholy" quality.

The "crowning" of Edwin's success was his recognition by the City of New York. A municipal committee along with the Governor of New York State planned to present Edwin with a gold medal on the night of his hundredth performance of *Hamlet*, March 22, 1865.

On March 20, 1865, John Wilkes plotted for the third time to achieve his own unforgettable "fame." Had he succeeded, it would have ruined Edwin's day of fame and honor and transformed it into a day of shame and disaster.

SIGNIFICANT EVENTS IN JOHN WILKES'S LIFE

John Wilkes's intense unconscious hatred was mostly directed at his brother Edwin who was an alternate for both his real and fantasy-life father. Edwin was five-and-a-half years older than John Wilkes. From the time of John Wilkes's birth until he was eight or nine, Edwin was consistently the oldest male at home and must have appeared to John as a father as well as a brother. Edwin occupied the double dais of a rival heir and substitute father. However, when Edwin was fourteen years of age, he replaced Junius, Jr., as his father's touring companion—a role in which he was to guard his father against excessive drinking and its ensuing difficulties. This tour also served as a period of apprenticeship in acting. During the next four years, from the age of nine to thirteen, John Wilkes, with no older male about, was like a fatherless boy, always playing wild games.

In the spring of 1852, John Wilkes, age fourteen, was completing a year at a large boarding school, kept by the Quakers in Cockeysville. The elder Booth intended to buy a farm nearby and thus provide a home and future occupation for his two younger sons, John Wilkes and Joseph; he thought that no other sons of his would become actors. Consciously he wanted none of his sons on the stage, but all his actions indicated that he was shaping the theatrical careers of his two older sons.

That same year, Junius, Jr., who was now a theater manager on the West Coast, induced his father to accompany him back to California to seek new theatrical horizons. Edwin, age nineteen, now an established professional actor in his own name, was persuaded to join them. Such a drastic move, going from the East to the West Coast, in those days carried with it the implication of a permanent change. The family was now split. The father, in a theatrical unit with the older brothers, headed for San Francisco; the other domestic unit, with John Wilkes as the eldest male, his mother, two sisters, and younger brother, remained on the Maryland farm. John Wilkes felt that he had been badly treated and neglected and that he was not accepted as a man and an actor by his father. He complained bitterly to his sister Asia, "How shall I ever have a chance on the stage. Buried here, torturing the grain out of the ground for daily bread, what chance have I of ever studying elocution and declamation" (Clarke, 1938). He began to plan defiantly for himself, for his acting and subsequent fame. From now on, in every way and at every moment, his acting developed a stealthy, surreptitious, aggressive quality that persisted until the final day of the drama at the Ford Theatre.

At the end of the scholastic year, the parents were invited to a school picnic. Asia escorted her mother in place of the migrant father. The entertainment for the occasion consisted of planned recitations by the students. One of the pupils recited Othello's declamation. Then, to the surprise of his relatives, John Wilkes mounted the stage as Shylock and, as Asia put it in her *Memoirs* (Clarke, 1938), "A master, who stood screened by the boys nearest the platform, read out Salarino's, the servant's and Tubal's lines, and Shylock had the stage to himself." This unannounced but carefully plotted first stage performance was to be repeated with even greater melodramatic flavor throughout his subsequent, if short, theatrical career.

This surreptitious quality tainted all the future theatrical undertakings of John Wilkes. He confessed his first professional activity in Baltimore, when he was seventeen, to his sister Asia, as if he were a criminal; he had originally pretended that he had to leave the farm for a few days on business. Outwardly the escapade had the style of a pleasant surprise, but it was inwardly structured as a stealthy, forbidden act. Asia reports the incident as follows: " 'Well, Mother Bunch, guess what I've done!' Then, answering my silence he said, 'I've made my first appearance on any stage for this night only and in big capitals.' . . . Mother was displeased as we to hear of this adventure. She thought it premature and that he had been influenced by others who wished to gain notoriety and money by the use of his name" (Clarke, 1938, p. 106). Wilkes's mother was overprotective in her reaction to her son's enterprise. As his adoring mother, she would find it hard to face the truth, for actually John Wilkes was taking advantage of the famous name of his father and brother and was seeking notoriety and money when it was "premature" for him to be starred at his "first appearance on any stage" considering his lack of training. He rebelled and competed as an actor with his father and Edwin.

As his stage career developed, he was described on one occasion as an "outrageous scene thief." He planned to confine his acting to the South because he "would never hope to be as great as father, he never wanted to rival Edwin but wanted to be loved by the Southern people above all things. He would make himself essentially a Southern actor" (Ruggles, 1953). However, his actions proved otherwise. As soon as Edwin Booth had gone to England in the summer of 1861, John Wilkes invaded his brother's theatrical territory. Eleanor

Ruggles writes in *Prince of Players* (1953), "When Edwin sailed for England, John saw his chance. He starred in St. Louis, in Chicago, then in Baltimore; and here in the city most associated with all the Booths, his posters proclaimed defiantly: 'I AM MYSELF ALONE!' "

JOHN WILKES'S ADOLESCENT
FANTASIES—FEARS AND WISHES

The Unlocked Book, written by Asia Booth Clarke, who died in 1888, was not released for publication until 1938. Asia had concealed the manuscript during her lifetime. Prior to her death she passed it on to a trusted friend whose daughter finally permitted it to be published. Asia had hoped that posterity would evaluate these memoirs of her brother John in the coolness of distance. She preserved for us the events, aspirations, and fears of his boyhood. She also preserved her mother's aspirations and dreams for him. All of these helped shape Lincoln's assassin.

Along with her own manuscript, Asia left "A Book of Cuttings," stamped "J.W.B.," containing a variety of newspaper clippings. The six articles she selected to save for the future from the multitude written about John Wilkes during her lifetime showed extraordinary intuition and perception. The most significant of this group is entitled, "His Schooldays, by a Classmate." It is merely signed "A Marylander" and is dated December 3, 1878, New York—thirteen years after the notorious crime. This article was actually a letter written in response to a newspaper article by John T. Ford, who had made a remarkable case for the theory referred to as John Wilkes's "Admiration for Brutus."[3] Ford felt that "the fact

[3] Wilson (1940) contends that John Wilkes was identified with Brutus. Unfortunately, I did not encounter this paper until just prior to my own publication. In his paper, Wilson formulates that the act of the paranoid John Wilkes Booth "constituted unconscious father murder but represented unconscious suicide as well."

that the public had made assassination respectable by ap-
plauding the chief actor in the play of Julius Caesar, was the
mainspring of his action."

The classmate from Maryland suggests that John Wilkes
was *not* playing Brutus. He concludes, "I believe instead of
following the Brutus idea, his thoughts were rather after
Washington, Bolivar and Leonidas—but his great boyish aim
would be accomplished. 'His name known in history, to live
forever'" (Clarke, 1938).

I think that the classmate has given us a meaningful hint
in his phrase "but his great boyish aim would be accomplished." Credit the "Marylander" for recording in this article
the boyhood fantasies, told him by John Wilkes, which are
crucial to our ultimate understanding. Their first meeting was
in 1852, at school. I quote further from the "Marylander"
(Clarke, 1938):

Morris Oram always looked forward to the law as his profession,
and in stating his views for the future his ambition was to be
a greater orator than Daniel Webster, and a more profound
lawyer than Reverdy Johnson, while Booth thought only of
being a man admired by all people. He asserted that he would
do something that would hand his name down to posterity
never to be forgotten, even after he had been dead a thousand
years. Booth and Oram had red clay pipes, with reed stems
about a yard long, and when they with their pipes lay on the
ground, these daily conversations were always in order. Our
opinions of the future were freely discussed. I recollect when we
asked Booth how he expected to acquire such greatness and
notoriety as he was constantly talking of. One of his answers
was: "Well, boys, I'll tell you what I mean. You have read about
the Seven Wonders of the World? Well, we'll take the Statue
[Colossus] of Rhodes for example. Suppose that statue was now
standing, and I should by some means overthrow it? My name
would descend to posterity and never be forgotten, for it would
be in all the histories of the times, and be read thousands of
years after we are dead, and no matter how smart and good

men we may be, we would never get our names in so many histories."—On another occasion when the same subject was discussed, I recollect he said, "I wish there was an arch or statue at the mouth of the Mediterranean Sea across the Straits of Gibraltar, with one side resting on the rock of Gibraltar and the other on an equally prominent rock on the coast of Africa. I would leave everything and never rest until I had devised some means to throw it over into the sea. Then look out for history, English, French, Spanish, and all Europe, Asia and Africa would resound with the name of John Booth. I tell you it would be the greatest feat ever executed by one man."

Reckless of Consequences

While speaking, his whole soul appeared to contemplate with satisfaction the future he had drawn.

Oram said, "Billy, suppose the falling statue took you down with it, what good would all your glory then do you?"

His answer was: "I should die with the satisfaction of knowing I had done something never before accomplished by any other man, and something no other man would probably ever do."

The fantasies of this fourteen-year-old boy amaze us when we realize how thoroughly they were enacted a dozen years later, when they had been long forgotten by their weaver.

The destructive fantasies of smashing both the Colossus of Rhodes and the arch spanning the Straits of Gibraltar belong to the current events in John's life. He related these fantasies to his young friends some time after his father and two older brothers had left for the Northwest Coast. (As we noted before, John felt that, as his brothers before him, he had come of age and was permanently bypassed by his father in his rightful turn to accompany him and become an actor.) The migration of the theatrical elders was undertaken by steamer. In those days there was no Panama Canal. The "Illinois" left New York, steamed past Mexico, and landed at Colon. There they "poled up the Chagres River to Gorgona." Here they "mulebacked" through the jungle across the Isthmus, finally landing in Panama City on the Pacific. They boarded ship, sailed north, and arrived in San Francisco on July 28, 1852.

The route of their voyage is pertinent to John Wilkes's fantasies. The Straits of Gibraltar lie between the continents of Europe and Africa, between the Atlantic and the Mediterranean, as the Isthmus of Panama lies between North and South America and separates the Atlantic from the Pacific. In his fantasy, John Wilkes created an imaginary land arch spanning the Straits of Gibraltar, similar to the Isthmus of Panama. The dangerous jungles of the isthmus, where his father and brothers could easily have perished, were transformed into the fantasied arch for which he would devise "some means to throw it over into the sea."

What is hidden behind these fantasies are the murderous wishes against his father and Edwin. Junius Brutus, Jr., also a father figure to John Wilkes, entered little into John Wilkes's unconscious hostility since Junius was so much older and had been away from home during John Wilkes's entire formative childhood years. Furthermore, he never became the theatrical rival to John that Edwin was. In his daydreams John willed the destruction of his male elders because he felt they had abandoned him and destroyed his dreams to become an actor like them and with them.

The Colossus of Rhodes, the sixth wonder of the world, existed about 300 B.C. on the Island of Rhodes. It stood 105 feet high, 50 feet short of the Statue of Liberty, and was, like our statue, a harbor statue. It is said to have stood at the entrance to the island's harbor, and the figure of Helios, the worshiped sun-god, stood with his legs straddling the harbor's entrance. Again we note that John Wilkes's fantasy dealt with structures which were gateways to water voyages. The dangers of both the sea voyage and the jungle of the isthmus which threatened his father and brothers were displaced onto distant waters. The statue of Helios, the sun-god, represents an un-equivocal, universal symbol in man's unconscious for the father. Thus, again, John Wilkes's fantasied destruction intended the destruction of his father and his fatherlike brother Edwin.

The part of the fantasy in which the statue falls on him as he destroys it anticipates a curiously accurate preview of his capture and death subsequent to his assassination of the President.

In the twelve intervening years between the boyhood fantasy and the act of murder, the life of John Wilkes Booth was a series of enactments dictated by the long-repressed but lively fantasy. With Lincoln destroyed like his "statue," John died as he had promised, "with the satisfaction of knowing I had done something never before accomplished by any other man and something no other man would probably ever do."

THE NATURE AND ORIGIN OF
JOHN WILKES'S FANTASIES

John's fantasies were provoked by, but did not originate from, his father's adventures to California. Some explanation for both the basic origins of John's fantasies and the fuel for their enactment are found in Asia's *Memoirs*. She tells us (1938, pp. 43–44) that "his mother, when he was a babe of six months old had 'a vision' in answer to a fervent prayer in which she imagined that the foreshadowing of his fate had been revealed to her and as this incident was more painfully impressed upon her mind by a 'dream' when he had attained manhood, both vision and dream were familiarized to me by frequent repetition. . . . The oft-told reminiscence was put into this form and presented to the mother on her *birthday*; the lines claim no other *merit* than affording an explanation of her vision:"

THE MOTHER'S VISION[4]

'Tween the passing night and the coming day
When all the house in slumber lay,
A patient mother sat low near the fire,
With that strength even nature cannot tire,
Nursing her fretful babe to sleep—
Only the angels these records keep
    Of mysterious Love!
One little confiding hand lay spread
Like a white-oped lily, on that soft bed,
The mother's bosom, drawing strength and contentment warm—
The fleecy head rests on her circling arm.
In her eager worship, her fearful care,
Riseth to heaven a wild, mute prayer
    Of foreboding Love!
Tiny, innocent white baby-hand,
What force, what power is at your command,
For evil, or good? Be slow or be sure,
Firm to resist, to pursue, to endure—
My God, let me see what this hand shall do
In the silent years we are tending to;
    In my hungering Love,
I implore to know on this ghostly night
Whether 'twill labour for wrong, or right,
For—or against Thee?
                        The flame up-leapt
Like a wave of blood, an avenging arm crept
Into shape; and COUNTRY shone out in the flame,
Which fading resolved to her boy's own name!
God had answered Love—
    Impatient Love!
                (Clarke, 1938, pp. 44–45.) [Italics mine—P. W.]

This is the terrible vision of John's destiny, written as a
poem for the mother's birthday by sister Asia when she was
eighteen and John sixteen. The vision implies an early death,
an act of brave but bloody violence, in the name of his country.

[4] Written 1854, June 2nd, by A. B. (Asia Booth) Harford Co., Md.

However, its morality is in doubt—"for wrong or right," "For —or against Thee?" Asia further tells us, "Mother and I often talked of her 'vision in the fire' and of her 'awful dream' . . ." (pp. 90–91). John Wilkes was not spared from hearing this "talk" and became intensely preoccupied with its content.[5]

We have recounted how John Wilkes, at thirteen, had un-expectedly recited Shylock at school. Immediately after that performance, he could hardly wait to show his sister Asia his written version of "what he called 'his fortune' which a Gipsy . . . had told him a few days since. 'See here,' he said, 'I've written it—but there was no need to do that, for it is so bad that I shall not soon forget it.' "

The fortune read: "Ah, you've a bad hand; the lines all cris-cras. It's full enough of sorrow—full of trouble—trouble in plenty everywhere I look. . . . You'll die young, and leave many to mourn you, many to love you too, but you'll be rich, generous and free with your money. You're born under an unlucky star. You've got in your hand a thundering crowd of enemies—not one friend—you'll make a bad end, and have plenty to love you afterwards. You'll have a fast life—short, but a grand one. Now, young sir, I've never seen a worse hand, and I wish I hadn't seen it, but every word I've told is true by the signs. You'd best turn a missionary or a priest and try to escape it" (Clarke, 1938, pp. 57–58). The fortune had not ceased to trouble him, and at intervals, through the course of the few years that summed up his life, frequent reference was sadly made to the rambling words of that old gipsy in the wood of Cockeysville.

Asia had no understanding that the constant talk between her mother and herself in his presence affected him. She naïvely accounts for his gullibility of the gipsy's story because

[5] John Wilkes was fourteen when he spun his fantasy of fame in which he destroys the Colossus of Rhodes; Asia's poem, written when he was sixteen, was the culmination of the years of talk about his mother's vision in the fire in which John Wilkes will do an act "for evil or good."

"this seed of an inherent superstition [was] kept alive by early associations with Negroes, whose fund of those stories, legends and ill-omens never knew exhaustion" (1938). She could not see that his mystical and fatalistic attitudes stemmed from her own and her mother's visionary attitudes. This interplay between John and the two women became structured within his psyche. He consciously shared in their anxiety for him as if the vision were his own; indeed, it became part of himself.

THE NATURE AND ORIGIN OF
HIS MOTHER'S DELUSION

His mother's "vision" was actually a visual hallucination and her preoccupation with its contents throughout the years represented its gradual transformation into a fixed delusion. The symptom was masked in the disguise of a mother's conventional dreams, hopes, and anxieties for her child's future. A mother's intense anxiety about a child, even when not overtly expressed, rarely fails to become the child's own anxiety. In the earliest phase of ego development, the infant feels himself and the outside world as one. In the normal development of the infant's ego, his self-representation becomes completely separated from that of his parents and the world about him within the first year of life. Recent psychoanalytic investigations show that in mental illness the representation of the parent remains fused with the self-representation, as it had been originally. Consequently, in psychotic behavior, the individual often enacts incorporated psychotic aspects of a given parent, but feels the actions as exclusively his own (Jacobson, 1954).

Such an organization of John Wilkes's delusion can be recognized from his last words, quoted by Ruggles: "He . . . opened his eyes and moved his lips to shape the words, 'Tell . . . Mother.' Then he fainted again. When he came to he

finished his sentence. 'Tell . . . Mother . . . I . . . died . . .
for . . . my . . . country.'" His dying utterances expose the
structure of his delusion to have been a part of his mother's
delusion embedded within him. This is not to imply that
Mary Ann shared her son's terminal political delusion in
which he hatefully saw Lincoln as a reigning king. As a
matter of fact, she was prone to share Edwin's views and was
somewhat pro-North and pro-Lincoln. Actually, the Booth
family homestead was in northern Maryland where it was
quite common to have pro-Northern feelings. Whenever John
Wilkes talked bitterly against Lincoln, his mother felt helpless,
uncomfortable, and concerned.

Why did his mother develop this symptom at this particular
time, when John Wilkes was six months old?

Mary Ann and Junius Brutus Booth had shortly before
suffered the loss of three children: four-year-old Frederick,
their fifth child; Elizabeth, the sixth child; and their fourth
child, Mary Ann. These deaths occurred within the span of a
few weeks. The father developed an agitated depression and
was cared for by his wife, whose troubles as a bereaved
mother were compounded by the burden of her husband's
temporary derangement. The next year, in 1836, the whole
family went to Europe, where the father had a theatrical tour.
Here their third child, eleven-year-old Henry, died of small-
pox. But Mary Ann had more burdens in store. She became
concerned that the world might learn that she was not the
legal wife of Junius Brutus Booth.

During this trip, the elder Booth was blackmailed by his
brother-in-law, Jimmy Mitchell, who had been a kitchen boy
in the Booth home before he married Booth's sister. Mitchell,
a drunk, the father of eight children, was always desperate for
funds. He threatened exposure of Booth's first marriage and
thus attempted to extort money from the well-to-do actor.
To escape these unpleasant experiences, the Booths gladly returned to America.

"Home again in Maryland, Booth sent his sister the where-withal to leave her husband and join him at the farm with her eight children. But all ten Mitchells, including Jimmy, came, and the unsavory tribe of Mitchell children . . . scuffled and snapped like scabby puppies over Booth's chosen refuge. Their father bullied their mother, wouldn't work, was constantly in liquor . . ." (Ruggles, 1953). Thus, in 1837, Mary Ann had to live in a household in which her illegal union with the elder Booth was constantly in danger of being exposed to her children and the world.

That year Mary Ann became pregnant with John Wilkes. No previous pregnancy had been associated with any misfortunes, such as the deaths of four children and the threatened exposure of her illicit life. These trying conditions and qualms of conscience disturbed Mary Ann throughout her pregnancy and subsequent birth and first months of John Wilkes's life. In the midst of this suffering she experienced her intense hallucinatory "vision."

A few years ago in a clinical study I described "a woman, who would occasionally visualize, whenever there was a severe exacerbation of her obsessional symptoms, the image of the muscular arm of her father threatening her with physical punishment" (Weissman, 1954). It was then shown that the avenging arm represented an early internalized image of a disapproving father. We recall that in the vision of Booth's mother

> The flame up-leapt
> Like a wave of blood, an avenging arm crept
> Into shape. . . .

Mary Ann Booth's evoked image of the avenging arm speaks directly of her pangs of conscience. These unfortunate circumstances led to the development of her significant vision and subsequent delusion, which had such tragic repercussions on the life of her son and our nation.

THE ENACTMENT OF THE DELUSION

Granted that John Wilkes had a paranoid delusion derived from his mother's delusion, which developed when he was an infant; granted that his delusion contained a deep unconscious hatred for his fatherly brother Edwin—"Prince of Players"—which found its transfigured representation in Abraham Lincoln; granted that this transformation into a psychotic hatred of Lincoln became possible via the coincidence of the President's re-election; granted that the assassination was an outgrowth of his geographic adolescent fantasies of Rhodes and Gibraltar with well-hidden death wishes against his traveling father and brothers, with everlasting fame as the reward for his "heroic" deeds. What distinguished him from the multitude of people in the history of the world who have had similar delusions about ruling men displaced from "father and brother," with similar unconscious death wishes against them and desires for undying fame and notoriety? Why did they rarely commit an act of Cain, but rather lived out their lives, in spite of their murderous thoughts, in mundane mediocrity, undistinguishable from other citizens? What made John Wilkes enact his fantasies with such brazen indifference for his life?

His bravado and unconcern were rooted in his wild childhood play as he "stormed through the woods on horseback, screaming his throat dry at invisible enemies and whirling a Mexican sabre over his head . . . and his adoring mother saw in his escapades the germ of heroic deeds" (Ruggles, 1953)—and we see the germ of his final murderous act.

His mother enjoyed his enactment of their mutual visionary fantasies, although his wild play went beyond the normal boy's warlike games. The mother's sanction and timorous admiration of his wild nature and behavior nurtured the expansion of his future wild delusion, culminating in the act of murder. This special state of sanction from his mother, who shared in her "vision" his patriotic delusion "for my Country," distinguished him from the run-of-the-mill paranoid psychotic who believes his dreams but does not enact them; consequently, Booth shot Lincoln.

THE AFTERMATH

Fourteen years later, on the eventful anniversary date of April 14, 1879, Edwin Booth began a four-week engagement in Chicago. On the night of April 23, while playing Richard III, he was shot at three times, but was not hit. It is said that Edwin "rose at the third shot, walked to the footlights and pointed out to the audience the would-be assassin as the pistol was again levelled at his head. At the trial which followed, the man was proved to be insane, and he has ever since been confined at the asylum at Elgin, Illinois" (Ruggles, 1953). What terrible memories and perhaps uneasy stirrings must have been mobilized in the unconsciously intended victim of Lincoln's murderer!

Edwin Booth died on June 7, 1893. "Booth's funeral was held two days later at the Little Church around the Corner. . . . As Booth's coffin was being carried out of the church after the Episcopal service to the sonorous 'Dead March' from Saul —in the same moment by an eerie coincidence, three stories of the Ford Theatre in Washington, where Lincoln had been shot by John Wilkes Booth and which since had been made into government offices, collapsed with a splintering roar, killing over twenty persons" (Ruggles, 1953).

The life story of John Wilkes Booth ends as it was lived, with a mystical and unfathomable event. It was as if the dying Ford Theatre in the end confessed that it was intended to house and symbolize the murder of Edwin Booth, and in its place was staged an historical tragedy—the assassination of

Lincoln—with the leading role in both dramas played by the notorious and visionary actor, John Wilkes Booth.

POSTSCRIPT

This psychoanalytic study of an historical American tragedy was written prior to the most recent historical tragedy—the assassination of President Kennedy by Lee Harvey Oswald. Although these two events are separated by a century short of two years the twenty-four-year-old Oswald and the twenty-six-year-old Booth had in common, besides their unsuccessful infamous lives, many psychological and developmental features in their early youth and childhood which become obvious through this study.

Among several differences, Oswald, not an actor, was an unscholarly truant from both school and his country, but an avid reader. The lonely killer of Kennedy was driven by his delusional impulses which he silently executed from a window high in the Texas School Book Depository, entrenched in a fortress of stored books. The slayer of Lincoln, for better or worse, was inherently an actor. His psychotic delusion and murderous impulses never parted from the world of theater. Booth had to execute his delusion in the guise of a drama enacted off and on the stage of the Ford Theatre before an audience.

III

The Dramatist's Psychobiography
and His Plays

8

O'Neill's Conscious and Unconscious Autobiographical Dramas

THERE ARE SIGNIFICANT correlations between certain manifestations in Eugene O'Neill's dramas and specific features in his personal life. These correlations will be demonstrated in two plays: *Desire under the Elms* and *Long Day's Journey into Night*. The former reveals unconscious autobiographical experiences that resemble in content and structure the conscious autobiographical material of the latter play. The implications of both modes of expression and content—conscious and unconscious—will be examined insofar as they are related to variations in the status and quality of O'Neill's creativity in these different periods of his life. The specific features of O'Neill's oedipal conflict as reflected in his life, his choice of profession, and his writings will be studied.

BIOGRAPHY AND CONSCIOUS
AUTOBIOGRAPHICAL DRAMA

It is quite unique for a major dramatist to use the material of his conscious biography in an "unaltered" form for the purpose of writing a play. It becomes more valuable than unique to those of us who are interested in studying the nature of artistic creative imagination from the psychoanalytic viewpoint. In such a study, it is revealing when one examines the biographical material which the dramatist has consciously selected for his personal drama and then notes the significant material which he may have unconsciously omitted. Because *unconscious* autobiographical material is often the natural raw material on which a dramatist draws, it is a rare opportunity to study the status of his creativity during an era in which he calls on his *conscious* biography as the source for his new play. It is somewhat analogous to the creative mood of a painter who is occasionally absorbed in a self-portrait.

Unlike such a painter, O'Neill intended his self-portrait as a major creative achievement in his career rather than as an artistic exercise. O'Neill's intense preoccupation with this personal theme resulted in a modification of his pattern of immediate production and publication after the play had been written. This change in his pattern of communication occurred during an uncharacteristic, protracted period of years of non-communicativeness about all the plays written in this era.

The dramatist who bequeathed this unusual but creatively arranged material to us also bestowed on America its citizenship in the world of drama; and through his own works and their inspiration to others he has achieved for America the position of the capital of modern drama. For this extraordinary drama, O'Neill's expressed wish was that it be neither published nor exhibited during his lifetime and for twenty-five years after his death. To so modify the aim of artistic communication in this manner is uncommon; it deviates sharply from the aim of artists in general and from O'Neill's at all other times. Communication is an essential aspect of every artistic creation: communication and artistic creation are the symbiotic synonym of art. As a matter of biological fact, ordinarily O'Neill was so anxious for communication that in 1913 he induced his father to pay the full publishing cost of his first unproduced plays, which are referred to as "The Thirst Volume." It is also interesting and related to the modification of O'Neill's aim of communication that he subsequently repudiated these plays to the extent that they "will never be reprinted with O'Neill's permission" (Clark, 1947, p. 49).

Long Day's Journey into Night was written in 1940, during the noncommunicative twelve-year period between 1934 and 1946—noncommunicative in that no new play was produced or published during this period. This is to be viewed against a background in which O'Neill started to write plays in 1913 and uninterruptedly produced and published at least one play a year until 1929, then one in 1931, one in 1933, and the last before the "dry" period in 1934. In 1946, *The Iceman Cometh* was produced. A 1947 production of his last play, *A Moon for the Misbegotten,* failed to reach Broadway; it was published in 1952, the year before he died at the age of sixty-five. The two last-mentioned plays were written during the noncommunicative period and were conceived by O'Neill as "part of an interlocking series of four plays" of which *Long Day's Journey into Night* is the last and *A Touch of the Poet*[1] is the third. In the midst of this period, O'Neill was preoccupied with, plagued by, and enslaved by a monumental undertaking referred to as "The Cycle." The Cycle in its final

---

[1] *A Touch of the Poet* was first produced in Stockholm. Clark places the play in the series of four. It is more likely one of the partially destroyed Cycle plays.

form was to be a series of nine plays which carries the beginning back to 1775.

> The Cycle goes back to my old vein of ironic tragedy (*Mourning Becomes Electra, Desire Under the Elms, The Great God Brown,* etc.)—with I hope added psychological depth and insight. The whole will be a unique something, all right, believe me if I can ever finish. . . . I have to think in terms of nine plays and a continuity of family lives over a span of 150 years while I am writing each play. But given time and health I can do it. What I would like to do is not have any production until the whole thing is finished . . . productions are only nerve wracking interruptions to me—"show business"—and never have meant anything more. The play, as written, is the thing, and not the way actors garble it with their almost-always-alien personalities (even when the acting is fine work in itself) (Clark, 1947, p. 144).

Writing for production and theater are now referred to in the derogatory declamation—"show business." Dramatic writing is now dissociated from its totality ("the play as written is the thing"); and as for the actors ("almost always alien"), it is implicit in all this that the audience is also temporarily discarded. The formerly loved actor ("even when the acting is fine work in itself") is now a hated object, and so is the audience, which he stated in one form or another would not be sympathetic to his current writing, particularly the autobiographical drama. The interlude of this perplexing transformation of O'Neill's attitude toward the presentation of his plays coincides with a period of personal illness, the nature of which is obscured by both the biographer (Clark) and the autobiographer (O'Neill). Is it neurological (Parkinson's) or is it psychiatric (depression, phobia, "stage" fright) or is it both, intertwining with each other?

It is germane to our problem of artistic communication that the consciously biographical drama was created midstream during this otherwise protracted noncommunicative period—

a period in which this consciously withheld creation coincides with an unconsciously noncommunicative state. It goes without saying that psychoanalysis views artistic creations as a form of sublimated activities.[2] Thus O'Neill's biographical drama as well as the whole period must be examined in terms of psychoanalytic criteria for sublimation.

In connection with this play, disturbances and impurities exist in the fulfillment of the sublimated aspects of both aim and object. The aim of communication—giving to a love object and exhibitionism—has a detouring rather than direct discharge. O'Neill's inability to permit this play to become immediately available, or, for that matter, during his lifetime, indicates a disturbance in regard to the libidinal and exhibitionistic aims of this creation. His attitude was unwarranted since the play's publication and production have been received by critics and public as a major artistic achievement and revived the memory and restored the appreciation of his much earlier accomplishments. O'Neill's expectation of an unsympathetic response by the public also proved to be grossly miscalculated. The public has felt the deepest empathic compassion for his struggle with life. His "love object, the world," did not forsake him; he had forsaken it.

Since this was a conscious prohibition, we would conjecture that, as with all mortals, there would be a conscious reason. In 1946, a public interview was held preliminary to the production of *The Iceman Cometh*. O'Neill revealed that he had written a play about real lives (*Long Day's Journey into Night*), and, in devious detours to direct surmisals that this was autobiographical, he refused to say any more except that it could not be released because one of the characters was still alive.

[2] Freud's original description of sublimation is that of a successful ego defense in which instinctual drives are modified in their aim or object or both, thus permitting their adequate discharge. If we add to these prerequisites the factor of valuation (that is, the degree of creativeness and the capacity for communication), we are more precisely in the area of artistic creative functioning.

I have been unable to avail myself of any other direct remarks about the play except a comment by his widow that he felt the American public might be unsympathetic to the contents of the personal revelations. As for indirect but revealing statements, in 1926, when he was cooperatively interviewed by Barrett Clark, who was undertaking the task of a biographical study of the now famous dramatist, O'Neill wrote:

> You see, when you speak in the script of my having helped on the details of it, you make me a bit responsible, so I've waded right in, even to the extent of suggesting word changes which I thought better expressed the truth. . . . When all is said and done—and this is, naturally, no conceivable fault of yours—the result of this first part is legend. It isn't really true. It isn't I. And the truth would make such a much more interesting—and incredible!—legend. This is what makes me melancholy. But I see no hope for this except some day to shame the devil myself, if I ever can muster the requisite interest—and nerve—simultaneously! (Clark, 1947, p. 7).

Thus what O'Neill said fifteen years before he finally wrote his autobiographical play would serve as a more revealing and explanatory introduction—both to himself and to us—than the dedicatory letter to his wife which appears in the published play. This interview and communication with Barrett Clark took place during the time O'Neill was involved with the first production of *Desire under the Elms* at the Greenwich Village Theatre—a play he had recently completed in 1924.

We also intend to demonstrate that this same play, *Desire under the Elms*, is the unconsciously written biographical play that is most similarly structured to the conscious autobiography, *Long Day's Journey into Night*.[3] We further intend to

[3] I have used "biographical" and "autobiographical" loosely and interchangeably. The posthumous play is autobiographical in a special sense. In the representational sense, it is more his family's biography. However, as we know from so many of O'Neill's plays, his heroes are the haunted embodiments of the members of his family. Thus, as we learn about the members of his family, we begin to know the hero. In this sense the material becomes autobiographical.

show that the unconscious autobiography, *Desire under the Elms,* belongs to and is part of a healthy or effective creative era in the artist's life and that the conscious biography belongs to a disturbed or less effectual creative period. It is hoped that our efforts will contribute to the understanding of the nature of a given creative talent and the factors favorable or detrimental to its enhancement.

O'Neill's prediction that there would be a day "to shame the devil myself" is a retrospective and prospective, unrestricted utterance with unconscious significance, applicable as well to the unconscious autobiography *Desire under the Elms* with which he was no longer preoccupied creatively. It applied to the contemplated conscious autobiography which was still too far removed from being realized to necessitate disguising what he had to say. *Desire under the Elms* was subjected to moral investigation by city officials during its first New York production, but this set of circumstances did not perturb the author. On the other hand, the author's own moral censure of *Long Day's Journey into Night* is evidenced by his remark that he would have to muster his nerve to write it and by his express wish that it be made public posthumously.

We have yet to discover what aspects of the play caused O'Neill to become neurotically disturbed in the sphere of the sublimated exhibitionistic and libidinal aims of communication to the world. We would guess that consciously O'Neill felt disturbed at revealing to the world his mixed feelings of hatred and love toward his father. More poignant and painful to himself must have been the necessity to expose his mother's drug addiction. This disclosure promoted unconscious guilt and led to the deviation of the aim to show his work to the world. Since he was unusually disturbed in the course of writing such a highly personal play, one is not surprised that he was equally out of balance on this occasion as to whom he was writing the play for. Though an artist may customarily dedicate a given work to a beloved person, O'Neill went far beyond this with

Long Day's Journey into Night. In his dedicatory letter to his wife, O'Neill *gives* to her his sorrowful play, which he tells her he created in tears and in blood. He did not intend to exclude the literal meaning of the word "give"; the written play, unproduced, actually became the possession of his widow. Whether a work is or is not dedicated to a person, it is implicit that the world is the object to which the artist wishes to communicate. Knowing this to be his ultimate aim, O'Neill correctly predicted that this particular creative gift to the world could not be executed directly by his own ego.

What lies beneath O'Neill's uneasiness in revealing his mother's morphine addiction? In studying *Long Day's Journey into Night,* we discover that the father, James Tyrone, Sr., the older brother, James, Jr., and O'Neill himself, called Edmund in the play, learn early in the one day of the play that the wife and mother, Mary Tyrone, shows absolute indications that she is again succumbing to the horrifying drug addiction from which she has had a happy reprieve for the past few months. The dramatic revelation in the play is the struggle in the observing members of this family to deny to themselves and to each other that this is as inevitable as the day's journey into night. O'Neill shares with us the most painful aspect of her status—the stage of addiction in which she reaches complete withdrawal from reality. That state is depicted in the final scene of the play as ultimate tragedy and hopelessness, as Mary Tyrone moves about in a soft soul-searching somnambulism that bypasses any recognition of her bereaved ones. O'Neill has counterstructured the unfolding of his mother's tragic day with the unfolding of his own tragic day—a day in which he learns that he has tuberculosis and must go away to a sanatorium. Here he repeats a similar rhythm of dramatic revelation in the observing members of the family to deny to themselves and to each other the nature of his illness, which again is as inevitable as night following day.

In this exquisite interplay of the two tragedies, the mother is unified with the father and brother in their struggling denial of the inevitable nature of O'Neill's illness, as O'Neill is unified with his father and brother in a hopeless denial of the unfolding fate of his mother. In this portrayal, the author has shown the identification between his mother and himself. In each case, O'Neill is the most ardent of the three in denying his mother's illness, as his mother is the most intense of the three in denying her son's illness. The play resolves itself with the unmistakable finality of both illnesses and the tragedy ends with his mother's successful and complete withdrawal from her needful son at the moment of his greatest despair. By way of a minor matter, a major implication is substantiated by the fact that O'Neill obscured the first names of himself and his mother, whom he calls respectively Edmund and Mary (her real name was Ella), whereas his father and brother remain James and James, Jr., as in real life. The implication is that beyond the identification with each other (of which more will be said later), the characters Edmund and Mary continued to be unconscious enigmas to O'Neill, which may be at the core of the explanation as to why this strange biography was useful as a major artistic drama.

O'Neill himself gives us a subjective description of his enigmatic unconscious identification. In the latter half of the same letter (written in 1926 to Barrett Clark) that was quoted earlier, he comments further on the possibility of a future autobiographical drama, "And I myself might not be good at writing it; for when my memory brings back this picture or that episode or that one, I simply cannot recognize that person in myself nor understand him nor his acts as mine (though objectively I can), although my reason tells me he was undeniably I"[4] (Clark, 1947, p. 8).

[4] This is a clear description of the status of objects transformed into unconscious identifications and simultaneously arranging themselves within the ego in self-representations and object representations serving to confuse his identity.

Beres (1959), in a methodological study of the analyst's contribution to biography, wisely warns us that "the psychoanalyst must be cautious in his use of letters, memoirs, autobiographical novels—and even actual autobiography, insofar as all of these may have the quality of screen memories." This is vividly demonstrated in O'Neill's autobiographical drama, *Long Day's Journey into Night,* as the following dramatic example will illustrate. The play is set in the year 1912, when O'Neill was twenty-three. He is characterized by himself as a young man who in the few previous years (1910–1911) had been away from home, seeing the world by sea, and working at intervals all over the world. He then returns to the States. In the winter prior to the time of the play he had worked in his father's theatrical stock company. In the spring he gets a reporter's job on the local New London newspaper. He still works there on the one day of the play, when he is reunited with his parents and brother at the family summer house—an annual occasion. He is further depicted as a small edition of his actor brother, Jim, age thirty-three, who drinks heavily and spends his plentiful unemployed time and unearned money visiting prostitutes. Thus we have in the play a portrayal of two apparently unmarried men, carelessly unconcerned and uncommitted to the present and the future. In the play, James, Sr., the father, constantly reproaches his sons, particularly the elder, for their lack of responsibility and lack of direction. We are then quite surprised (in spite of Beres' quoted warning) to learn from Clark's book that Eugene O'Neill—Edmund in the play—was married in 1909, became the father of a son, and was subsequently divorced in 1912, the year of the play's setting. While almost all the other facts in the play are biographically and chronologically true—that is, the sea voyages, the acting in his father's company, the reporter job, and so forth— the gross omission (repression?) of a highly significant aspect of relevant biography is noteworthy, and is particularly important when the author's self-revelation aims at self-understanding. This distorted self-portrait points to a screen memory that serves the purpose of repressing painful data. Apparently his biographer, Clark, identified with this repressing and distorting screen memory. He failed to correlate the simultaneity of the two lives and actually isolated them as if they belonged to different eras. Clark writes of the marriage: "The married life of the young couple lasted only a short time. The marriage, characterized laconically as 'a mistake,' was finally ended by divorce in 1912" (1947, p. 13). This is Clark's only reference to the marriage. He even omits her name from the index of the book.

Of the "seeing the world and sea-voyaging saga" which began in 1909 (the year of his marriage) through 1910 (the year of the birth of his son) and 1911, Clark writes:

> His bumming instincts, however pronounced, were not altogether vicious; he was not a hopeless failure. He had simply not found himself. On the other hand, he was no literary chap in search of copy. He bunked with the outcasts because he was himself something of an outcast—he worked when he had to—when he could find a job—in order to pay for board, room and liquor, and on occasion for such crude forms of entertainment as he could find near the wharves or in the vicinity of Buenos Aires. He was "seeing life" with a vengeance (Clark, 1947, p. 15).

Not a word by the biographer that his hopeless searching, his feelings of failure, his drinking were in any way related to the unhappy state of his marriage in which he was away from his wife and newly born son and which as yet had not been resolved by the finality of divorce. Clark treats these two aspects of a single period of his life as if they were two isolated eras.

In the autobiographical play, the author completely obliterates the existence of the marriage. He portrays himself as a young, irresponsible man of twenty-three, who failed at college, had odd jobs in business and acting, searched and traveled the world, begins to find himself in newspaper work but

still drinks and cavorts, and is still uncommitted. I would conjecture that all this was more than a simple deliberate omission
thirty years later when he wrote the play. This was a screen
memory of himself and was brought about by specific mechanisms, characteristic for O'Neill and significantly related to his
other writings. It is self-evident that the obliteration of his
marriage, fatherhood, and divorce were brought about by
suppression, repression, isolation, and denial. The identification
between O'Neill and his mother contributes to this psychic
omission. The two are perceived as mutual images of each
other. Both are depicted in the play as falling ill with finality
on the given day. Both mother and son deny to themselves
each other's illness with the greatest intensity. The play un-
folds a picture of Mary in which she reveals what she had
wanted to be all her life (her ego-ideal). We quote her last
speech with which the play ends, when she states in a drug-
derived hypnotic trance (O'Neill, 1956):

> I had a talk with Mother Elizabeth. . . . I told her I wanted to
> be a nun. I explained how sure I was of my vocation that I had
> prayed to the Blessed Virgin to make me sure, and to find me
> worthy. I told Mother I had had a true vision when I was praying
> in the shrine of Our Lady of Lourdes on the little island in the
> lake. I said I knew as surely as I knew I was kneeling there, that
> the Blessed Virgin had smiled and blessed me with her consent.
> But Mother Elizabeth told me I must be more sure than that,
> even, that I must prove it wasn't my imagination. She said, if I
> was so sure, then I wouldn't mind putting myself to a test by go-
> ing home after I graduated, and living as the other girls lived,
> going out to parties and dances and enjoying myself, and then if
> after a year or two I still felt sure, I could come back to see her
> and we would talk it over again. I never dreamed Holy Mother
> would give me such advice! I was really shocked. I said of course
> I would do anything she suggested but I knew it was simply a
> waste of time. After I left her, I felt all mixed up, so I went to
> the shrine and prayed to the Blessed Virgin and found peace
> again because I knew she heard my prayer and would always

love me and see no harm ever came to me so long as I never lost my faith in her.

(She pauses and a look of growing uneasiness comes over her face. She passes a hand over her forehead as if brushing cob-webs from her brain—vaguely.)

That was in the winter of senior year. Then in the spring some-thing happened to me. Yes, I remember. I fell in love with James Tyrone and was so happy for a time.

(She stares before her in a sad dream. Tyrone stirs in his chair. Edmund and Jamie remain motionless.)

FINAL CURTAIN

The full content of Mary's unfulfilled wishes and ideals is most significant to our psychoanalytic biography of O'Neill, because in this image O'Neill has portrayed himself. Like his mother who barely remembers her marriage, O'Neill com-pletely represses his own in his self-portrayal as Edmund. O'Neill depicts himself, denying his path of love, marriage, and paternity, as his mother denies hers in her utterances. His drinking and wanderings serve to make him forget his com-mitments to earthly life, as his mother's addiction and som-nambulance rendered her unaware of her husband and chil-dren. And it now seems that his tuberculosis, for which he has to go to a sanatorium, as his mother goes to one for her addic-tion, will again remove them from their earthly life and at-tachments. What O'Neill has his mother say of, and do to, her marriage, which was irreconcilable with her ideal, O'Neill, by identification, makes of his own marriage—a state of non-existence.

Thus the mother's addiction and the son's tuberculosis are conscious symbols of their unconscious identification. Although their illnesses were factually if not chronologically correct, O'Neill has done more than merely report them. It is part of his artistic achievement that he has arranged them in a juxta-position in which his mother's relapse into addiction and his own illness are simultaneously brought into absolute existence

on a given day. It is more than likely that these two chronic
pathological states revealed themselves over a more protracted
period. Their artistic arrangement in the play coincides with
the state of unconscious affairs, that is, the identification between mother and son. The son and the mother were bound
together in their wishes and ideals to renounce earthly pleas-
ures and responsibilities.

Clark, the biographer, tells us that O'Neill's health did not
break down until December 1912. The time of the play is "a
day in August 1912." Thus O'Neill has already abridged four
months in his life, probably unconsciously, to bring his personal tragedy in juxtaposition to his mother's tragic day—an
event occurring several months earlier. Perhaps, after all, the
actual accurate dates are not so prosaic. Eugene O'Neill entered Gaylord Sanatorium on Christmas Eve, 1912, the anniversary of the birth of Christ, son of the Blessed Virgin, Mary—
his mother's created name in the play. It is not pseudoanalytic
to reconstruct that entering a sanatorium on Christmas Eve for
tuberculosis would feel like the renunciation of life and would
provoke a religious re-evocation of becoming the child of God.
We must remember that O'Neill's choice of Christmas Eve was
his own, although unconsciously determined. His illness was
not so acute—actually he was ambulatory and had been working until the illness was diagnosed. This unconscious enactment by O'Neill in real life on Christmas Eve is identical in
its embodiment with the speeches of "Mother Mary" in the
final utterances of the play. It now becomes self-evident that
the choice of the name Mary for his mother was not a meaningless matter to him. We have only to remember that in *The Great
God Brown* the hero Dion Anthony is a fusion of Dionysus and
St. Anthony. But more of this later.

To authenticate the biographical data, Clark reports that
George Jean Nathan's mother attended the same convent in
Cleveland as Eugene O'Neill's mother. Nathan's mother used
to tell of O'Neill's mother "that the girl was strikingly beautiful

and was looked up to by the students and teachers alike as the most pious girl in the place." This validates the observation that in real life she received and felt more self-esteem from her piety than from her beauty as a woman. Clearly, O'Neill, in portraying his mother, captured this unconscious ideal of purity and piety which was in conflict with her role throughout womanhood of lover, wife, and mother.

It was necessary for the author to communicate, portray, and explain to himself and the world that his mother's addiction aimed toward a regressive wish to become a child—in her case, a child of God. The author does not and perhaps cannot elaborate the similar unconscious wish since it is his own. His tuberculosis is a self-revealing symbol that spells out withdrawal from, and renunciation of, a normally active life. At this point, we might restate what was said earlier—the characters Edmund and Mary (Eugene and mother in real life) continued to be unconscious enigmas to O'Neill. This circumstance, we believe, made it possible for this strange biography to become a major-ranking artistic achievement.

Some final comments are in order regarding the silencing of the play by the author. The omission of his marriage and fatherhood must have contributed to the conflict of revealing this play. The use of direct, identifiable biographical material, necessitating such a gross omission for an artistic expression, produced a dilemma for the creator concerning his identity.[5] The artist's internal conflicts are, on the one hand, treated by part of the ego in the usual ways and result in typical solutions, such as neurotic symptoms, sublimations, inhibitions, reaction formations, whereas the other part of the artist's ego utilizes the conflict by the combined efforts of talent and sublimation for the purpose of aesthetic achievement. In the given case, O'Neill was dealing directly with biographical material. This factor undid his capacity for ego dissociation and pro-

[5] Glover (1956) has demonstrated a dissociation of the ego which, according to Beres (1959), is particularly characteristic of the artist's ego.

duced the hybrid of an aesthetic creation with a neurotic inhibition of communication to the public—its normal object.

In the literal sense, the play was given to his wife rather than merely dedicated to a loved person and properly given to the world, as is usually done. Greenacre, in her study "The Childhood of an Artist" (1957), describes the design of the creative artist's object relationships. She demonstrates the duality of the artist's love object—first the usual individual love object, and, in addition, the collective love object or, as she aptly puts it: "the love affair with the world." These two types of object relationships have the qualities and the range of "collective alternates." She states (p. 58): "Such love affairs with the world occupy varying relationships with the individual love relationships, sometimes one being at the expense of the other, at other times or in other individuals appearing as quite separate or complementary attachments. But generally the more powerfully demanding one is that of the world." I would extend this duality of the object relationship of the artist to a corresponding duality of his own identity—a personal identity and a world (artistic) identity, both sensitive to similar unconscious strivings.[6] Usually the artist creates from his world identity for the collective love object. To create from his personal identity may produce a deviation toward the goal of the more personal love object and less toward the collective object. The aesthetic product may then be subject to more stringent restrictions, for example, in the area of communication, because the prohibition for the personal identity is usually more severe than it would be for the collective one.[7]

[6] The development of Stanislavski's "personal" and "artistic" ego has already been described (see Chapter 6).

[7] Greenacre (1957, p. 68) has also considered this from the viewpoint of the distribution of libido in the artist: "When the polarity of the personal sexual investment is not appreciably diminished and displacement has occurred too massively, then the collective love affair also assumes too much of the personal conflict. It is then subject to the same hazards, usually derived from the castration conflict, which have existed in the

Thus in *Long Day's Journey into Night* we find that O'Neill's artistic identity was encroached on by a more personal identity in his new role of conscious autobiographer. Other impurities, aided by *his* physical illness, invaded his identity of the "pure" artist during the period of a dozen years which his first biographer Clark aptly described as a "temporary retirement." During this silent period O'Neill contemplated the plan of writing nine plays about a family, beginning in 1775 and extending the continuation of this family's existence to the present with meticulous regard for chronology. Such an orientation would be more relevant to a conscious biographer or a sociologist than a dramatist. The changes in O'Neill's artistic identity seem indeed to have obstructed the great dramatist and his capacity for communication.

BIOGRAPHY AND BECOMING A DRAMATIST

The biographical fact of O'Neill's tuberculosis is central, not only to the autobiographical play, but also to the biographical crossroad of the subsequent development of O'Neill as an artist and a man. Therefore it may be useful to see how O'Neill viewed himself at that time. In 1919, O'Neill wrote an autobiographical sketch for the *New York Sun,* from which the following is excerpted. "My health broke down, my lung being affected, and I spent six months in a sanatorium thinking it over. It was in this enforced period of reflection that the urge to write first came to me. Then next fall—I was twenty-four—I began my first play—*The Web.*"

He subsequently wrote of this period in the *Journal of Outdoor Life,* in 1923: "Undoubtedly the inactivity forced upon me by the life of a san [sanatorium] forced me to mental

personal sphere. The site and nature of the displacement will further determine the character of the symptomatic invasion of the creative activity."

activity, especially as I had always been high-strung and nervous temperamentally."

It becomes apparent that O'Neill saw himself as having had
six months to cure his tuberculosis and the same six months to
be driven to become a writer. His becoming a dramatist was
evidently psychically more complicated than the mere decision
to become one. It was more complicated than transforming an
active physical life into an active mental life, although the
latter contains a plausible piece of the total truth. One need
only read his play, *The Straw*, to become familiar with O'Neill's
attitude toward his illness. Via Stephen Murray, the young
tubercular newspaper man, we learn that tuberculosis was the
only deliverance from the dull, dire, deadly, and dreary doings
of a small town's significant days.

O'Neill's father had always badgered him to settle down and
make a living. At any rate, the secondary gains of his illness
were to escape the feelings of guilt he might otherwise have
had in abandoning his father's wishes. This conflict between
his father and his own wishes, between earning a living and a
more esoteric life, had been raging ever since he was expelled
from Princeton at seventeen, if not before. He was expelled for
throwing a beer bottle through the window of President
Wilson's house.[8] The significance of this has all the qualities
of a cliché, but the ensuing events of the next few years force
us to recognize the hostility he had displaced from his father
onto the university president. His subsequent passive submission to his father in consequence of his violent collegiate outburst and ousting can already be seen in the next two years
during which he worked as secretary of a mail-order business
in which his father had an interest.

[8] O'Neill perpetuated this dramatic account of his expulsion. Actually,
while drinking, he disrupted the home of the railroad stationmaster near
Princeton. This was reported to the university's president. O'Neill was
suspended only for six weeks, but also failed to take his final exams.

After this the pattern of alternate aggression and submission toward his father set in with a machinelike regularity. In 1909, he went off on a gold-prospecting tour to Honduras. O'Neill says of this venture, "It was my very first trip on my own. I expected to do a lot of jungle shooting." He returned in 1910, to the paternal subservience of assistant manager of his father's theatrical company. After this he rebelled with a sea voyage of "sixty-five days on a Norwegian barque" which landed him in Buenos Aires where he took odd jobs. Of this period he writes, "I landed in Buenos Aires a gentleman so-called and wound up a bum on the docks. Another trip from Buenos Aires to Durban and back ending in complete destitution on the beach—terminated by my signing as an ordinary seaman on a British tramp steamer bound home for New York" (Clark, 1947, p. 14). He tenaciously held on and lived at the waterfront for a few months, and then had one last fling at sea. A last spurt of the rebellion took him from New York to Southampton and back to New York. On his return, he gambled and won a lot of money, had a wild drinking party and days later, "When O'Neill regained consciousness, he found himself on a through train with a ticket for New Orleans. Why New Orleans? No one knows. On his arrival in New Orleans he learned that his father was there, playing the ever-popular Monte Cristo" (Clark, 1947, p. 17). Clark treats this as mere coincidence. But we are not surprised to learn that O'Neill now subserved his father as a minor actor in the latter's theatrical troupe—always a new job under his father which disguises the repetition of the subservience. This leads us to the summer of 1912, when he took a job as cub reporter in New London, the city in which his father owned a home for many years. A few months later he developed tuberculosis, which was the compromise and the termination of his acts of rebellion and submission toward his father. Again we must remind ourselves that this period of conflict coincides with his unsuccessful marriage from which a son was born. We note with amazement that this unhappy incident is completely avoided by his biographer and by the autobiographer, although not suppressed. It is never intertwined with O'Neill's struggle with, and resignation toward, his father who frequently admonished the young O'Neill as to the kind of life he should lead.

The alternation of aggressive rebellions and passive submissions is clearly part of O'Neill's oedipal conflict. This aggressive rebellion included his unconscious wish to outdo and remove his father and have his mother as a sexual object. The passive submission included a surrender of his masculinity and becoming a passive feminine love object like his mother as a punishment for his aggressive strivings. These statements are not made glibly; they are borne out in full detail in O'Neill's dramatic characters. For instance, in *Desire under the Elms,* the unconscious autobiography, the youngest of the household, Eben, replaces his dead mother as "cook and housekeeper" for the father; in his rebellion against the father he becomes the lover of the latter's last wife and fathers her child. That this episode is related to the personal conflict of O'Neill with his own father becomes apparent in *Desire under the Elms* in which young Eben represents O'Neill and Cabot represents his father.

One wonders about his father, the hard-working, penurious parent. In his autobiographical play, O'Neill tells us more about his father, who confesses to the son that he is really unhappy about his unfulfilled ideals. The temptation to earn a great deal of money through a repetitious repertoire of a single play, *The Count of Monte Cristo,* which he did year in and year out, had robbed him of the potential of developing into a full artist. The elder O'Neill never forgot that Edwin Booth had told him that he could play Othello better than the great actor himself could. The father unconsciously furthered the dramatist's struggle against himself. He always welcomed his son home and helped him. He sent him to Harvard to study in Baker's "Forty-Seven" playwriting class. He subsidized the publication of his earliest unsuccessful plays. He offered to direct his son's play *Before Breakfast* at the Provincetown Theater in 1916, when Eugene sought his father's advice.

In *Long Day's Journey into Night,* O'Neill also portrays his father's lifelong escape into drink, which helped him drown his feelings of depression caused by the disappointment of his frustrated artistic ambitions. As the father haunts local bars seeking solace, the young son takes longer strides into the world, seeking his place in the sun or in the shadow to which as yet he was neither committed nor designated.

The father's unconscious ideal of pure acting and the mother's unconscious ideal of purity of purpose in life (asexuality) are significant determining identifications that O'Neill developed and maintained in his subsequent life as an artist. Many other factors in his life cemented and shaped his artistic career. Greenacre expresses the conviction that, in the development of talent, identifications play a significant role and simulate inheritance. "Fortunate is that creative child or youth who has available within his own family individuals suitable for these identifications and reinforcements of his own creative needs"[9] (Greenacre, 1957, p. 66). During his earliest years of life, O'Neill's family were all associated with the theater. Moreover, until the age of seven he heard endless dramatic tales from his Scottish nurse.

However, the crucial determinant (which always has the appearance of being accidental or "fate") for the developing dramatist was certainly his "touch of tuberculosis." The ensuing physical inactivity forced him into mental activity. Thus O'Neill tells us that his neurotic conflicts were enacted in his rebellious travels and his capitulating homecomings—charac-

[9] Stanislavski's fortunate opportunities for such identifications have been elaborated (see Chapter 6).

teristic of his aggression and submission to his father. In psychoanalytic work we usually find that when these conflicts are not confined to fantasy life but for various reasons (such as tolerance of the ego) are acted out, the patient as well as the analyst find it extremely difficult to halt their continued enactment. This was the task confronting O'Neill when tuberculosis forced inactivity on him, thus enabling him to displace his energies onto mental activity. However, his acting out could never be restricted to a personal fantasy life. Many of his plays deal with characters and actions which are identifiable with his own uncontrollable enactments. The rich, vivid variations of his short-lived period of acting out are preserved in the variations of characters and themes in his dramas. More to the point, we often find our dramatist barely disguised on stage in many of his plays.

Thus his playwriting is a new solution for expressing his rebellion by its contents. Furthermore, this was certainly not a way to earn a living, as his father had demanded. O'Neill was bitterly disappointed and never forgave his father for considering sending him to a public sanatorium since his father could well afford the expense of private care. O'Neill's intense bitterness was an expression of his frustrated unconscious wish to be supported and controlled by his father. It may be a social paradox—but not a psychoanalytic one—that the young man who bitterly enacted symbolic deeds of becoming independent of his father, protested with equal bitterness his father's inadequate support during his illness. These variations verify the unresolved ambivalence in the relationship with his father.

Tuberculosis provided the compromise: on the one hand, he was being taken care of; on the other, he could shift his rebellious acts to such sublimated dramatic enactments as his early sea voyage plays and his early plays of parental and inner conflict. This compromise was perhaps of lifelong duration. O'Neill lived the life of a tubercular much beyond the six-month period required for his cure. The pattern of the six months became

the pattern of a lifetime. For a year after his discharge he lived
with a family in New London, continuing the regimen of the
tubercular patient. This pattern was still discernible during
the next several years when he lived in Provincetown. Life was
maintained in an endless therapeutic regimen.

O'Neill sees himself emerging as a dramatist as a result of a
contemplated decision reached during a contemplative period.
We prefer to see the playwright born as a result of a dynamic
psychic conflict rearranging itself into physical illness and creative sublimations. Perhaps of even greater psychoanalytic significance in understanding O'Neill, the man, was that his falling
ill and his sublimated activity were essential to his identification with his mother. Her illness forced her into a neurotic
retreat (which simulated a sublimated religious retreat). However, the pursuit of the total man O'Neill is beyond our horizon.
We shall be satisfied if we can uncover fragments of the formation of the artist. As it is with many artists, O'Neill's early life
was a painful emotional struggle until he found himself as a
dramatist.[10]

No psychobiographical study of O'Neill can ignore the fact
that his dramas embody an amazing amount of psychoanalytic
insight, often related to his own specific conflicts.[11] For example, his portrayal of the members of the Mannon family in
Mourning Becomes Electra finds confirmation in the most recent concepts of mourning. This play was written in 1931—

[10] Greenacre notes the frequency of such emotional crises in the lives
of artists. She points out that when creative talent is still in a state of
potentiality and if "for any reason channels of outlet are blocked, states
of frustration and blind frenzy with very slight provocation may arise.
The best description I know of this is Helen Keller's autobiography, in
which she gives a picture of her inner explosiveness before her need to
communicate could be channeled expressively after the illness which cut
off both sight and hearing" (1957, p. 69).

[11] Wittels (1944) felt that O'Neill worked with "a profound knowledge of Freud's incest complex." Peck (1935) recognizes O'Neill's capacity to portray "obscure psychological problems" and to "reveal fundamental realities of human life."

antedating our fuller formulation on the dynamics of mourning by many years.[12] Nevertheless, his is not the mastered knowledge of the scientist, as has often been implied. In his attempts to understand himself, his insight is mundane. It is only in his created characters that he approximates exquisite psychoanalytic elaborations of personality structure.

BIOGRAPHY AND THE UNCONSCIOUS FAMILY AUTOBIOGRAPHICAL DRAMA

Desire under the Elms

In the first part of this study, we attempted to understand the unique utilization of direct biographical material for an aesthetic dramatic creation. It was concluded that O'Neill's conscious contrivance of telescoping into one day the simultaneous unfolding of his mother's drug addiction and his own tuberculosis was an artistic and dramatic method of presenting a family drama, which was particularly poignant in view of the strong identification between mother and son. In studying the chronological accuracy of the biographical data and the autobiographical drama, we find that in both O'Neill is portrayed as an unmarried young man of twenty-three when in fact he had been already married for two years, fathered a son, and was approaching the termination of this marriage. We have assayed this as beyond artistic license. O'Neill utilized artistic license in pushing back the date of his illness four months to coincide with his mother's breakdown, since this matter is properly dated in his self-supervised biography. Although his marriage is correctly dated in the biography, it is

---

[12] O'Neill created the mournful Lavinia (*Mourning Becomes Electra*) as if he understood the latest concepts of mourning as they were developed by Dr. Edith Jacobson (1954) in which the mourner introjects the lost love object into the object- and self-representations of his ego as well as its concomitant introjection into the superego. For further details see Chapter 11.

isolated, abbreviated, completely dissociated and disconnected from the dramatic doings of the coinciding period. It is treated like O'Neill's screen memory of himself.[13]

In psychoanalysis, the biographical data would be the conscious life history with its great gaps that the patient would tell us early and easily enough. The conscious autobiography—or the "personal myth," as Kris (1956) has aptly put it—would be analogous to the subsequent emotional recounting of the life story, but still not disclosing the forgotten fantasies and facts. Then the patient, with increasing intensity and a limited utilization of free association, directs himself to an understanding of his unconscious conflicts. In analogy, an artistic creation, regarded as an unconscious biography, becomes the free associations and the royal road to our writer's unconscious—a road leading to the reconstruction of specific experiences, both factual and fantasied.

Our purpose at this point is to utilize one of O'Neill's significant achievements, *Desire under the Elms,* as a reciprocal tool to reconstruct specific experiences in his life and to demonstrate how its otherwise obscured or repressed contents were only made available in this aesthetic accomplishment. Our effort is not to be confused with the thoroughgoing work of a psychoanalysis, which aims at reconstructing as many infantile, childhood, and later experiences as are clinically possible in any given case. It would be incorrect to imply that a complete study of all the writings of O'Neill—or for that matter, the total artistic output of any other artist—would lead to a total psychoanalytic reconstruction that would in any way approximate clinical analysis. Studies of applied psychoanalysis frequently assume, explicitly or implicitly, that the totality of the artist or the man becomes approachable through the all-inclu-

[13] A screen memory may be likened to a collage. Fragments of various memories from different periods of life are unified into a single memory which seems to make sense but serves the purpose of obscuring from consciousness the full details of one or more past unpleasant phenomena.

sive study of his works. It is more likely, however, that many of the individual creations of a given artist utilize the same conflicts repeatedly.

A summary of the plot of *Desire under the Elms* is indicated. The play is set in the early summer of 1850. Ephraim Cabot, age seventy-five, a New England farmer, a religious man with a concept of a severe God, returns to his home with an attractive, thirty-five-year-old bride, a young widow, as his third wife. Abbie has married Ephraim to secure a home for herself. Ephraim has two sons from his first wife—Simeon, age thirty-nine, and Peter, age thirty-seven—and a younger son, Eben, age twenty-five, from his second wife. Both wives have died. The two older sons, on learning from Eben that their father was en route with his new bride, decide to make their way to California in search of gold. Eben induces the two brothers to assign to him their rights as heirs to the farm for $600, which he stole from his father's hiding place. We are informed that the father and the two older sons work the farm, while young Eben keeps house for the family in place of his dead mother. Ephraim regards young Eben as soft and weak, like the boy's mother, whereas the two older brothers see Eben as a tower of strength and determination, not unlike their father.

With the permanent departure of the two older brothers, the play confines itself to the lives of Eben, Ephraim, and Abbie. Eben looks on Abbie as a designing intruder who will rob him of his inheritance. Abbie is attracted to Eben. She wants Ephraim to die and leave her the farm. She induces the father to believe that she could conceive a child of his. In his enthusiasm, Ephraim promises her that their child will become sole heir to the property. Abbie then deliberately seduces Eben for the purpose of having a child, and, in the process, they fall in love with each other. Eben then feels the power and revenge against his father whom he hates. In the consummation scene, the seduction occurs in Eben's mother's special room. Eben's dead mother sanctions the love act, encourages Eben to love and trust Abbie. Eben's love for Abbie transforms itself from a filial love to a sexual one. The son intensifies his revenge by telling his father that he, Eben, is actually the father of the newborn child. The father counters with a blow, telling Eben that Abbie had only pretended to love the young man in order to become heir to the property by giving Ephraim, the old man, a son. This revives Eben's original hatred of Abbie, and he decides to run away. Then Abbie kills the baby to prove her love for Eben. Momentarily Eben thinks that she had killed the father. Eben is reassured by her act that she loves him. Then Eben seeks out the police and confesses voluntarily that he is an accomplice to the murder and is prepared to be punished with Abbie. The final scene shows Abbie and Eben being taken away, happy, united, and victorious in their love and crime.

An explanation of the title of the play rounds out the mood and theme of the play. This can best be accounted for by quoting O'Neill's introductory stage directions concerning the house: "Two enormous elms are on each side of the house. They bend their trailing branches down over the roof. They appear to protect and at the same time subdue. There is a sinister maternity in their aspect, a crushing jealous absorption. They have developed from their intimate contact with the life of man in the house an appalling humaneness. They brood oppressively over the house. They are like exhausted women resting their saggy breasts and hands and hair on its roof, and when it rains their tears trickle down monotonously and rot on the shingles."

The intensity of this description has always impressed me as one written by a man who had been recently in the midst of the most intense mourning for his mother. Evidence for this was not attainable from direct biographical sources. Subsequent investigation revealed that O'Neill's mother and only brother were dead by the year 1923. His father died in 1920. The play was written in 1924. Thus the preconditions for writing an unconscious family biography and personal autobiography were much the same as they were in 1940, when O'Neill wrote the conscious family biography and personal autobiography, *Long Day's Journey into Night,* namely, that all concerned were dead.

The family situation in the two plays is identical. In *Long Day's Journey into Night* there is first his mother (age fifty-four), who is described as still having "a young graceful figure, a trifle plump, but showing little evidence of middle-aged waist and hips, although she is not tightly corseted." The father is sixty-five years, the older brother, thirty-four, and O'Neill himself is twenty-four. In *Desire under the Elms,* written in 1924, there is the father, aged seventy-five (in 1923, had he lived, O'Neill's father would have been seventy-six years old). Abbie, the stepmother, attractive and thirty-five years old, is certainly in the image of his mother. The two older brothers, thirty-nine and thirty-seven, who appear briefly in the play, are portrayed in a twinlike singularity representing unconsciously and biographically O'Neill's older brother and another aspect of his own self. Finally, Eben, aged twenty-five, represents O'Neill (unknown to himself) with his usually unallowable unconscious wishes. The fact that the characters in these two plays are not represented identically does not mean that we are merely juxtaposing matters of slight similarity and overevaluating their identity. The characters in a created play—a product of the unconscious—should be treated like the manifest content of the characters in a dream or fantasy; their latent meaning can be identified only by associations of similarity. To strengthen our contention that, for example, O'Neill's father and Ephraim Cabot are identical, it might be pointed out that in both biographical dramas they are portrayed as older men who are powerful, patriarchal, and penurious. Both men have an intense passion for property. In each play, in almost identical dialogues, it is said about each of them that they would buy the sky if it were property. The author's

images of the two fathers, real and created, spring from a
single source.

A similar identity can be demonstrated between O'Neill's
mother in the family play and Abbie. Both seek and demand
intensely a home from their husbands. Mary complains that
they have always lived in second-rate hotels, and Abbie tells
Eben about her desperate longing for a home. The brothers,
Simeon and Peter, chronologically represent O'Neill's older
brother who is in his thirties when O'Neill is in his twenties.
In their brief appearance, aspects of their histories are more
parts of O'Neill's life than his brother's. Thus Simeon, thirty-
nine, tells us how at the age of twenty-one he lost his wife
Jenn. Jenkins is the maiden name of O'Neill's first wife, to
whom he was married when he was twenty-one. Simeon and
Peter both leave to seek gold in California, as O'Neill did in
1909 when "he set out on his gold-prospecting trys to Honduras." In addition, there is the identity of Eben and O'Neill—
they are, respectively, twenty-five and twenty-four in the biographical plays. However, the matter of being a father to a
son is handled very differently in the two plays. Whereas in the
conscious autobiography O'Neill's fatherhood is completely
obliterated by powerful defense mechanisms, in the unconscious drama he is a father in violation of the most intense
taboo known to man. Subsequently he obliterates his fatherhood by accusing himself of an uncommitted crime. This pro-
vides us with an opportunity to examine the vicissitudes of
an unconscious conflict in the personal life of the artist.

A life situation (marriage, fatherhood, and divorce) about
which there has been an unconscious conflict is treated in
personal life with complete suppression and repression of
both its contents and affects, respectively. It reappears in a
creation, unknown to the creator, for what it is—a part of his
own biography. Under these conditions, it becomes possible
for the artistic part of the ego to elaborate the total content of
the unconscious conflict with all its painful affects. The crea-

tion has the complete content and pain, whereas the life situation is devoid of either content or pain.

The unfolding of Eben's conflicts can be organized into a constellation or a design of an oedipal situation and its fantasies. On the one hand, Eben is his father's rival, first with his real mother and then with his stepmother. He had won the love of his mother at the expense of his father. For the fulfillment of this wish he suffers the punishment of surrendering his masculinity by adopting the passive feminine life of his mother: he becomes his father's housekeeper, as his mother had been. When Abbie enters the picture, the old conflict is revived; he wins her sexually and fathers her child. His punishment for this is the loss of his child, the loss of the farm, and imprisonment. He is unable to grow beyond his sexual feelings for his mother and his death wishes toward his father. Thus he is destined to failure in resolving his oedipal strivings.

Our conclusion would be that O'Neill's life situations are mirrored in the image of his unconscious counterpart, Eben, and that O'Neill's lovemates are reflected in the image of Abbie and Eben's mother—a maternal and sexual object rightfully belonging to the father. Further, the role of being father to a real child belonged to the image of Abbie's baby— a child that cannot live and be recognized as long as Ephraim lives—the unconscious image for O'Neill's father. Also, the unconscious identification with his mother's ideal of purity and worldly abstinence contributes to the surrender of parenthood. In the final moment of *Desire under the Elms,* Eben and Abbie are seen united (identified with each other) in a "child-destroyed" punishable love, reminding us again of Edmund (O'Neill) and Mary (his mother) in the conscious biographical drama.

We can now better understand why O'Neill never saw his first son, Eugene, Jr., until the boy was ten years old, in 1920. Not until then—the time of his father's death—could O'Neill recognize his son as his own. Until then O'Neill is denied his paternity, as Eben is denied his child. In 1920, when Eugene, Jr., was ten years old, O'Neill went to see him for the first time. He then became interested in his son and began to participate in plans for his education and general care. He was also able to establish some relationship with his son, who grew increasingly fond of him.

This is not to be construed to imply that O'Neill was now able to assume the full role of a father. The death of his father was an essential circumstance, momentarily undoing the severest prohibition against having a child. There is much evidence that O'Neill had to struggle all his life with the same conflict in connection with the subsequent children from his second wife. Recent newspaper accounts of and interviews with his children clearly establish that O'Neill held himself apart from his children throughout his life, while at the same time he made sporadic though short-lived efforts to recognize and relate to them. At the end of his life, he remained unreconciled to them, and they were not recognized as his rightful heirs.

As to O'Neill's relationship with women, it is generally conceded that much unhappiness prevailed in his marriages. It is fairly clear that O'Neill tended to idealize a loved woman to the point of desexualization. In his life and in his created characters that unconsciously portray himself, there is a brief enactment of mature sexuality—that is, love, marriage, and children—which then regresses to a desexualized idealization of the loved woman accompanied by a regressive abandonment of the child or children. This regressive path was often followed by establishing relationships with prostitutes, who also became desexualized, and was limited to relationships of a mother's nurturing love for a son and the son's love for a comforting mother. As with the regressive abandonment of a child, the regressive surrender of a loved woman is self-directed by the living, punishing father and the identification with a virginal mother.

One wonders whether O'Neill's father in real life was much

different from Ephraim, the created prototype. Considerable evidence is available that the father was as morally severe and restrictive to O'Neill and his brother as Ephraim was to Eben and to the other sons. The elder O'Neill made every effort to merge his sons into his own life and to make them subservient to himself. In *Long Day's Journey into Night*, James, Jr., the elder son, bitterly complains that the father forced him to become an actor against his will. Not until O'Neill developed tuberculosis did his father begrudgingly help him achieve his own ambition—to become a dramatist. Prior to this, his father always encouraged him to work under him as a secretary in his business, an assistant manager, or as a totally minor actor in his play. It would seem that he encouraged the passive subservience of his sons. For Eugene, the early sea voyages and endeavors to make his own way were suffered with an atmosphere of parental excommunication. Neither in the play nor in biographical material is there evidence that the elder O'Neill encouraged his sons to pursue their self-directed desires for mature achievements and mature manhood.

In *Desire under the Elms*, O'Neill chose to set his conflicts in a family of hard-working, primitive, God-fearing people. In this respect too, Ephraim resembles O'Neill's real father, who was an uneducated boy and supported his family from the age of ten. Certainly, O'Neill's choice of a primitive family to mouth the primitive conflicts of the play was also determined by his great talent to construct families appropriate for his dramatic conflict.

In *Desire under the Elms*, as in *Long Day's Journey into Night*, the character of the woman (Abbie or his mother) remains an unconscious enigma to the author, in sharp contrast to the realistic portrayals of the father. We cannot fail to recognize that the author intends Abbie to be much more than an attractive stepmother. She is linked with the symbols of long-endured suffering motherhood—the elm trees. She is linked with Eben's mother who loved her son and was more devoted to him and her stepsons than to her husband. This is a composite concept, similar to what O'Neill contended with in his own life in his relationships with women. O'Neill's mother's unconscious ideal of chastity and purity became his own unconscious ideal of womanhood and manhood. The contribution of his mother and father to the formation of his ego-ideals and his conscience gives the personal stamp to many of the unconsciously determined creations of O'Neill.

Engel concluded about O'Neill that "sequestering himself, he distilled from modern life the futility, the emptiness, the chaos, and left out the particulars of external events. Yet, preoccupied though he was with the universal and the abstract, he continually revealed the thinly disguised particulars and concrete facts of his personal life" (Engel, 1953). Engel subsequently gives evidence that he evaluates the appearance of the thinly veiled personal life in O'Neill's works as a consciously controlled activity. He is of the opinion that if O'Neill had been born a generation earlier, he would have been a hackneyed dramatist, rewriting a meaningless version of *The Count of Monte Cristo* for his father. I would rather think that if O'Neill rewrote this play, he would—by necessity of overdetermination of unconscious conflicts—write it in the vein of his powerful tragedies, as he transformed the Aeschylean trilogy of *The Furies* into a more tragic *Mourning Becomes Electra*.

O'Neill's sense of tragedy—referred to as his sixth sense—was a result of his psychic conflicts. As I said earlier, O'Neill did not decide to become a dramatist. He was driven to it.

9

Shaw's Childhood
and *Pygmalion*

IT WOULD BE MOST VALUABLE for the study of creative imagination to record Shaw's conscious intentions in writing *Pygmalion* as we search for his unconscious motivations. It will be noted that whatever he had in mind consciously will be matched subsequently with evidence from his unconscious imagery. A recurrent theme appears in almost all his previous plays and was destined to reappear in some subsequent plays. Such repetitions have the stamp of unconscious imagery and differentiate it from conscious imagery which all artists use as part of their skill and technique.[1]

In Shaw's preface to *Pygmalion* he writes that one of the purposes of the play was to pay tribute to those men who contributed to the study of phonetics and who had greatly influenced Shaw in his early adolescence and adult years through their personal relationships with him. He begins with Alex-

[1] In the next chapter, we shall encounter a recurrent prostitutional theme in Tennessee Williams' heroines.

ander Melville Bell,[2] the father of Alexander Graham Bell, inventor of the telephone, and then goes on to Alexander J. Ellis and Tito Pagliardini. His prototype for Henry Higgins, to whom he wanted to pay a personal tribute, was his contemporary, Henry Sweet. The latter's spirit of revolt against convention added the necessary ingredients for a Shavian dramatic character. Shaw further tells us that were it not for the great phoneticists like Sweet it would not be possible to create great actresses who most often come from humble origins and whose native dialects are transformed by their mastery of first-rate speech.

Shaw tells us that in his play we can find some autobiographical aspects. More precisely, autobiographical to Shaw means someone like Henry Sweet whom he knew in his midtwenties, or someone connected with his journalistic career or Fabian Society activities. He remained unaware that autobiographical character creations like Eliza Doolittle and Henry Higgins were derived from his early childhood memories and fantasies; the original models for his characters were his mother and her vocal teacher Vandeleur Lee.

Examined from a psychoanalytic angle, the theme of Shaw's *Pygmalion* reveals unconscious reflections on psychobiographical data from his early personal and family life. The same early experiences shaped Shaw's distraught emotional state from the time he began to write the play until its first production was launched. Instead of fully enacting his troubled state, he confined its contents to creative enactments within a new drama; to do this the playwright had to successfully dissociate himself from his unconsciously determined personal conflicts. Shaw, the aknowledged literary genius, drew on the appro-

[2] The earliest Bell to influence Shaw was Chichester Bell, who was lodging in the same house with Shaw in Dublin after his mother left for London. Shaw studied Italian with him and was introduced to physics, pathology, and Wagnerian music.

priate Galatean myth which became the living protoplasm for the plot of *Pygmalion* and an essential ingredient in the play's communicativeness.[3]

SYNOPSIS OF THE PLAY

Pygmalion is a play in five acts in which Shaw presents a romance between a young cockney flower girl, Eliza Doolittle, and a middle-aged bachelor phoneticist, Henry Higgins; Higgins attempts to make a lady out of her. He wagers Colonel Pickering, a somewhat older colleague, that within six months he will succeed in passing her off as a duchess at a fashionable party. During the period of Eliza's re-education she lives in the home of Higgins along with Pickering. Eliza's father, Mr. Doolittle, appears through the play as a lighthearted, ineffectual, and sham protector of his daughter's morality. Higgins' mother, Mrs. Higgins, is the ardent promoter for a marriage between the flower girl and her son. Following a preliminary and precarious tryout in the society of Higgins' mother, the final test is carried through successfully at an ambassador's party. By Act IV, Eliza has triumphed; Higgins is satisfied but restless for another adventure. Eliza has been transformed into a lady and now demands love and respect from her creator. The bewildered Higgins appears to be vaguely and indecisively in love with her. The play ends in ambiguity as to the final outcome of the future relationship between the hero and heroine.

[3] Giovacchini (1957) has examined Shaw's capacity for communication in which he compares it to the analytic process of interpretation. Erikson (1956) has examined the formations of Shaw's identities of "snob," "noisemaker," and "diobolicalone" which he feels were significant for the power of his ego to integrate his "ripened capacity." Erikson describes Shaw as an outstanding individual "who labored as hard on the creation of a world-wide public identity for himself, as he worked on his literary masterpieces."

PYGMALION'S CHARACTERS CREATED
FROM SHAW'S CHILDHOOD

The qualities of Eliza Doolittle find their counterpart in Shaw's mother (also named Lucinda Elizabeth, from which we assume Eliza is derived) in many significant areas. As Eliza dedicated her life to the development of her speaking voice, so did Shaw's mother put her total energy into the mastery of her musical voice. As Eliza transgresses conventionality by living with Higgins and Pickering during the period of her education in speech, so in real life Shaw's mother lived in an even more complicated *ménage à trois* with her music teacher Vandeleur Lee and her husband, along with her three children, so that she could further her vocal and musical career. When Shaw created Eliza he also endowed her with an aptitude and talent for the piano and singing which charm her educators.

As Eliza struggled to raise her social position, so did Shaw's mother, both as a young girl and young woman. With the aid of her maiden guardian Aunt Ellen, she laid plans "for the conquest of a well-appointed peer." In Shaw's postscript to *Pygmalion* he envisions Eliza married to the ineffectual Freddy (a secondary character in the play) and continuing her intense relationship with Higgins. He forecasts the possibility of Eliza and Freddy living under Higgins' roof, much the same as Shaw's mother and father lived under Vandeleur Lee's roof.

Examining these circumstances it becomes clear that Henry Higgins is unconsciously cast in the mold of Lee, who undoubtedly was a father figure for Shaw. Lee was the dominating male in the Shaw household, having readily displaced Shaw's father in Shaw's mother's respect and affection. In his writings Shaw speaks of his mother's disillusionment in his father when she discovered that he was a heavy drinker; she threatened to leave him at the very beginning of the marriage. Although they did not actually live in the same house until Shaw was ten years old, Lee appeared as a complicating factor very early in the marriage of Shaw's parents, probably at the time of Shaw's infancy. It can be assumed that Shaw's oedipal conflict centered not only in the usual drama of father, mother, and son, but was additionally complicated by Lee and his mother's admiration for the latter.

Lee's mastery over Shaw's mother via voice training was the area of choice in which Shaw could exploit his own fantasies to win his mother. With but a slight switch from vocal music to speech, Higgins becomes a disguised compromise (unconsciously determined) between the literary speech-making Shaw and the voice-training Lee; Higgins is in pursuit of the malleable Eliza, the created prototype for Shaw's mother. Further evidence that Vandeleur Lee was a hero to the young Shaw (between the ages of six and nine) is to be noted in Shaw's intensely excited reactions and overdevotion to General Robert E. Lee's participation in the Civil War. During this time Shaw avidly followed the bulletins of the General's campaign. This was one of Shaw's childhood recollections. Shaw commented: "Lee was undoubtedly one of the world's great military strategists; and although Wellington is one of my idols as a soldier, I am inclined to believe that Lee was his superior as a strategist" (Henderson, 1956). Shaw's identification with the General extends itself to an identification with the "weak child," the South, in its rebellion against the "parental" North.

Henry Higgins, then, is the created character fused from Shaw's oedipal fantasies and from his memories of the successful activities of his parental rival Vandeleur Lee. In *Pygmalion*, a realistic version is molded into the character of Colonel Pickering, a benign, older accomplice and colleague.

Shaw's childhood and early adult life bear testimony that he identified himself with Lee. For example, some of Shaw's famous practices in abstinence (such as his vegetarianism) were imitative of Lee, who believed that brown bread and open windows were indispensable safeguards against all ills. Shaw's oedipal conflict with Lee must have been intensely vivid when Shaw's mother broke up the family and with her two daughters followed Lee to London, deserting her husband and fifteen-year-old son, Bernard Shaw. Five years later Shaw rejoined his mother in London and resumed his complicated relationship with Lee. Shaw's first job in London was as a "ghost writer" for Lee, as a music critic and pamphleteer. Thus the literary genius, Shaw, came to his true course via a long-standing identification. Shaw explains his part in re-writing Lee's book (*The Voice*):

> I set to work to provide this and had drafted a good deal in shorthand when Lee's sudden death put an end to the project; and my career as a pseudo-Lee closed forever—Let no Shaviotralrous professor of literature therefore hereafter dig up and announce it as a newly discovered masterpiece. The hand is my hand; but the soul of it was Lee. He was a genius in his way, but not in my way (Henderson, 1956).

Shaw declares this episode as the termination of his "Lee career." But his emotional involvement with Lee continued and reappeared in Shaw's created characters. Henry Higgins is a case in point.[4]

---

[4] Greenacre (1957) has emphasized the significance of the fact that many artists have talented fathers with whom the future artists can identify. In Shaw's case, Lee, as a gifted father figure, seemed to impede as well as aid Shaw's creative progress. After Lee's death in 1886, Shaw, now past thirty, began to write for himself but retained the need to offer his writings in the name of someone else (see, e.g., his pseudonym Corno di Bassetto, *London Music*, 1888–1889). The need to be someone else was never thoroughly shed by Shaw. Bentley (1957, p. 101) comments on Shaw's first two plays: "Shaw took up a couple of plays by less skilled

The counterpart for Eliza's father, Mr. Doolittle, is structured on the life of Shaw's maternal grandfather, Walter Bagnal Gurly. In *Pygmalion,* Mr. Doolittle is a widower with a grown marriageable daughter whom he neglects in the pursuit of solving his own personal problems. In the play, Mr. Doolittle dramatically announces his plan to marry his common-law wife, while Eliza is in the midst of the most intense struggle about her feelings concerning marriage, love, and Henry Higgins. A similar event took place in the life of Shaw's mother at an age corresponding to Eliza's; her widowed father, Walter Gurly, suddenly announced he would marry again; this announcement shocked all his relatives. He had been penniless and heavily in debt to his deceased wife's brother and sister, who were also burdened with the upbringing and marital concerns of Gurly's neglected daughter, Shaw's mother. In reaction to her father's remarriage, Shaw's mother suddenly announced her own marriage to Shaw's father, whom the family considered a most unsuitable suitor. Similarly, Shaw's *Pygmalion* ends on an ambiguous note as to Eliza's next move in the solution of her life problems, as she learns of her father's marriage. So involved was Shaw with Eliza's life that he wrote a protracted postscript to the play in which he spelled out the heroine's future as if she were a real person. It is significant for our purpose to establish the (unconscious) identity of Mr. Doolittle (Eliza's father) and Mr. Gurly (Shaw's maternal grandfather) in order to further the evidence that Eliza Doolittle is the created representative of Shaw's mother in childhood. Finally, the character of Mrs. Higgins, the hero's mother, again has her counterpart in Shaw's mother—but this time as a realistic portrayal of her as a woman in her sixties, when Shaw himself was in his early forties. Shaw conceived the character of Eliza in 1898 (age

---

and more conventional hands—William Archer's *Rhinegold* and Janet Achurch's *Mrs. Daintry's Daughter* and by 'inverting' the characters arrived at *Widowers' Houses* and *Mrs. Warren's Profession.*"

forty-two) and did not write the play until 1912 (age fifty-six).[5]

CREATED CHARACTERS AND
CURRENT LIFE

Until this point we have only accounted for a one-dimensional unconscious representation of the characters in *Pygmalion*. We shall now demonstrate that Shaw tended to re-enact his early object relationships either in current real relationships or in the creation of his play characters. Thus "acting out" in real life was used interchangeably with the creation of play figures. Henry Higgins is a composite of Shaw between the ages of forty-two and fifty-six, coupled with his childhood fantasies and his identification with Vandeleur Lee. Mrs. Patrick Campbell is the Eliza of Shaw's current life, as his mother was in childhood. The fusion of past and present object relationships into a single created character will be viewed from the perspective of Shaw's ego capacity for creativity. At one moment Shaw would be overwhelmed by enactment in personal relationships (derived from early experiences) which gave his life dramatic color; at another moment he could extricate himself from these enactments by creating a character that represented both the early and the current object. This creative transformation diluted the excessive feelings (libidinal and aggressive) he invested in the love object. The energies were redirected to the created love object where the excessive expression was more appropriate. In a letter to Mrs. Campbell, Shaw wrote, "I looked at the piano and I said, 'Good God! fancy listening to *that* when I can listen to her.' Is this dignified? Is it sensible? At my age—a driveller—a dotard! I will conquer this weakness or trade in it and write plays about it" (Dent, 1952).

---

[5] Shaw's father was fifty-six when he was permanently deserted by Shaw's mother.

In 1897 Shaw wrote to Ellen Terry that he had an idea for a play for Mrs. Patrick Campbell. *"Caesar and Cleopatra* has been driven clear out of my head by a play I want to write in which he will be a West End gentleman and she [Campbell] an East End donna in an apron and three orange and red ostrich feathers" (Terry, 1931). Fifteen years later Shaw wrote this character as Eliza Doolittle. The enactments in this play, inspired by and written for Mrs. Campbell, occurred simultaneously with the romance in real life between Shaw and Pat Campbell. The personal relationship concluded with a defeat for Shaw, whereas the play ends in an unresolved finale with appropriate aesthetic ambiguity.

Henderson (1956) in a chapter entitled "Joey and Stella" (Shaw and Campbell) writes of this relationship.

> Was this merely epistolary courtship with the *arrière pensée* of winning her for the Liza role? Or was he enamored, infatuated with this somewhat faded beauty, a lioness with very sharp claws always but slightly sheathed? Who shall say? The threads were so entangled, the motives—sex amorism, coquetry, jealousy—so commingled with managerial plans, histrionic and dramatic ambitions, the temperaments of the principals so aggressive, self-assertive, egoistic, vain, mischievous—that even the most expert psychoanalyst would be baffled by the task of unraveling the web.

I concur with Henderson as to the difficulty of the problem. Add to this Shaw's written comment to Mrs. Campbell when she was about to publish her autobiography: "It will be hard enough on her [Charlotte], as it is, to see her husband as the supreme ass of a drama of which you are the heroine. Pity that it must be dramatized; but the thing itself cannot be put into words." Shaw at age seventy-five commented on the affair and compared it to his correspondence with Ellen Terry. "Ellen did get down on paper a series of letters which brought her out with flying colors from a correspondence with so artful a practitioner as myself. The whole thing was on paper; it was a correspondence with nothing else; it was literature. But the Stella–G.B.S. [Joey] idyll was acted, not written; it was not on paper and is not literature" (Henderson, 1956).

Shaw first became entranced with Mrs. Pat Campbell in 1897, after hearing her play the piano and sing. Later he stated, "I am convinced that Mrs. Patrick Campbell could thread a needle with her toes as rapidly, as prettily—as she can play an arpeggio." Here we note the link between the voice and music that we had seen in Shaw's early relationship to his mother. When Shaw wrote *Pygmalion* for Mrs. Campbell in 1912, his mother was eighty-two and had suffered a severe stroke. His wife, Charlotte, became afflicted with severe asthma and was less able to take care of herself or Shaw; she frequently had to be sent away for cures. Shaw had married Charlotte in 1898, when he was suffering from tuberculosis of a foot bone and had been bedridden for some time. He was preoccupied with fears of dying since his sister, Agnes, two years older than himself, had died of tuberculosis at the age of twenty-two. Thus the beginning of his marriage had more of a nursing atmosphere than a healthful one, particularly since Shaw also broke his arm during the first two weeks of the marriage and was thoroughly incapacitated. In the subsequent relationship his wife served him mainly in a maternal role. It is little wonder that, threatened by the loss of his real mother and his substitute one (Charlotte, his wife), unconscious sources were activated to re-create and re-evoke the early mother image in artistic and personal enactments, respectively. It is to be remembered that Eliza Doolittle becomes important to Higgins for such purposes as keeping his appointments in order, buying his clothes and food, and putting out his slippers. When Shaw's mother died in February 1913, Mrs. Campbell became increasingly significant to him. Two letters to Mrs. Campbell (Dent, 1952, pp. 90–91) reveal much of the unconscious stirrings within Shaw. They establish links between Shaw's feelings in childhood for his mother and his current feelings toward Mrs. Campbell. The link between Eliza and Mrs. Campbell is established by Shaw's denial of grief over the death of his mother. The first letter was written five days prior to her death.

> 10, Adelphi Terrace, W.C.
> 14th Feb. 1913

> Stella: I must break myself of this: there is some natural magic in it, some predestined adorability for me in you, that makes me quite reckless when I am within reach of you. It is the dark lady the child dreamt of. . . .
>
> So, oh Stella don't ever let me lose it. Don't let me hurt anyone to whom I am bound by all the bonds except the bond of the dark lady to the child. . . . Oh that loathesome but necessary conscience. And oh! this wild happiness that frees me from it!
>
> I saw you first in a dream 43 years ago. I have only just remembered it.

> G.B.S.

Obviously Shaw never knew Mrs. Campbell at the time of the dream. When Shaw wrote this letter he was between fifty-six and fifty-seven years of age and Mrs. Campbell was forty-seven. He would have been thirteen years old at the time of the remembered dream and his mother would have been forty years old. There is little doubt that his present erotic feelings for Mrs. Campbell were related to a repetition of an erotic oedipal dream about his mother during puberty.[6]

The second letter, written three days after the death of Shaw's mother, links Eliza Doolittle to his personal relationship with Mrs. Campbell and shows the connection between

---

[6] During puberty there is a normal resurgence of the original fantasies belonging to the infantile oedipal period. The revived erotic wishes are more threatening after puberty when they are more likely to be accompanied by ejaculatory masturbation. This concern would be especially applicable to someone like Shaw whose early manhood and subsequent married life appear to have been sexually monastic.

Mrs. Campbell and Shaw's mother. Mrs. Campbell became his exclusive confidante regarding his mother's death. The letter indicates that Shaw's wife did not attend the funeral services for his mother. Shaw's defensive denial of grief over his mother's death is to be noted.

> The Mitre, Oxford
> 22nd February 1913

What a day! I must write to you about it, because there is no one else who didn't hate her mother, and even who doesn't hate her children. Whether you are an Italian peasant[7] or a Superwoman I cannot yet find out; but anyhow your mother was not the Enemy.

Why does a funeral always sharpen one's sense of humor and rouse one's spirits? This one was a complete success. No burial horrors. No mourners in black snivelling and wallowing in induced grief. Nobody knew except myself, Barker and the undertaker. . . .

I have many other things of extreme importance to say but must leave them til Monday. . . . If you are gone when I call I shall hurl myself into the arena and perish.

And so goodnight, friend who understands about one's mother and other things.

> G.B.S.

It might be well to clarify the nature of Shaw's object relationships as they were rearranged by his creative career. By 1897 (age forty-one), Shaw had become a recognized playwright, if not yet an outstandingly successful one, and had developed his personal relationships in the theater, particularly with leading actresses. In the few preceding years he established a correspondence and professional friendship with the great Ellen Terry (who was eight years his senior and

---

[7] This is a reference to Mrs. Campbell's origins; she was partly Italian and partly English. Shaw was similarly preoccupied with Eliza Doolittle's social origins.

looked much like his older sister, Lucy, who dabbled in music, acting, and writing). Shaw became increasingly aware of his new powers and began to create plays for the great actresses. To create for them was to create them (Galatea) and to possess them. Viewed from his oedipal situation with Vandeleur Lee, who won his mother from his father with his musical genius, Shaw's unconscious fantasies formed the basis for an ambition for writing for actresses.

Shaw had an intense need for a mother to care for him physically. This need was intensified by the fact that Shaw's mother had been indifferent to and neglectful of his physical and emotional needs when he was a young child. Shaw has poignantly described this lack in his mother in many communications. In particular, he emphasized his mother's complete disinterest as to whether or not her children received any food whatsoever. Shaw's need for a woman who would care for him physically was gratified through his marriage to Charlotte. Nevertheless, Shaw adored and worshiped his mother. He accounts for the development of this overvaluation with psychological insight. In his *Preface to London Music* (Shaw, 1956), he writes, "I hated the servants and liked my mother because on the one or two rare and delightful occasions when she buttered my bread for me, she buttered it thickly instead of merely wiping the knife on it. Her almost complete neglect of me had the advantage that I could idolize her to the utmost pitch of my imagination and had no sordid or disillusioning contacts with her."[8]

It is clearly established that the early neglect by his mother promoted the perpetuation of the omnipotent and omniscient mother image. This image would be projected onto the real mother who then became indispensable and idolized. Small

---

[8] A fine example of literary artistic expression finds its counterpart in psychoanalytic concepts. Freud (1959) has described how the hungry infant hallucinates with gratification the mother's breast. The process is perpetuated during somewhat later stages of development in which the very young child attributes omnipotent qualities to the absent parent.

wonder that Galatea became the common symbol for Shaw's
ego-ideal of a mother, i.e., his created Eliza and his concept of
Mrs. Pat Campbell. Shaw could wish for a maternal nurturing
woman and an overvalued, omnipotent, idealized woman.
What was not permitted to Shaw was a mature sexual relationship. It is well known that his previous adult life (until age
forty-two) showed little sexual activity and that his marital life
followed the same pattern. An overwhelming amount of material on this aspect of Shaw's life is available in essays, biographical, and autobiographical writings. We shall restrict ourselves to that which is relevant to Shaw's creative talents,
particularly in drama, and more particularly to *Pygmalion.*

Shaw has let it be known that he first had sexual intercourse
at the age of twenty-nine. He related his revulsion to sexuality
to the proximity of the sexual and excretory organs. Hence,
Shaw's inhibitions in sexual intercourse are unconsciously
molded by castration fears (i.e., dirty vagina). Most likely his
most severe sexual conflicts, in view of his monastic manhood
and marriage, would have been in the area of ejaculatory
masturbation. Further determinants for his sexual inhibitions
are suggested by the previously quoted erotic dream which related to his mother. His description of himself at the time of his
wedding reveals an incapacitated (castrated), nonsexual man
who surrenders his love object to his parental rival.

> I was very ill when I was married, altogether a wreck on crutches
> and in an old jacket which the crutches had worn to rags. . . . I
> had asked my friends Mr. Graham Wallas of the London School
> Board and Mr. Henry Salt, the biographer of Shelley and De
> Quincey, to act as witnesses. The Registrar never imagined I
> could be the bridegroom, he took me for the inevitable beggar
> who completes all wedding processions. Wallas who is consider-
> able over six feet seemed to him to be the hero of the occasion
> and he was proceeding to marry him calmly to my betrothed,
> when Wallas thinking the formula rather strong for a mere wit-
> ness hesitated at the last moment and left the prize to me (Hen-
> derson, 1956).

In a letter to Beatrice Webb, Shaw writes further of his marriage.

> I found my objections to my own marriage had ceased with my objections to my own death. This was the main change; there were of course many other considerations which we shall probably discuss at some future time. Possibly one of them was that the relation between us had never until then completely lost its inevitable preliminary character of a love affair. She had at last got beyond that corrupt personal interest in me . . . by the way, the dates of the foregoing history are the marriage, 1st June, the move to Hindhead, 10th June, the arm fracture, 17th June (Henderson, 1956).

Shaw's incapacity from tuberculosis of the foot was "not enough"; it had to be compounded by an arm fracture which left him completely helpless during his "honeymoon."

Shaw was in pursuit of the Uranian Venus, the classic love of the aesthete. In the Galatean myth, Venus sanctions the womanhood of Galatea for its creator, Pygmalion. Shaw had no quarrel with the world in its pursuit of direct sexual gratification (giving the misleading impression that it was true of him), but his major personal pursuit was a desexualized aesthetic one. Throughout most of his life, his ego was master of the situation and he was able to desexualize and sublimate his erotic interests in women, which always had the outer form of a love affair. Occasionally he was overwhelmed by uncontrollable sexual urges. A love affair at fifteen, a sexual relationship ending his virgin state at twenty-nine, and the erotic outburst toward Mrs. Campbell at fifty-seven are outstanding moments. The first and the last episodes were mobilized under the threats of the loss of his mother.[9] The threat of his own death from tu-

---

[9] The first incident was at the time of his mother's final separation from his father with whom he was left, not seeing his mother for the next five years; the last incident was at the time of his mother's final illness and subsequent death.

berculosis mobilized the intense need for a "nurturing mother,"
which Shaw consciously recognized (almost completely) and
converted into his sudden need for marriage. In his explanatory
letter to Beatrice Webb he continues,

> It was now plain that I must go away to the country the moment
> I could be moved and that somebody must seriously take in hand
> the job of looking after me. Equally plain, of course, that Char-
> lotte was the inevitable and predestined agent appointed by
> Destiny. To have let her do this in any other character than that
> of my wife would have involved our whole circle and interests
> in a senseless scandal (Henderson, 1956).

Shaw permanently resolved his needs for being mothered
through this marriage. His needs for an omnipotent mother
shaped the variations and inconsistencies in Shaw's personal
and artistic careers. His relationship with Mrs. Pat Campbell
(as with many previous actresses) belonged to the area of his
creative "love affair with the world." At one moment such a relationship would be the stimulus for a new creation (play,
essay, or criticism) and seek its appropriate universal audience;
at another moment the omnipotent object would be wanted
personally and exclusively. At most times these two attitudes
were fused in a confusing fashion. At various times, whenever
Shaw was threatened with the loss of the maternal, nurturing
object, the more unrealistic, fantasied, omnipotent ideal would
be activated and projected onto a real object and pursued. When
Shaw at fifteen was deserted by his mother for five years, he
fell in love with a young girl who was somewhat older than
himself, with the same uncontrolled intensity and idolatry that
was characteristic of his brief outburst (between May and
August 1913) in relation to Mrs. Campbell following his mother's death and wife's illness. In all his life his relationships
with women never approximated this special, intense quality
as on these two occasions.

Shaw's intense emotional distress at this time was compounded of confluent misfortunes in both his personal and professional life. Along with Mrs. Campbell's protracted delay (for about eighteen months) in deciding to appear in the English version, her personal rejection of him via her marriage to George Cornwallis-West compounded his narcissistic injuries which deepened the denied hurts of the loss of his mother and his incapacitated wife. Because Shaw was keenly aware that his plays were severely criticized and belittled in England as too talkative and too much in the style of essays, he avoided an English world premiere for *Pygmalion* and arranged to have it appear first in Vienna and Berlin. Thus we can better understand the precarious state of Shaw's ego at this time.

Pygmalion had its world premiere in Vienna in September 1913, and became an immediate commercial success. A few months later, early in 1914, Shaw succeeded in obtaining Mrs. Campbell for the Eliza Doolittle role. The play was overwhelmingly successful in its London production. Winning Mrs. Campbell for the leading role and the play's great success probably undid the severe injuries that Shaw had sustained and spared him from a crippling depression. His artistic and personal "lives" became less confused and each assumed more reasonable proportions. Shaw, as well as his various biographers (Ervine, 1956; Henderson, 1956; Pearson, 1942), remained confused as to how and why the bizarre (Stella and Joey) incident ever took place. Although they all acknowledge Shaw's overinvolvement with Mrs. Campbell, both Shaw and his biographers failed to be impressed by the significance of the death of Shaw's mother. They forgot that Shaw's capacity to change "tragedy into trivia" (an identification with his father) was a defensive denial mechanism, useful for creative purposes but not necessarily sparing Shaw the deep suffering displaced onto enacted substituted situations. Similarly, the capacity of turning "tragedy into trivia" pervades the atmosphere of the play *Pygmalion*. Born from sources which were painful enough to render them unconscious, the deep-seated conflicts are treated in a light-hearted fashion and style.

SHAW'S UNCONSCIOUS DETERMINANT IN THE CREATION OF *PYGMALION*

The first conscious image (inspiration) for *Pygmalion*, written in 1912, occurred to Shaw in 1897, some fifteen year earlier. I requote the passage of his confidential communication to Ellen Terry. "*Caesar and Cleopatra* has been driven clear out of my mind by a play I want to write in which he will be a West End gentleman and she an East End donna" (Terry, 1931). The psychoanalyst would readily surmise that the unconscious core of *Caesar and Cleopatra* could not be so easily done away with. What had happened to Shaw was that a new artistic "idea" had substituted for the former "idea" of *Caesar and Cleopatra*. Both "ideas" were related to the same unconscious image. In his "unconscious drama" he was recasting Caesar as the West End gentleman, Henry Higgins. Both originated from his childhood drama in which the fantasied heroes were determined by his oedipal rival, Vandeleur Lee. Similarly, he transformed Cleopatra into Pat Campbell as the East End donna, Eliza Doolittle, from the repressed childhood image of his mother, his oedipal object. In *Pygmalion*, Shaw moved to a personal theme from a historical one in *Caesar and Cleopatra* without, however, changing the theme of the unconscious conflicts.

A careful examination of Shaw's early plays reveals that a number of them deal with the same unconscious conflict. Bentley (1957), in an excellent comparative examination of Shaw's *Plays for Puritans* (*The Devil's Disciple, Caesar and Cleopatra,* and *Captain Brassbound's Conversion*) puts it succinctly: "The play is a neat five-act structure in which Caesar is the Shavian protagonist, Cleopatra the Shavian antagonist. Caesar is the teacher, Cleopatra the pupil. So far there is nothing to surprise the reader of *Candida, The Devil's Disciple* and *Captain Brass-*

bound's Conversion" (p. 113). Bentley might well have added
Pygmalion to his list. In this, of course, Higgins is literally the
teacher and Eliza Doolittle the pupil. Bentley then adds, "But
although Cleopatra, like Marchbanks, Anderson and Brassbound, grows up as much as she is capable of doing—she begins as a mere child and under Caesar's influence becomes a
woman—her capacities are limited. She is of a lower nature
and her growth, to use the metaphor of the play itself, is from
a kitten to a cat" (p. 113). The characterization of Cleopatra
has been almost literally transformed into the uneducated Eliza
of lower class origin. Higgins, like Caesar, refuses "to avenge
himself and refuses to make love." The identical nature of the
"unconscious theme" of both plays could have determined the
similarity of their construction. The first three acts elaborate
the story of Caesar's and Higgins's education of Cleopatra and
Eliza, respectively. In the last two acts of both plays, Cleopatra
and Eliza are fully educated and the conflict between protagonist and antagonist ends the play.

The major plays of Shaw's first decade as a dramatist, particularly the *Plays for Puritans*, are not the end of his elaborations of the same unconscious images utilized in his most
"personal" play, *Pygmalion*, written at the end of his second
decade as a playwright. Shaw never freed himself from the
irritating demands of these unconscious images. Another decade passed and Pygmalion appeared again as an actual character in *Back to Methuselah*. In this latter play, written in 1921,
the character Pygmalion attempts to assemble a mechanical
man, as Henry Higgins created Eliza.

It might appear rather presumptuous to Shavian admirers
to portray Shaw as a man with limited insight into his own
dramas, in view of Shaw's reputation as one of the great
music critics and his equally great reputation as an art critic.
Bentley (1957, pp. 100–101) accounts for this with intuitive
insight.

If Shaw is not, like Johnson, a great literary critic, it is because
he is preoccupied (unconsciously, as he might say) with his creative work. He has nothing to say *about* it precisely because he is
busy *doing* it. When he does talk about it, he often gives evidence
of good natural taste but seldom knows what to say. The old
dichotomy of form and content only makes matters worse for him.
Because his feeling for form and technique is natural and undifferentiated he talks always about content and advises his biographer to do the same when discussing the Shavian life work. If we
want to know, then, just what actually happened to the Problem
Play in Shaw's hands, we must disregard the legend that he is explaining everything in his prefaces and look at the plays for ourselves.

I thoroughly agree with Bentley. Whatever the extent of his
analytic capacities were as an art and music critic, music and
art were not his modes of creative communication, as drama
was. However, Shaw stood apart as an extraordinary, sensitive
recipient of the artistic communications in other art forms.

THE WORLD'S INTERPRETATION OF
PYGMALION VERSUS SHAW'S

If Shaw had his blind spots to the unconscious derivations of
his own dramas, they were particularly pronounced in his interpretation of *Pygmalion*. Much as he tried to influence his
biographers to view his dramas as well as his life in his way,
they deserted Shaw in the unique case of *Pygmalion*. His biographers joined the opposition—the directors who have staged
it and the audiences who have witnessed it—and through the
years have been left with the overwhelming impression that
Eliza will marry Henry Higgins. On this matter Shaw's biographer, St. John Ervine, remarks, "The end of the fourth act as
well as the end of the fifth act deny the laboured account of
the flower girl's future and all sensible persons assume that she
married Henry Higgins and bore him many vigorous and intelligent children" (1956).

The first incident in the "battle of interpretations" between Shaw and the world began with Beerbohm Tree's original London production of *Pygmalion* in 1914. Tree chose to interpret the last moment of the play with the symbolic gesture of Henry Higgins throwing a bouquet of flowers to Eliza, to imply a future marital union between hero and heroine. This infuriated Shaw to the degree that he wrote a manifestolike postscript to the play, spelling out in dictatorial blueprints the only possible conclusion to the lives of his created characters, Higgins and Eliza, in which he commands more than proves that they could not marry each other. The most recent incident in this battle of half a century is the case of *My Fair Lady*, the transformed musical version of *Pygmalion* which has been described as one of the finest musical plays of the century.[10] In this version the marriage of Higgins to Eliza is clearly implied. Although we question the artistic value of such an overt implication and relish Shaw's more ambiguous finale, we would still psychoanalytically question the significance of Shaw's obstinate inability to envisage the subsequent union between his hero and heroine.[11]

The intensity of Shaw's response to such a minimal aspect of the play provoked him to write the postscript in 1914. Ever

[10] Shaw intended a tribute to phonetics in *Pygmalion*. Voice in the form of the spoken word was the accentuated characteristic of the created Eliza and was unconsciously derived from his musical mother. In all probability the fortunate coincidence of *Pygmalion's* conversion from a drama into a musical may have augmented its communication in the new (but unconsciously original) form. Music meant much in Shaw's life and must have been absorbed into his own creations. Bentley (1957, p. 98) says, "For Shaw music and message are not only two separate arts. They are also two sides of the one art of literature, the great poets being musicians, the useful poets being evangelists."

[11] Stein (1956) regards Eliza as a phallic-equated woman and questions if marriage between Higgins and Eliza could be a happy one. He views Higgins as a created character, unrelated to Shaw himself or any other unconscious autobiographical derivative from the author's life.

since it has been a companion piece to the play in all subsequent publications, as though Shaw intended it as a safeguard against any future productions that might dare to interpret a successful livable union between Henry and Eliza. Paradoxically enough, in spite of the awe for Shaw, subsequent productions continued to challenge his interpretation with thoroughgoing success. Such facts give credence to the concept that the artist's possession of his works (created love objects) ends with their creation; subsequently they become the property of the collective world for whom they were intended from the beginning.[12]

Shaw's blind spots are now understandable, but his narrow dictatorial postscript to *Pygmalion* still needs scrutiny. Certainly Shaw's intellectual and artistic superiority could well tolerate the multiplicity of meanings that could be evoked by an artistic creation. In fact, Shaw avoided a final solution for *Pygmalion's* hero and heroine in order to enrich his romantic drama with poetic poignancy. We would surmise that the similarity and proximity between *Pygmalion's* Higgins and Eliza and Shaw's "personal romantic drama" between Mrs. Campbell and himself must have been the unconscious as well as the surface explanation for Shaw's rejection of a solution in which creator and pupil go on to a marital and therefore sexual union. It is also a denial of sex relations between his mother (pupil) and Lee (teacher), As he had to renounce and subsequently denounce his erotic pursuit of Mrs. Pat Campbell in defense of his marriage, so he had to denounce the final union of his hero and heroine. The morality that intervenes between Higgins and Eliza (for Shaw) is the morality which operates for their unconscious prototypes; Shaw the child (Higgins) was bound in an unresolved oedipal romance with his mother (Eliza). The world could not know the unconscious origins of Higgins

---

[12] A similar process was demonstrable in the creative works of Eugene O'Neill (see Chapter 8).

and Eliza and thus demands their proper union. The members of the world to whom Shaw gives his characters have often solved and bypassed their own oedipal loves and see no reason why a love based on the prototype of the mother cannot be fulfilled.

THE APPROPRIATENESS OF
THE GALATEAN LEGEND

There are at least three versions of the Galatean legend and myth. In pseudoclassical mythology one finds the more commonly known version that was utilized in Shaw's play. Pygmalion used to worship his statue Galatea for hours at a time. Venus permits the statue, loved by Pygmalion, to become a woman. Shaw's long-standing hero worship of Ellen Terry and then of Pat Campbell is much in the style of the Galatean myth. By his presence, by his creations, and by his correspondence, the adored "Galatean" actresses were transformed into gracious sounding boards for his scintillating person. In the life of a genius or one of high creative talent, it has been postulated that there is a division of love feelings (libidinal cathexis) shared between the personal object and the collective object. It has been further postulated that throughout the life of such a gifted person there may be a frequent redistribution of libidinal investment from the personal object to the collective one and vice versa (Greenacre, 1957). The possibility suggests itself here that the state of desexualized feelings (libido) which is essential for a "romance with the world" is subject to alterations (due, for example, to personal deprivation, loss of a loved one, and so forth) and then becomes resexualized in both aim and object. We may view Shaw's life history as a case in point.

In 1898, Shaw became infatuated with Pat Campbell—an "object of the world" as famous actresses are likely to be. His sexual attachment was immediately neutralized into a created image for an artistic future production when he fantasied her as an East End donna in a play. During the next fifteen years of his life, all this remained in abeyance until the period of Shaw's mother's final illness. As we have shown earlier, this event evoked the childhood images of his mother and mobilized him to create Eliza, with the transitory object of Mrs. Campbell—a conscious desexualized "world" object—as the inspiration. After the completion of the play (1912) and after the death of his mother, the sexualized "altercation" between Shaw and Campbell (Stella and Joey incident) occurred. One would conjecture as to the outcome of Shaw's artistic career had Mrs. Campbell gone along with his "acting-out" incident and agreed to marry him.[13] Would he have dispersed his need for a creative romance with the world which until then produced dramas and might now produce only personal gratification?

The conflict between personal relationships and "the romance with the world" is worthy of further investigation in psychoanalytic studies of highly creative persons. The creations of the artists are often the rearranged responses to the primal object (mother's breast) expressed in aesthetic forms. It is no wonder that the artist's created object—steeped as it is in the early maternal object—is often embellished with his own omniscience and omnipotence, as Galatea was by Pygmalion, as Eliza was by Henry Higgins, as Mrs. Campbell was by Shaw, and, finally, as Shaw's mother in his childhood was so embellished by him. Henry Higgins is saturated with omnipotence which he projects onto Eliza and then returns to himself, in the same way that small children in normal development attribute such omnipotence to their parents and then reassign it to themselves as they dethrone the parents. The following excerpt from the closing moments of Act IV in *Pygmalion* illustrates this clearly. Liza has soured on Higgins, wants to be herself again and return what belongs to him.

[13] It is of course questionable whether Shaw would have stood by his own proposal of marriage had Mrs. Campbell agreed to marry him.

LIZA: (Drinking in his emotion like nectar, and nagging him to provoke a further supply) Stop, please. (She takes off her jewels) Will you take these to your room and keep them safe? I don't want to run the risk of their being missing.

HIGGINS: (Furious) Hand them over. (She puts them into his hands) If these belonged to me instead of to the jeweller, I'd ram them down your ungrateful throat. (He perfunctorily thrusts them into his pockets, *unconsciously decorating himself with the protruding end of the chains*) [Italics mine—P.W.] (1948, pp. 258–259).

Shaw has chosen to symbolize omnipotence via the borrowed jewels; what Higgins has consciously given to Eliza he now undoes and unconsciously assigns to himself. In Shaw's *Pygmalion*, the godlike quality is the final property of Henry Higgins. Like Higgins, Shaw is often Galatea as well as Pygmalion.

But the omniscience and omnipotence that Shaw projected onto his love objects were overdetermined. Had he not been the endowed man he was, he would still have been subject to an immature (pregenital and oral) fixation in his object relationships because of the negligent quality of his mother's attitude toward him in infancy and early childhood. It is a common clinical experience that when an infant is not gratified with satisfactory early loving and nurturing care by the mother during the period of normal development in which the child and parent are interchangeably omnipotent, the world of omnipotence does not recede into the background. Throughout the child's development into adulthood he retains his self-image of omnipotence and is driven in pursuit of a love object onto whom he can project these feelings. Had Shaw been artless and average, he would still have had to cope with an unresolved problem of childhood omnipotence. Unaided by a creative talent and outlet, his life would have remained an unwritten drama about *Pygmalion*.

IV

The Created Characters and Their Psychoanalytic Value

10

A Trio of Tennessee Williams'
Heroines:

The Pyschology of Prostitution

IN THE EARLY 1940's, a young playwright appeared on the scene with acclaimed creative gifts, particularly for the portrayal of psychopathological character. Thus in this period the world became familiar with Tennessee Williams' play *The Glass Menagerie* and shortly thereafter with the now-famous character portrayal of Blanche DuBois in *A Streetcar Named Desire*.

In 1942, a man of the theater and arts made public Freud's hitherto unknown and unpublished paper, "Psychopathological Characters on Stage" (1942), which was written in 1904. In an accompanying essay, Max Graf wrote: "Freud gave it [the paper] to me, and I now submit it to a world in which the ideas of Freud have become part of the spiritual air we breathe" (1942).

In this early study, Freud recommends that the character in psychopathological dramas reveals in an ambiguous form the struggle of unconscious impulses toward consciousness. He emphasizes the essential nature of ambiguity in this art form. Kris and Kaplan (1952), expanding on Empsom's essay (1931) on ambiguity in poetic language, develop the conception of art "as a process of communication and re-creation in which ambiguity plays a central role." Thus we have brought together analytic observations on psychopathological drama, on the use of poetic language, and on art in general. This may be particularly fruitful here, since Tennessee Williams is both poet and dramatist. His plays, even when not written in verse, are regarded as essentially approaches to character by way of poetic revelation. Intending to focus on his character creations, we are suddenly and simultaneously struck by the superimposed impressions and implications of his poetic language. It is self-evident that his poetic dramas express higher levels of artistic creation.

One distinction from the current breed of dramatists of psychopathology to be noted in Williams is his uncompromising completeness of portrayal. Williams' characters are not always favorably responded to by audiences.[1] However, there is rarely a lack of emotional response in either his critics or supporters. There is also rarely a moment in the unfolding of his plays in which one is not "in the grip of his emotions, rather than capable of rational judgment."[2] If our dramatists of today would heed the requisites suggested by Freud sixty years ago, the goal of true artistic achievement would be much closer for them.

We are indebted to Williams for a most unusual portrayal

[1] Perhaps this can be compared to the way the general public only likes and in some cases only understands a mild caricature of psychoanalysis and often shows its unhidden hostility and open fears of its real representation.

[2] In his paper, Freud (1942, p. 463) comments on the psychopathological drama as follows: "It appears to be one of the prerequisites of this art form that the struggle of the repressed impulse to become conscious, recognizable though it is, is so little given a definite name that the process of reaching consciousness goes on in turn within the spectator while his attention is distracted and he is in the grip of his emotions, rather than capable of rational judgment."

of a thirteen-year-old girl from a small Mississippi town who is a juvenile derelict. In this one-act play, *This Property Is Condemned,* the young girl, Willie, is seen living secretively alone in her condemned house, which her mother deserted by running off with a railroad man, one of the many who frequented her combined home and house of prostitution. The prostitutes had been Willie's mother and her idolized older sister Alva. Her alcoholic father disappeared shortly after the mother. Willie lived with Alva until Alva developed tuberculosis and died.

Thus, Willie sees the life of her dead sister Alva as a success story studded with scenes of many admirers who showered her with gifts. It is to be noted in Williams' characterization of deserted or deprived or depraved heroines that they seek both solace and sanction in fantasies that reconstruct their current or former activities into the ideal of the pretty Southern belle who has many young, handsome, and wealthy admirers. Likewise, in *Hello from Bertha,* the prostitute Bertha, who is suffering from a venereal tubal infection, clings to the memory of her affair with Charlie Aldrich, the hardware man from Memphis, with a fantasy in which he is an ever-loving figure who will rescue her from her plight. In *The Lady of Larkspur Lotion,* the bleached-blonde, forty-year-old, alcoholically delusioned prostitute who calls herself Mrs. Hardwick-Moore cannot pay her room rent in the French Quarter. Defensively and delusionally, she demands that her landlady rid the place of roaches and haughtily explains that there has been a delay in the quarterly payment which she regularly receives from the man who takes care of her Brazilian rubber plantation.

Running through the heroines of Williams' plays, the mixture of prostitute and prostitute fantasy is always present with artistic ambiguity, as are pride and poverty, social achievement and ostracism, and, finally, reality and fantasy. In Williams' plays, one is impressed with the thorough integrative ambiguity and the similar thoroughness of stringencies elaborated in the depiction of his psychopathological heroines.[3] Thus, Blanche DuBois is constantly contained in a portrayal of an exhibitionistic woman concerned with her appearance and clothes and with when she is seen and not seen. The heroine here is at each moment entrenched in the eyes of the author, the other actors, herself, and the audience as a woman who encompasses every variation and vicissitude of the fears and wishes of being looked at. To be looked at in admiration of beauty, in despair of waning youth, in the brutality of daylight, in the kindliness of night, or in the evanescence of cheap costume jewelry and summer frock is to be Blanche DuBois.

Beyond this clear-cut exhibitionist identity of Blanche DuBois, which makes her always believable and enactable, we must seek out Blanche in the deepest depiction of her inner conflicts, of her failing social adjustment, and of her final tragedy. Williams' heroines frequently meet the poignant pressure of unconscious strivings and catastrophic realities with a delusional denial of reality, as is demonstrated by the *Larkspur Lotion* heroine who awaits the harvest of her Brazilian rubber plantation. The characters' delusional denials become a part of Williams' inspirational point of departure as they regress into created fantasies of poetic ambiguity that are either spoken or enacted. His characters weave fantasies that unburden the momentary crisis, transform narcissistic injury into painless gratification, and devise schemes of secure eternities.

But what are Blanche DuBois' repressed wishes, struggles of conscience, and ego-ideals? What is her total adaptive adjustment? Where does she fit in our frail schemes which separate neurosis from psychosis? Is her prostitutional psychopathy immoral, amoral, or asocial? Williams approaches these questions

[3] It is noteworthy that actresses who have played Williams' heroines have often transformed their latent talents into performances of great achievement and recognition. In many cases, the already-accomplished actress seems to have added immeasurably to her status in the role of a Williams heroine.

in his stage direction when he refers to her as a neurasthenic personality. How much beyond Williams' own description we can carry this is a question.

Let us for the moment attempt to "psychoanalyze" Blanche DuBois and account for her promiscuous quasi-prostitutional life. Following the direction of the drama's plot, we might conclude that Blanche DuBois has unresolved oedipal wishes which culminate in her enactment of a single impulsive relationship with her brother-in-law Stanley and subsequently results in her complete breakdown and abandonment as punishment for the direct fulfillment of this wish. We could then account for her promiscuity as disguised but consciously enacted repetitions of the same wish. We could also state that her early, short-lived tragic marriage to a suicidal homosexual and her desperate attempts to retain the family plantation (which she states was ruined "as piece by piece our improvident grandfathers and father and uncles and brothers exchanged the land for their epic fornications—to put it plainly"), and finally her inability to subsequently undertake a functioning marriage as did her sister Stella—all these facts seem further variations of her unresolved oedipal situation. We might also conclude that sexual maturity (genitality) has been surrendered and reduced to exhibitionism and promiscuity, which became the regressed functioning levels of her sexual gratification.

But the methodology employed in the analysis of a created character cannot be so satisfactory as when employed in clinical psychoanalysis. For one thing, we cannot ask these characters or even the author to free-associate. Nor can we remove their resistances and analyze their defenses, dreams, and fantasies. There is no next moment when more of the unconscious can then be made available. We also have to deal with the limited historical material that the author has made available to us in a single session. It is particularly interesting that Williams' characters never relate much of their early child-

hood. Their lives seem to begin for them mainly in early adolescence, more rarely in puberty. The contents of infancy and
latency are well sealed. This effective omission of their early
childhood may have a strong correlation with the credibility of
their dramatic and colorful episodes of acting out.

Another difficulty confronting the analyst trying to "psychoanalyze" the created character is that the usual procedure
tends to reduce the creation to a more-or-less single ambiguity.
This is redundant to the essence of creativity, which, according
to Kris, should be a cluster of multiple integrative ambiguities.
We must bear in mind that the attempt to reduce creative material which shows preconscious elements to a specific unconscious meaning is to partake of the responses of any ordinary
member of an audience who comes away from an artistic creation with only a "personal" message.

Since "psychoanalyzing" Blanche DuBois offers only incomplete solutions to the understanding of her psychopathological
character, an alternative methodological approach suggests
itself. Since a created character originally belongs to the inspired ego of the author, we might examine other inspirational
emanations (in this case, other characters from other plays)
and search for common unconscious denominators. We have
already demonstrated that Blanche of *A Streetcar Named
Desire* has in common with the girl Willie of *This Property Is
Condemned* and Mrs. Hardwick-Moore of *The Lady of Larkspur Lotion* an identical major defense mechanism—the delusional denial of reality and of inner conflicts. This hints at the
idea that little Willie, Blanche, and Mrs. Hardwick-Moore are
derivatives of a single image in the author's unconscious.

We note that our trio of heroines has further in common
complete abandonment by friends and family; all three are
equally preoccupied and confronted with their lost home and
property. For the little girl Willie, it is her condemned home
to which she clings desperately; for Blanche, it is the lost battle

for her plantation called Belle Reve; and, for the deluded, disoriented Mrs. Hardwick-Moore, it is her Brazilian rubber plantation which is a mile from the Mediterranean and from which, on a clear day, it is possible to distinguish the white chalk cliffs of Dover—to this delusional home she adheres with the greatest tenacity.

To the growing bond of our trio, we might add the mutuality of their promiscuity and prostitution. To Willie, the future of having many gentlemen callers who will wine her, dine her, and be with her through the night is the heritage from her sister Alva. In a welcome ambiguity, we are never certain whether Willie has already filled the gap of Alva, since we are simultaneously uncertain regarding her knowledge of the sexual act itself. But Willie definitely tells us that the men who visited her mother's and sister's house were important guests, to be respected for their achievements in life. Blanche's promiscuity is portrayed in pictures of prostitution: her repeated intimacies with strangers in a cheap, disreputable hotel and the clamoring cries for her of the drunken soldiers from the nearby training camps on a Saturday night, to which she responds in this fashion: "I slipped out to answer their calls. Later the paddy wagon would gather them up like daisies— the long way home" (Williams, 1947, p. 139).

To the *Larkspur Lotion* lady, prostitution is a long-established profession. She deludes herself into the identity of a titled lady with a second-hand coat of arms who denies that she has male visitors with whom she quarrels over money for her services. Finally, our three heroines have a common fantasy of being rescued by the well-to-do admirer. For Willie, it is the freight superintendent, Mr. Johnson, "the most important character we ever had in our rooming house," with whom she goes steady and who buys her fancy shoes and corsages and takes her dancing every night. For Blanche DuBois, it is Shep Huntleigh, the college boyfriend—now an owner of oil wells in

Texas—who at the height of her breakdown and homelessness she fantasies has come to rescue her. For Mrs. Hardwick-Moore, the imaginary rescuer is the rubber king from the plantation.

With only the minimal sacrifice of creative reality, it is possible to see the thirteen-year-old Willie grown into the thirty-year-old Blanche DuBois, whom we have most recently seen ejected from her last refuge and institutionalized, emerging in a final scene of deterioration and hopelessness ten years later and older as Mrs. Hardwick-Moore, whose Belle Reve plantation becomes a Brazilian rubber plantation, whose oil king becomes a rubber king, and for whom prostitution has become a dismal reality.

Psychoanalytic literature also tends to coalesce its understanding of promiscuity and fantasies of prostitution.[4] Prostitution itself—as an institution, so to speak—has not been commented on. However, it could be said that, since fantasies are often enacted, we would find among prostitutes some who are enacting that which belongs to fantasy life. It is not assumed that all prostitutes arrive at this occupation via their fantasy lives. Environmental, cultural, and economic factors play important roles. However, the one patient I treated who had been a prostitute for a short period had enacted an integral part of her fantasy life. As we shall soon see, her history was not unlike those of Williams' prostitute-heroines.

For the moment, we shall pursue Williams' depiction of promiscuity, prostitution, and the prostitution fantasy in the given context—that related to these women clinging desperately to their childhood homes in their loneliness and fantasying that they will be rescued by a rich hero. Willie, in *This Property Is Condemned*, describes her home as follows:

[4] In analytic literature, promiscuity and prostitution are said to be related to early or severely repressed penis-envy, which gives rise to character traits of masculinity or vengeance toward men. Both traits give rise to fantasies of prostitution, and the vengeful type is related to promiscuity (Abraham, 1927).

We used to have some high old times in that big yellow house. Pianos, victrolas, Hawaiian steel guitars. Everyone played on something. But now—it's awful quiet (Williams, 1946, p. 201).

Later she declaims:

Tell him—the freight superintendent has brought me a pair of kid slippers—patent. The same as the old ones of Alva's. I'm going to dances with them at Moon Lake Casino. All night I'll be dancing an' come home drunk in the morning! We'll have serenades with all kinds of musical instruments. Trumpets an' trombones. An' Hawaiian steel guitars. Yeh yeh! The sky will be white like this (Williams, 1946, p. 205).

The young boy, Tom, asks her to expose herself as she had done for his friend Frank. Willie, refusing, explains: ". . . because I was lonesome then an' I'm not lonesome now. You can tell Frank Waters that." Willie thus demonstrates that her promiscuous enactments are related to her feelings of abandonment.

In *A Streetcar Named Desire*, Stanley questions Blanche regarding her millionaire about whom she unrealistically weaves ways and means of her rescue.

STANLEY: This millionaire from Dallas is not going to interfere with your privacy any?
BLANCHE: It won't be the sort of thing you have in mind. This man is a gentleman and he respects me. What he wants is my company. Having great wealth makes people lonely! A cultivated woman, a woman of intelligence and breeding, can enrich a man's life immeasurably! Physical beauty is passing. A transitory possession. But the beauty of the mind and richness of the spirit and tenderness of the heart—and I have all those things—aren't taken away, but grow! How strange that I should be called a destitute woman! (Williams, 1947, p. 145).

Blanche explains her promiscuity to Mitch, who wanted to marry her until he heard all about her. She confesses that her den of iniquity was a hotel called Tarantula Arms. She says:

> Yes, a big spider! That's where I brought my victims. [She pours herself another drink.] Yes, I had many intimacies with strangers. After the death of Allan, intimacies with strangers was all I seemed able to fill my empty heart with. . . . I think it was panic, just panic, that drove me from one to another, hunting for some protection—here and there in the most unlikely places—even at last in a seventeen-year-old boy. But somebody wrote the superintendent about it: "This woman is morally unfit for her position!" (Williams, 1947, p. 136).

From the angry accompaniment of a confession transformed into the quality of a first understanding, Blanche reveals to herself and to us that her promiscuity pleaded her intense panic and search for protection. Blanche then tells Mitch the meaning of her wanting him:

> You said you needed somebody. Well, I need somebody too. I thanked God for you, because you seemed to be gentle—a cleft in the rock of the world that I could hide in (Williams, 1947, p. 137).

In these poetic revelations, Blanche reveals that her promiscuity, her struggle for her home, and her fantasies of being rescued have the unconscious meaning of intense fear of aloneness and abandonment and wishes to be reincorporated in the mother.

Let us now turn to a consideration of my patient who temporarily became a prostitute. She was a twenty-nine-year-old unmarried salesgirl. She was considerably overwrought, overtalkative, and overdressed, with a tendency toward gaudiness and girlishness. Prior to coming to me, she had first been in a cultist type of therapy and later in a state hospital. She had lived on the estate of this so-called therapist with a group of other patients. She was both secretary to the therapist and a member of his group therapy or group living of one sort or another. She had relations with him which were confined to fellatio. She was encouraged to do this, since it was rationalized that it would be therapeutic to her fantasies in this controlled situation. She came well fitted to this role. On her discharge from a state hospital after one and a half years, she decided not to return home, but to make her own way. In her wanderings about town, she was picked up by a young Negro man with whom she established more of a liaison than a relationship, which in turn led to her becoming a member of a house of prostitution. In this occupation, she encouraged and accepted mostly the role of performing fellatio.

Her not returning home had the meaning to her that she could not go home because of her sense of shame for having been institutionalized and at being abandoned and rejected. Much in her mother's attitude toward her was correctly interpreted by her as abandonment and rejection. This rejection was a re-enactment of a state of affairs which existed since the patient was eight. At that time, the patient began to practically live in the house of a married woman who befriended her. Regarding the endless time she spent there, she was never questioned or disapproved of by her mother, who she felt completely rejected her to the extent that she was never disciplined or disapproved of for any straying from home. This relationship with the befriending woman continued until the age of seventeen. This does not confine the state of rejection by her mother to the age of eight. The patient felt that she was rejected from the beginning.

In a sketchy way, since created characters are our main interest, the abandonment and neglect, the loss of home and her struggles to attach herself to home and mother—first through a woman, then through the Negro man and the house of prostitution, and finally through the strange therapist and his group home—indicate her struggle to be rescued and to incorporate the mother via the masturbatory fantasies and acts of fellatio and promiscuity.[5] There is clearly a parallel in unconscious content among the patient, Willie, Blanche, and Mrs. Hardwick-Moore, although the patient's life is perhaps less dramatic and colorful, since the background of our scene is a tenement home in Manhattan rather than a decaying plantation in Mississippi. Again, we lack analytic finality, since this patient came in an acutely depressed state and was in need of shock treatment, so that history-gathering and analytic understanding were minimally applied in this situation.

It is only retrospectively concluded, in view of the hints from our dramatic heroines, that some significant connection existed between her abandonment, her loss of home (pre-oedipal mother), and the enactments of her masturbatory fantasies of promiscuity into a period of prostitution. What is usually considered a house of prostitution for this patient and perhaps many others in the same position is in fact a home of prostitution. What Williams has conveyed to us about such Southern belles in drama, Toulouse-Lautrec has portrayed in his paintings of the empathically considered Parisian *demimondaines* and is confirmed in biographical studies of the famous impressionist's life.

We can now evaluate the advantages of our two methodological approaches. The conclusions reached by each are of necessity generalized constructions. Since the material under consideration was not correlated with the psychobiography of the artist, both methods of study were equally inadequate.

Granted these limitations, what have we learned by "psychoanalyzing" Blanche DuBois—the school teacher who has struggled unsuccessfully to maintain her family estate and has been evicted from her profession and community and finds her last refuge in the home of a younger sister's husband with

---

[5] In her sexual enactments, the penis was unconsciously equated with the breast.

whom she has an affair which terminates in her complete breakdown? From this history, we reached conclusions about Blanche's unresolved oedipal situation. Her promiscuity represents an intense expression of her unresolved oedipal wishes with disguised, unconscious incestuous objects. Her regression to exhibitionism also enables her to enact oedipal wishes by means of a regressive instinctual displacement. Her fantasies of being rescued represent the wish for a powerful but desexualized father. But, not unlike our experience in clinical analysis, the presence of the ubiquitous and often pathological oedipal solution is not always the only problem or the essential therapeutic solution for any given individual.

The second methodological approach seems the more helpful in understanding the origins of our heroine's plight. More can be learned about Blanche DuBois by studying her characteristics and problems in common with those of Willie of *This Property Is Condemned* and Mrs. Hardwick-Moore of *The Lady of Larkspur Lotion.*[6] The simultaneous study of the three heroines enables us to conclude that Blanche DuBois' fear of loneliness and abandonment is probably based on a disturbance of early object relationship, in which she differs intensely from her sister Stella. This accounts for her incapacity to establish a permanent object relationship; for that matter, every relationship is but a transient negation in her search for an unattainable reunion with the preoedipal mother. Her promiscuity, her unending fantasies of being rescued, and the inevitability of her final failure are further evidence of this state of affairs. The direction of Williams' plots are neither unique nor original. The story is but the vehicle for the poetic, dramatic, and deeper unconscious communication. In these

---

[6] On this score, Beres (1959) states "that a person reveals himself by the choice of language, by recurrent phrases, metaphors, images or themes, is a recognized fact in psychoanalytic practice and has also been noted by literary scholars."

aspects of his portrayals, Williams communicates to us the repetitive and overdetermined message of his unconsciously derived creations of prostitute- and prostitutelike-heroines.

Agoston's (1948) study of psychological aspects of prostitution reveals some interesting correlation between our applied studies and his observations. He describes the pseudo-personality of the prostitute, which involves the denial of identity to escape her feelings of guilt. This is extended into telling fictitious personal tales. Helene Deutsch (1948) has pointed out the convincing "pseudologia" of her prostitute patient, Anna. One can readily recall the dramatic delusional denials of Willie, Blanche, and Mrs. Hardwick-Moore. Agoston then points out that, in all cases, there is an unresolved Oedipus complex and a "complete emotional rejection by both parents, usually in actual fact, with a partial element of fantasy."[7]

Our study of Blanche's story through the plot of the play clearly demonstrated the unresolved oedipal situation and the regression to exhibitionism. The study of the triad of prostitutional heroines through their introspective and self-descriptive utterances illustrates, not only regression and the rejection by parents, but the additional disturbance in object relationships with the concomitant fears of abandonment and the restitutional fantasies of being rescued by men—which represents being reunited with the preoedipal mother. Thus our investigation of Williams' heroines tends, not only to confirm previous clinical findings in the psychology of prostitutes, but also to extend the understanding into more basic aspects of ego-development and the nature of the object relationships in such cases. Accordingly, our two methodological approaches—the comprehending of the events in the plays and studying of

---

[7] Concomitantly, according to Agoston there is pseudo-regression to the oral/anal level in the guise of money-madness which conceals regression to the completely infantile level of exhibitionism, scopophilia, and enjoyment of magical power.

the fusion of the author's identical characters—give us both a longitudinal and dynamic perspective in our analytic evaluation.

It would be circumspect and limited to view Williams' *A Streetcar Named Desire* and indeed the other plays mentioned as exclusively psychopathological dramas. Freud, in his 1904 paper (Freud, 1942), classified drama into religious, character, social, psychological, and psychopathological categories. He writes: "Every combination of this situation with that in the earlier types of drama, that is the social and the character drama, is of course possible insofar as social institutions evoke just such an inner conflict, and so on" (p. 462). Thus Blanche DuBois' struggle against Stanley and the social community becomes in addition the enactment of a character drama and a social tragedy.

There are in applied psychoanalytic studies many technical pitfalls and limitations of sources and resources which block the road to the ultimate psychoanalytic goal—the study of creative imagination. It would appear that the happy combination of the study of the creations that are repetitively unconsciously determined and the study of an analytically complete biography of the creator, properly correlated, can give us the most scientific and accurate construction and interpretation.

In this connection, Beres (1959), in his search for valid methodologies for the biography of the artist, states:

> It is not necessary to assume that in every instance an actual experience is the source of the artist's creation. I refer to the capacity of an artist to identify and empathize with different emotional states and experiences which he need not have gone through. This capacity to identify with another's experience may be a primary requisite for any true artist, an essential component of his personality and a measure of his greatness.

This conclusion may turn out to be the most valid reason for studying psychoanalytically the biography of an artist. A separation between the creation and the artist's personal experience may prove to be a stamp of the greater artist. This may explain the often-noted phenomenon of the failure of an artist to repeat the promise of a single work. The resultant successful product may have had more to do with an intense personal experience than with the artist's inherent creativity. It is a question whether the difficulties in the psychoanalytic biographical studies of Shakespeare are really due to the obscurities of his person or to the obscure relation of his characters to his own person. Kris (1952), in his study of Prince Hal, states that Shakespeare's unique capacity to imagine conflicts may far "traverse the range of his own experience." In the case of Tennessee Williams, the wide range of his plays—*The Glass Menagerie, A Streetcar Named Desire, Rose Tattoo, Camino Real, Cat on a Hot Tin Roof,* and many others—may or may not be the contents of his conscious or unconscious experience.

Brooks Atkinson (1956), the renowned retired *New York Times* drama critic, once wrote:

> Mr. Williams is a gifted writer; he can vitalize the theatre with whatever theme he may be developing. Mr. Williams has ventured far afield since 1945, using the stage with greater virtuosity, developing power, mastering bigger canvases.

Again we note the description of Williams' creations in terms of another medium—painting. Atkinson contends that it is merely a matter of whatever theme Williams chooses to elaborate. On this point, we take issue. Our conclusions indicate that such choices are not conscious.

Like other artists, Williams may be able to evoke the primary process and a controlled ego-regression for the purpose of creative writing, but he is bound by the unconsciously determined nature of his characterizations.[8] Perhaps, with such

---

[8] Only in that way can Freud's requisite of the obscure revelation of the repressed impulse and Kris's requisite of aesthetic ambiguity be met.

unconscious images, Williams is constricted to the helpless future of continuing to write tragedies about psychopathological characters, which the public may or may not like.

It is my impression that Williams' creative talent has directed itself to an overdetermined path of portraying psychopathological characters. To substantiate such an impression, a psychobiographical study of him would be necessary. The superior quality of Tennessee Williams' creations are of direct interest to us as students of mental illness. They may provide us with ways and means of analytically understanding a commonly misunderstood type of psychopathology which is rarely seen on the analyst's couch.

11

Sophocles' Antigone:

The Psychology of the Old Maid

IN THE PRECEDING CHAPTER a trio of twentieth-century heroines deepened and augmented our understanding of the psychology of prostitution. In the present chapter we shall focus on Antigone, the heroine of a drama of the fourth century B.C., to enhance our knowledge of old maidenhood in modern psychological terms. Perhaps no better tribute can be paid to our great dramatists, like Sophocles, than to recognize the ageless truth and wisdom reflected in their legacy of created characters which have become our heritage.

By turning to Sophocles' drama *Oedipus* and other sources of this legend, Freud (1937) affirmed the universality of one of his earliest theories of man's psychosexual development, the Oedipus complex. Such affirmations were necessary at that time since there were no other psychoanalytic evidences to draw on. In the following sixty years, abundant psychoanalytic, sociological, and anthropological data have been accumulated in the literature to validate his formulations.

In the current flourishing Freudian era, there is hardly an area of psychoanalytic investigation about which a scientific

190

literature has not been amassed. Occasionally one comes upon a clinical area, such as the one under consideration—the psychology of the old maid—about which very little has been written in spite of the fact that such cases have frequently presented themselves for psychoanalysis.

During the clinical investigation of the psychosexual development of neurotic virginity and old maidenhood (Weissman, 1964), I was unable to find a substantial literature that dealt with this condition. Motivated by a need to overcome these obstacles and an interest in creative imagination in drama, it seemed justifiable to embark on Freud's historic modes of psychoanalytic investigation to validate clinical formulation on the psychology of these problems from literary and legendary sources. Therefore I chose for this study Sophocles' plays about Oedipus' own daughter, Antigone. Viewed from the angle of creative imagination, it will be demonstrated that when a great dramatist like Sophocles creates a character like Antigone, we can anticipate a psychoanalytically valid portrait which may serve as an aid to a more complete comprehension of the psychosexual development of old maidenhood.

ANTIGONE IN SOPHOCLES' *ANTIGONE*

The time and setting of the play follow the death of Antigone's father, Oedipus, when the two brothers, Eteocles and Polyneices, contend for the throne of Thebes. Polyneices attacks from Argos and batters at the seven gates of Thebes; Eteocles, supported by Creon who has been acting as regent, defends the city. In a great battle the two brothers meet face to face and kill each other. It is the morning after the battle; the dead, including the two brothers, still lie on the field. Creon, now undisputed ruler of Thebes, decrees that Polyneices, because he fought against his own city, shall be left to rot on the battlefield. Antigone, caught in a conflict of loyalties to her

brothers, her betrothed, Haemon, son of Creon, and to the
State, defies Creon's edict at the cost of her life.

The play begins as Antigone beseeches her sister, Ismene,
to join her in the defiant burial of their brothers. Antigone's
unconscious motives for having her sister join her is that all
the members of the family will again be united, but now in
death. Thus she would not have to endure the separation from
any member of the family, if she and her sister are both
sentenced to death. Antigone slowly exposes her motivation to
Ismene:

> How sweet to die in such pursuit! to rest
> Loved by him whom I have loved,
> Sinner of a holy sin, with longer time
> To charm the dead than those who live, For I
> Shall abide forever there.

In the second episode, an exchange between Antigone and
Creon further exposes Antigone's irrational conscious motivations to defy Creon's orders, as well as her unconscious wish
to be unified with the family:

ANTIGONE: There is no shame to reverence relatives.
CREON: And the other duelist who died—was he no relative?
ANTIGONE: He was. And of the same father and the same mother.
CREON: So, slighting one, you would salute the other?
ANTIGONE: The dead man would not agree with you on this.
CREON: Surely! If you make the hero co-honored with the
          blackguard.
ANTIGONE: It was his brother, not his slave, that died.
CREON: Yes, and ravaged our land
          While *he* fell as its champion.
ANTIGONE: Hades makes no distinction in its rites and honors.
CREON: The just and unjust do not urge an equal claim.
ANTIGONE: The crime (who knows?) may be called a virtue
          there!
CREON: Not even death can metamorphose hate to love.
ANTIGONE: No, nor decompose a love to hate.
CREON: Curse you! Find the outlet for your love down there.

Thus Antigone indicates that her loyalty to Polyneices is determined by her irrational devotion to the family unit. Since both brothers turned against their father, Oedipus, when he blinded himself, and Antigone remained with her father, her subsequent loyalty to either brother can only be understood as an unreasonable devotion to the family. Her attitude is an elaboration of her unconscious wish for mother–child unity. She accounts for these feelings in the following speech:

> Therefore, I can go to meet my end
> Without a trace of pain. But had I left
> The body of my mother's son unburied
> Where he lay—ah! that would hurt.

In the fourth episode, Sophocles gives us a climactic portrayal of Antigone's psychosexual development toward old maidenhood, her early maternal (preoedipal) attachments, her devaluation and incapacity for a finalizing heterosexual relationship and having her own child. She explains to Creon:

> On what principle do I assert so much?
> Just this: A husband dead another can be found,
> A child, replaced; but a brother lost
> (Mother and father buried too)
> No other brother can be born or grows again.
> That's my principle, which Creon stigmatized
> As criminal—my principle for honoring
> You my dearest brother. So taken,
> So am I led away; a spinster still
> Uncelebrated, barren and bereft of joys:
> No children to my name.

In the same speech, Antigone welcomes her death as a wedding union with the beloved of her family.

> Come tomb, my wedding chamber come
> You sealed-off habitation of the grave!

My many family dead, finished fetched
In final muster to Persephone
I am last to come, and lost the most of all
My life still in my hands. And yet I come
(I hope I come) towards a father's love,
Beloved by my mother; and by you
My darling brother—loved. Yes, all of you—
Whom these hands have washed prepared and sped
With ritual to your burial.

Thus Sophocles depicts his heroine with flawless understanding of her unconscious wishes in the play *Antigone,*
which he wrote at the age of fifty-five.

ANTIGONE IN SOPHOCLES'
OEDIPUS AT COLONUS

Thirty-four years later, at the advanced age of eighty-nine,
Sophocles wrote *Oedipus at Colonus.* It is remarkable with
what constancy the portrait of Antigone remains true to the
earlier characterization, despite Sophocles' personal involvement with this play.[1] Oedipus dies peacefully and happily at
Colonus; he is buried in a tomb known only to Theseus, King
of Athens. Antigone, bereaved by the separation, states, as she
does later at the death of her brothers: "Then take me there
and kill me too."

In his development of the character of Antigone, Sophocles
proceeds in the chronological design of a psychoanalyst. His
first portrayal of her, in the play *Antigone,* depicts her in the
full bloom of life. She is betrothed to Haemon, son of Creon,
and designed never to consummate a marital or sexual love.

In the play *Oedipus at Colonus,* written three decades later,

[1] Kanzer's study correlates Sophocles' personal life and the current
Athenian scene to the creation of the play. Seidenberg and Papathoma-
poulous were able to correlate King Oedipus' conflicts, as an aging father,
in this play to equally dramatic events as an aging father in Sophocles'
personal life.

Sophocles depicts Antigone in her younger years, dedicated to her blind father. Here he gives us some hints about her childhood development which overdetermines her unending maidenhood. The blind Oedipus sums up his daughter's life:

> Antigone here,
> Ever since she left the nursery and became a woman
> Has been with me as guide and old man's nurse—
> Unhappy child—
> Steering me through dreary wanderings;
> Often roaming through the tangled woods
> Barefoot and hungry;
> Often soaked by rain and scorched by sun;
> Never regretting all she missed at home,
> So long as her father was provided for.

In the prologue of this play, the flavor of the relationship between Oedipus and Antigone is quickly established.

> OEDIPUS: Yes help me down, look after the blind old man.
> ANTIGONE: If time can teach, I need no lessons there.

In the second episode, Creon, coming upon Oedipus and Antigone at Colonus, aptly describes their lives:

> A girl his single prop
> And she poor thwarted creature
> Fallen lower than I could ever dream she'd fall
> The muffled light of squalidness and dark,
> Well ripe for weddings but unwed, and waiting. . . . ah!
> For some thick-fisted yokel's snatch

Oedipus sings the praises of both his daughters: "Dear props of my life," to which Antigone alone replies, "And partners in pain," revealing the intensity of her union with her parent.

Sophocles makes it quite clear that Antigone is dedicated to all members of her family, not only to her father. In the fourth

episode, Polyneices comes for his father's blessing in his contemplated war on his brother, Eteocles. He is spurned by the
father who forecasts the killing of both brothers at each other's
hands. In spite of her devotion to her father, Antigone again
shows a strange loyalty to Polyneices, who plans to ignore
the father's prediction. She pleads with her brother to abandon
his plan. She demonstrates an enormous fear of being abandoned by the possible death of her disloyal brothers and
disregards the fact that as yet there has been no threat to her
father, to whom she is deeply attached.

> POLYNEICES: If I must die, I'll die.
> ANTIGONE: No, hear me—never you!
> POLYNEICES: Don't press me uselessly.
> ANTIGONE: But if you're lost what's left for me?

As Oedipus dies, Antigone, loyal daughter of the house of
Labdacus, dedicates herself to the future:

> Then if his will and wish be this
> Enough for us. So be it
> But send us back to Thebes
> Old Thebes so lost in legend
> There shall we stem (if stemming be)
> The coming blood bath of our brothers.

From the evidence of Antigone's attachment and devotion
to her father and her brothers, one would readily conclude that
her chaste and unwed state was attributable to her unresolved
oedipal attachment to Oedipus, Polyneices, and Eteocles.
However, a more microscopic and qualitative analysis of these
attachments may lead to the conclusion that they were not
truly or typically oedipal, and to the possibility that they were
extensions of a preoedipal attachment to the mother.

In a study of neurotic virginity and old maidenhood, I presented a case in which the patient showed an overt, intense

attachment to her father and brothers. Thorough analysis revealed that the paternal attachment was preceded by a prolonged phase of exclusive attachment to the preoedipal mother. These findings were then correlated to Freud's last contributions to female psychosexual development in which he showed that both the oedipus complex and the castration complex of the little girl were differently organized than those of the boy. A full review of Freud's three final contributions to female psychosexual development would be repetitive. Yet it becomes imperative to quote one of his comprehensive summations in his paper, "Female Sexuality" (Freud, 1961).

> I have made [the] observations which I propose to report here . . . which have led me to adopt a particular view of female sexuality. The first was that where the woman's attachment to the father was particularly intense, analysis showed that it had been preceded by a phase of exclusive attachment to her mother which has been equally intense and passionate. Except for the change of her love object, the second phase has scarcely added any new feature to her erotic life. . . . The second fact taught me that the duration of the attachment had also been greatly underestimated. . . . Indeed we had to reckon with the possibility that a number of women remained arrested in the original attachment to the mother and never achieved a true change-over towards men. . . . Everything in the sphere of this attachment to the mother seemed to me so difficult to grasp in analysis—so grey with age and almost impossible to revivify—that it was as if it had succumbed to an especially inexorable repression. But perhaps I gained this impression because the women who were in analysis with me were able to cling to the very attachment to the father in which they had taken refuge from the early phase in question.

Since the preoedipal attachment to the mother is so obscured by the intense attachment to the father in thoroughly investigated psychoanalytic cases, it becomes comprehensible that the evidence for a preoedipal fixation on the mother in a created character, such as Antigone, may be meager but significant (Freud, 1961). Sophocles tells us that "Antigone here, ever since she left the nursery and became a woman has been with me as guide and old man's nurse—unhappy child." In the clinical case of old maidenhood it was demonstrated that the fixation on the preoedipal mother led to a regressive retreat to the oral stage of the nurturing mother. In her childhood longings she showed a preference for nurturing care from her mother; as an adult she manifested the same wish in her relations with men. The wish for a nurturing relationship is often reversed and the child becomes the donor where it once was the recipient. So it was with Antigone, who leaves the nursery and becomes nurse to her father.

Kanzer (1948), in his study of "The Passing of the Oedipus Complex in Greek Drama," interprets Oedipus' wanderings with Antigone as a renewal of his dependent relationship on the mother after his blindness had absolved his crimes. According to Kanzer's interpretation, the father–daughter relationship is a reversal of generations. Thus he sees Antigone involved in a mother–dependent child relationship with her father, Oedipus. The reversal of roles for Antigone must of necessity originate from her own dependent preoedipal attachment to her mother. In his later study on "The Oedipus Trilogy," Kanzer (1950) fluctuates in his evaluation of Antigone. Within the same study he sees Antigone's defiance of Creon's orders as "a continuance of the oedipal theme"; later he evaluates it as a "love of family represented by Antigone."

Goethe (Eckermann, 1930) criticizes Antigone's speech in which she declares that she would die for a brother but not for a husband or child since the latter can be duplicated and a brother cannot. He finds these lines unbefitting the character of a tragic heroine who would defy a royal edict to protect the honor of her family (*die Familienpietät*). As was shown elsewhere, this is one of the many contradictions in Antigone's character. However, as analysts we are not surprised to find that psychosexual regressions to infantile omnipotence may be sublimated to external acts of omnipotent heroism. Thus Joan of Arc, the maid of Orleans, who would tremble at a sexual encounter with any one man, could fiercely do battle with armies of men in the service of God and her country.

Sophocles gives us more clues to the early maternal (pre-oedipal) quality of Antigone's oedipal attachment, which was extended to all members of her family, and her wish for union and nurturing love. She welcomes death. "I am last to come, and lost the most of all/My life still in my hands./And yet I come . . ./towards a father's love,/Beloved by my mother, and by you/My darling brother—loved. Yes all of you/Whom these my hands have washed prepared and sped/With ritual to your burial."

If one imagines the Oedipus legend somewhat reversed, so that Oedipus kills himself and his mother-wife Jocasta blinds herself and wanders homeless, one could believe that Soph-ocles might have created Antigone as the loyal and devoted daughter who would nurse her cursed mother and who would wish to die with her. Thus her reactions would be identical with either suffering parent.

Another clue to Sophocles' clear characterization of Antig-one's early maternal (preoedipal) fixation is to be discerned in his differentiation of the two sisters, Both daughters are loyal to their father but with distinct differences. Ismene does not nurse her father during his wanderings. She does not be-come his eyes or "his single prop" or his "partner in pain." In a beautiful counterpoint, Oedipus' speech about Antigone as the unhappy child who "left the nursery" ends with his love and gratitude toward Ismene:

And you, my daughter
Once you used to sally forth
Slipping past the Theban sentinels
With all the news of oracles about your father.

You were my faithful spy
When I was driven from the land
But Ismene, what new message do you bring your father?
What new mission made you leave your home?
You are not empty-handed—that I know
You've brought me something—something I can fear.

Thus Ismene, who also loves her father, served him as a loyal mature mate or daughter who has her own home. She gives evidence of a more mature oedipally derived love. When Oedipus dies, Sophocles does not have Ismene say that she too wants to die, like Antigone. In *Antigone*, the heroine beseeches Ismene to join ranks with her and bury their brother. Loyal as Ismene is to her father and sister, she sees no sense in Antigone's wish to die for her dishonorable brother. Her wish is to live, to be forgiven, and perhaps fulfill her own life. She tells Antigone:

Sister, please, please! Remember how
Our father died, hated, in disgrace,
Wrapped in horror of himself, his own
Hand stabbing out his sight. And how
His mother-wife in one twisted off
Her earthly days with cord. And thirdly how
Our two brothers in a single day
Each achieved for each a suicidal
Nemesis
And now, we two are left
Think how much worse our end will be than all
The rest if we defy our sovereign's edict
And his power. Remind ourselves that we
Are women, and as such not made to fight
With men. For might unfortunately is right
And makes us bow to things like this and worse.
Therefore shall I beg the saints below
To judge me leniently as one who kneeled

To force. I bend before authority
It does not do to meddle.

Ismene is bound to her father by a deep but rational childhood love. Antigone, heroine that she is, is bound by a deep
attachment to all the members of her family, good and bad,
rooted in her small child's irrational attachment to a preoedipal
mother.

The significance of Antigone's lifelong nursing of her father
has been evaluated as an outcome of her preoedipal attachment to her mother with a regressive oral wish for a nurturing
mother. Via a reversal of her parent–child role, nursing and
nurturing became the central aim of Antigone's relationships.
A similar setting is to be found in the historical Breuer-Freud
case of Elizabeth v. R. (Breuer & Freud, 1947). Her situation
is described as follows:

> First, the patient's father died, then the mother underwent a
> serious operation on her eyes and soon thereafter a married sister
> succumbed to a chronic cardiac affection following childbirth.
> Our patient had taken part in all the afflictions, especially in the
> nursing care of the sick.

Earlier I suggested that if the Oedipus legend were modified
so that Oedipus died and a blinded Jocasta were to live, one
would expect Antigone (like Elizabeth v. R.) to spend her life
nursing her mother. In a fascinating applied psychoanalytic
study, "Daughters Who Tend Their Fathers—a Literary Survey," Seidenberg and Papathomapoulos (1962) have compre-
hensively examined all the significant works of literature that
deal with this theme. Following the conclusion of Breuer and
Freud, in "Studies in Hysteria" they attempt to show that there
is a recurrent theme of "hysteria" in young girls following the
illness and death of a father whom they had actively nursed.
They also demonstrate that these daughters tend to remain

unwed and welcome the nursing role toward their father, because of an oedipal wish "to win out over mother (at last having father to oneself) in the classical oedipal struggle."[2] Finally, they suggest that the nursing females, described in ancient and in nineteenth-century literature and in the Breuer-Freud case histories, are cultural and sociological reflections of the inferior status of womanhood which are rarely found "today in our progressive culture."

Though one must agree with their observation that such tending daughters tend to become hysterical old maids, some of the subsequent conclusions remain dubious. Antigone, as written by Sophocles, does not fall ill with hysteria after the prolonged nursing of her father, although had she been destined to live longer she might have. The conviction that an oedipal tie to the father accounts for the attachment is based only on the obvious devoted relationship to the father and does not account for the nursing theme that haunts these daughters, as it did Elizabeth v. R., in their relationships with all members of the family. Unfortunately, the authors chose to follow Freud's earliest formulation on the female oedipal complex and ignored his final, radically changed formulation on these matters in his last contributions.[3]

Since this study concerns itself exclusively with Sophocles' created character, Antigone, as a preoedipal old maid, no attention has been paid to other famous old maids in literature.

[2] The authors suggest that "father-nursing daughters may be motivated from lifelong anger and vengeful desires toward the dominating males in the family derived from the masculine complex and penis envy" (Seidenberg & Papathomapoulos, 1962).

[3] The authors state that the desire for the role of nursing may also arise out of hostile, vengeful motives toward the father, gratified in being witness to his demise. We are told that these wishes are a manifestation of their masculinity complex and penis envy. Again, if one follows Freud's later contributions to female sexuality, the hostile vengeful wishes of the masculinity complex and associated penis envy are preoedipal rather than oedipal and are mainly directed at the phallic mother, extended on to the father only as a secondary surrogate.

Such heroines as Mlle. Cormon in Balzac's *Old Maid* and Rebecca in Ibsen's *Rosmersholm* seem to have been created in the same design of conscious paternal attachments and unconscious preoedipal fixations. The maiden, Antigone, who has the identical neurotic conflicts of her nineteenth-century counterparts, can be seen today in socially and culturally acceptable roles. The Antigone of today will be found in various roles of a lifelong dedicated personal aide to either a famous man or woman, and to the respective families.

Thus the ancient dramatist Sophocles and the modern Williams, members of a creative brotherhood in existence for over two thousand years, have created characters which illuminate our current psychoanalytic insights about the old maid and the prostitute, which lie at opposite poles of the spectrum of the psychosexual development of the female.

12

O'Neill's Electra:

The Psychology of Mourning

DISSATISFIED WITH THE VARIOUS dispositions of Electra by Aeschylus, Euripides, and Sophocles in their interpretations of the Agamemnon tale, Eugene O'Neill selected the same figure as the central character in his play *Mourning Becomes Electra*, based on the Greek legend. In his working notes O'Neill commits himself to create a drama in which he can "give to the modern Electra figure (Lavinia) in the play a tragic ending worthy of character." He wanted to convey "a modern tragic interpretation of classic fate without benefit of gods—for it must, before everything, remain [a] modern psychological play—fate springing out of family life."

O'Neill's sense of tragedy, often referred to as his sixth sense, seems to stem from his tragic personal life. In our psychobiographical study of O'Neill we have seen that he was unconsciously forbidden to enjoy a happy fulfillment of family life and fatherhood.[1] From this design of his own destiny, he was sensitive to an original artistic understanding that Electra was not fated to "peter out into undramatic married banal-

[1] See Chapter 8.

ity." He then recreated her as an eternally haunted character, as he himself was. So personal was O'Neill's empathy that he (New England-bred) could only envision Electra's tragedy in terms of Lavinia Mannon, a New England character of the latter half of the nineteenth century. Although he has deprived us of the universality of the original legendary images, his more personal and contemporaneous transformation of the legendary characters has enriched them with more flesh and blood and vitality than they originally had. We can readily feel a personal identity with O'Neill's more contemporary alternates.

O'Neill was a contemporary spokesman for his generation. The late twenties and thirties were imbued with the new discoveries of Freud. Man's fate and destiny were reshaped and re-evaluated by artists as well as scientists in the context of this new knowledge. O'Neill's *Mourning Becomes Electra* succeeded in its mission to mirror the mood of his era and "before everything remain [a] modern psychological play."

Intending only to depict her accurately in a modern psychological drama, he succeeded in creating a portrayal of Electra (Lavinia) as the embodiment of the process of mourning. His creation of this key figure, entrenched in mourning, antedates by more than twenty years and confirms the latest psychoanalytic concepts on the psychology of mourning. O'Neill's characterization of Electra dovetails with the most recent concepts of mourning with its complicated mechanism of introjecting the lost love-object into the object representation and self-representation in the ego and the concomitant introjection into the superego, as developed by Dr. Edith Jacobson in 1954.[2] With such thoroughness did O'Neill portray Lavinia and the other mourning members of the Mannon family.

We agree completely with O'Neill in his rebuttal to Clark's accusation that the play was patterned too precisely on Freud and Jung. O'Neill (Clark, 1947) writes:

[2] See footnote 1 in Chapter 8.

I don't agree with your Freudian objections. Taken from my author's angle, I find fault with critics on exactly the same point —that they read too damn much Freud into stuff that could have been written exactly as is before psychoanalysis was heard of. Imagine the Freudian bias that would be read into Stendhal, Balzac, Strindberg, Dostoievsky, etc., if they were writing today! . . . Authors were psychologists, you know, and profound ones before psychology was invented. And I am no deep student of psychoanalysis.

O'Neill was too sensitively hurt in this discussion of scientific plagiarism to take any satisfaction in the more plausible view that his creation and the science of psychoanalysis verified and complemented each other.

His letter continues,

In short I think I know enough about men and women to have written *Mourning Becomes Electra* almost exactly as it is if I had never heard of Freud or Jung or the others. . . . As far as I can remember of all the books written by Freud, Jung, etc., I have read only four and Jung is the only one of the lot who interests me. Some of his suggestions I find extraordinarily illuminating in the light of my own experiences with hidden human motives.

Sievers, in his book *Freud on Broadway* (1955), feels that O'Neill was reluctant to acknowledge indebtedness to any source but original creativity and that the author was not objective on this score; further, that "Freud illuminated O'Neill's own experiences." We take issue with Sievers' evaluation and tend to agree with O'Neill. Sievers has failed to take into account that an artist's biography must consider his social milieu and thus he will tend to utilize consciously the *au courant* symbols of his environment. Beres (1959) warns us that the conventional use of symbols must be distinguished from the specific individual significance. The use of a conventional symbol—be it Freudian, Jungian, masks, or asides (preconscious thoughts) in a conscious or preconscious way—

must be separated from the use of the symbol in unconscious ways that are in the service of securing a mode of discharge for repressed psychic drives.

It is interesting that Jung had such an appeal to O'Neill. This verifies Beres' contention that Jung is particularly attractive to the "literary dilettante in psychoanalysis." Beres (1959) states that this "romance" comes about because Jung denies the importance of specific aspects of psychic structure and treats art as "a vision"—"a genuine primordial experience" —which arises from a "collective unconscious." This concept usually finds favor with artists because it permits them to conceive of the unconscious in an isolated fashion, but it tends to keep biography apart from the artist. The tendency of the artist to form a legendary illusion about his own identity goes well with a theory like Jung's, which relegates the aspects of psychic structure to an insignificant role.[3]

O'Neill used similarities in appearance, masks, make-up, and aside dialogues merely as technical symbols originating from *conscious* psychoanalytic concepts which would be intelligible to his audience. This can be clearly discerned in reading O'Neill's "Working Notes and Extracts from a Fragmentary Work Diary," for the play *Mourning Becomes Electra*. However, the *unconscious* revelation in this trilogy is to be found in this diary as O'Neill struggles to clarify to himself the meaning of the title that he chose before writing the play. He writes: "Title—Mourning Becomes Electra—that is—in old sense—it befits—it becomes Electra to mourn—it is her fate—" O'Neill excludes the "new" sense of the word (that is, to identify) to be or become mourning. This is preserved, as it is for all artists, for unconscious revelation. O'Neill intended to convey "a modern tragic interpretation of classic fate without benefit of gods—for it must, before everything, remain modern psychological play—fate springing out of family."

[3] Kris has described the frequent appearance of the legendary image of the artist.

O'Neill here demonstrates his primitive and naïve psycho-analytic knowledge. He is unaware that the power of the family fate is as representative of man's superego as the power of the Greek gods is representative of the superego of the classical Greek tragic hero. However, his plays of mourning do not fail to unfold an artistic awareness of such psychological processes in spite of himself. For example, Lavinia (Electra) becomes the full embodiment of her mother Christine (Clytemnestra) only after she contrives to bring about her mother's death. Then she fully becomes the enactment of her mother. She then re-enacts the sinfulness and tragedy of her mother as if they were of one identity. Lavinia introjects into her own ego the identity of Christine and enacts her mother's life; she hates and punishes herself in this new identification—as she formerly hated and punished her mother in life. In O'Neill's blueprint, the tragedy is based on the unfolding of family fate. In his aesthetic creation, *Mourning Becomes Electra*, Electra is given a new and proper portrayal which had been diluted in the Greek tragedy.

O'Neill's artistic sensitivity, rather than his direct scientific sensitivity, is illuminatingly illustrated in his working notes:

> Greek plot idea—give modern Electra figure (Lavinia) in play tragic ending worthy of character. In Greek story she peters out into undramatic married banality. [O'Neill did not note that the Greek word "Electra"—*A-lektra* means the "Unmated."] Such a character contained too much tragic fate within her soul [the psychoanalyst would say due to an identification within her ego] to permit this—why should Furies (superego, conscience) have let Electra escape unpunished. Why did the chain of fated crime and retribution ignore her mother's murderess?—a weakness in what remains to us of Greek tragedy that there is no play about Electra's life after the murder of Clytemnestra. Surely it possesses as imaginative tragic possibilities as any of their plots!

An affirmation that O'Neill's idea that mourning was becoming to Electra evolved itself unconsciously into Electra becoming one with mourning. And so he wrote the play—although he conceived it more limitedly.

This again verifies Freud's 1904 (1942, p. 463) formula for a psychopathological drama; it is worth quoting again:

> It appears to be one of the prerequisites of this art form that the struggle of the repressed impulse to become conscious, recognizable though it is, is so little given a definite name that the process of reaching consciousness goes on in turn within the spectator while his attention is distracted and he is in the grip of his emotion, rather than capable of rational judgment.

Thus Freud's formulation seems to be a condition applicable to the dramatist as well. Be it the psychopathological drama of Eugene O'Neill or Tennessee Williams, Freud's rule remains a fruitful formulation.

V

A Psychoanalytic View of
the Crises in Creativity
in Modern Theater

13

The Crisis in Creative Criticism:

Homespun versus Dynamic Psychology

PRIMARILY IN THE ACADEMIC world, the organized bodies of criticism of history and art have unsuccessfully resisted the strength, the pressures, and the endeavors of psychoanalysis to contribute to the orientation of their fields of study. Currently, die-hards continue to express bitter protests against new concepts, although progressive leaders of criticism welcome psychoanalytic orientations.

Dr. William L. Langer (1958, pp. 283–284), in his 1957 inaugural presidential address to the American Historical Association, stated that he would use the occasion

> not so much for reflections of the past achievements of the profession as for speculation about its needs and its future—that is, about the direction which historical study might profitably take in the years to come. . . . We are all keenly aware of the fact that during the past half century the scope of historical study has been vastly extended. . . . There is, however, still ample scope for penetration in depth, the "newest history" will probably be more intensive and less extensive. I refer more specifically to the urgently needed deepening of our historical understanding through exploitation of the concepts and findings of modern psychology.

And by this, may I add, I do not refer to classical or academic psychology, which, so far as I can detect, has little bearing on historical problems, but rather to psychoanalysis and its later developments and variations as included in the terms "dynamic" or "depth" psychology. . . . Despite this general and often profound intellectual and artistic reorientation since Freud published his first epoch-making works sixty years ago, historians as a group have maintained an almost completely negative attitude toward the teachings of psychoanalysis. Their lack of response has been due, I should think, less to constitutional obscurantism than to the fact that historians, as disciples of Thucydides, have habitually thought of themselves as psychologists in their own right. . . . Viewed in the light of modern depth psychology, the homespun, common-sense psychological interpretations of past historians, even some of the greatest, seem woefully inadequate not to say naïve. Clearly the time has come for us to reckon with a doctrine that strikes so close to the heart of our own discipline. . . . I call your attention to the fact that for many years young scholars in anthropology, sociology, religion, literature, education and other fields have gone to psychoanalytic institutes for special training, and I suggest that some of our own younger men might seek the same equipment. For of this I have no doubt that modern psychology is bound to play an even greater role in historical interpretation.

In 1956, Leon Edel (1957), who more recently was awarded a Pulitzer prize in biography, delivered the Alexander lectures at the University of Toronto on literary biography. In one of these lectures he remarked:

We have looked into the relations between biography and criticism and seen that the biographer is committed at every turn to the act of criticism. And now I should like to examine the newest and most significant of all the biographer's relationships, his as yet uneasy flirtation with psychology. It would be somewhat more accurate to speak of it as psychoanalysis rather than psychology. . . . The answer to the misguided use of psychoanalysis is not to close our ears but to ask ourselves: how are we to handle this difficult material while remaining true to our own discipline—and avoid making complete fools of ourselves? Critics who babble of the Oedipus complex and who plant psychoanalytic clichés higgledy-piggledy in their writings do a disservice both to literature and psychoanalysis. . . . Modern literary biography is a delicate and humane process of great complexity, as complex as life itself, involving wide-ranging curiosity and search, critical analysis, psychological insight and a quality of sympathy between biography and subject. . . . To arrive at this view, the biographer has to unite the qualities of critic and psychoanalyst. By penetrating more deeply into the life it is possible to penetrate more deeply into the work.

Edel here emphasizes a view held by Ernest Jones concerning the contribution of psychoanalysis to criticism in art. Jones (1949) wrote:

A work of art is too often regarded as a finished thing-in-itself, something almost independent of the creator's personality as if little would be learned about the one or the other by connecting the two studies. Informed criticism, however, showed that a correlated study of the two sheds light in both directions, on the inner nature of the composition and on the creative impulse of the author. The two can be separated only at the expense of diminished appreciation, whereas to increase our knowledge of either automatically deepens our understanding of the other.

Lesser, in his book *Fiction and the Unconscious,* points out that the real issue for the critic "is not whether to use psychology but what kind of psychology to use." Should it be a continuation of the homespun, "common-sense" psychology that literary criticism has always employed or will it be replaced by a scientific depth psychology—such as psychoanalysis? In support of the latter, Lesser (1957) states, "No 'common-sense' psychology yet employed in criticism has been helpful in explaining the unconscious sources of the behavior of literary characters or the unconscious sources of literature's appeal. In my opinion, every mode of analyzing literature should take cognizance of the fact that literature speaks to the unconscious."

Lionel Trilling (1950), the noted literary scholar and critic, credits psychoanalysis "as the only systematic account of the human mind which deserves to stand beside the chaotic mass of psychological insights which literature has accumulated through the centuries."

Hence psychoanalysis, a scientific system of the human mind, is entitled, not only to the role of collaborator, but also to the role of evaluator, interpreter, and critic of the unorganized mass of psychological insights to be found in literature and its creators, especially of the romantic era.

This does not sanction the oft-practiced procedure by psychoanalysts who, in their investigations of the arts for evidence of psychological content and psychoanalytic correlation between the life of the artist and his work, extend their authority to critical and judgmental evaluation of the aesthetic aspects of art. The aesthetic evaluation of art properly belongs to the critic, whether he is analytically oriented or not. Valid psychological contributions by the psychoanalyst or the psychoanalytically minded critic should augment aesthetic appreciation.

Thus, as art progresses in the expression of man's unconscious and his inner world, the critic should become increasingly aware of the scientific laws and body of knowledge of the internal psychic world that psychoanalysis has evolved. Freudian psychoanalysis has gradually been incorporated into the fields of medicine, psychology, anthropology, education, and the arts.

Of Freud himself it has been written that "he has in large part created the intellectual climate of our time" (Freud and the Arts, 1956) and that we live in a world "in which the ideas of Freud have become a part of the spiritual air we breathe"[1] (Graf, 1942). It would be worthwhile to review Freud's direct

[1] The critic of *The New York Times*, Brooks Atkinson (not the critic of today but of yesterday) once humorously remarked that Freud must bear the responsibility of persuading the average man that he is an expert on human nature.

contributions and his tribulations in the direction of fusing criticism and psychoanalysis. In such an historical perspective we may not only recapture the creative qualities inherent in psychoanalytically oriented criticism but discern a design for its future development.

Freud's first published biographical criticism is his famous study of *Leonardo da Vinci and a Memory of His Childhood*. He had been preceded in this sphere by his disciple Sadger, who had made similar studies of Conrad, Lenau, and Kleist. Freud's monograph met with more than the usual amount of disapproval, although he had anticipated this critical hostility in his comments in Chapter VI of this same study. His reflections on these matters are worth quoting, since they shed light on the beginnings of a struggle, which still exists, for the recognition of psychoanalysis in the field of criticism (Freud, 1957, pp. 130–131).

> It would be futile to blind ourselves to the fact that readers today find all pathography unpalatable. They clothe their aversion in the complaint that a pathographic review of a great man never results in an understanding of his importance and his achievements and that it is therefore a piece of useless impertinence to make a study of things in him that could just as easily be found in the first person one came across. But this criticism is so manifestly unjust that it is only understandable when it is taken as a pretext and a disguise.
>
> Leonardo himself, with his love of truth and his thirst for knowledge, would not have discouraged an attempt to take the trivial peculiarities and riddles in his nature as a starting point for discovering what determines his mental and intellectual development. We do homage to him by learning from him. It does not detract from his greatness if we make a study of the suffering which his development from childhood must have entailed, and if we bring together the factors which have stamped him with the mark of tragic failure.

Freud correctly anticipated the false objections to the nature of his only pathographical study of a creative genius. The predicted misunderstanding, because of the striking novelty and the startling conclusion of his study of Leonardo, led to a flood of pseudopsychoanalytic writing in the 1920's, which brought Freud's approach into disrepute and has continued until the present day to discourage serious scholars and critics from examining the contents of authentic psychoanalytic studies. The trend of the 1920's has not abated. The pseudopsychoanalytic study of the lives of important people, particularly of those living, is a popular pathological literary pastime and now floods our theaters, our movies, our television sets, as well as our bookshelves.

Freud points out that psychoanalytic discoveries have wounded mankind's idealization of its heroes as well as man's self-esteem in the same way that Copernicus' discovery destroyed man's concept of his central position in nature and Darwin's work undid man's concept of his divine origin in nature. Similarly, the discovery of the unconscious displeased our philosophers since it ended the exclusive exaltation of the conscious intellect. The displeasure specifically incurred from philosophers could be extended to include abstract thinkers in any field, especially such intellectual leaders as critics and historians in the various arts.

Whatever immediate unpleasant repercussions developed upon the publication of the Leonardo study, it eventually received recognition as a superior and original artistic criticism. Meyer Schapiro (1956), the art historian, concluded that Freud was able, "thanks to his theory and method, and perhaps even more to his deep sympathy for the tragic and the problematic in Leonardo, to pose altogether new and important questions about his personality, questions which were unsuspected by earlier writers and to which no better answer than Freud's has yet been given."

Criticism that incorporates psychoanalytic insight may well be called creative criticism. Freud intuited his insight of Leonardo from a patient who "seemed to have the same con-

stitution as Leonardo without his genius." He then obtained a
book on Leonardo's youth and confirmed his impression. That
the monograph on Leonardo was more in the nature and style
of a creative work rather that a prosaic scholarly study is attested to by the evidence that the inspiration for the work occurred more than a decade before it was written. Freud first
remarked to Fliess in 1898—eleven years prior to his study—
that, "perhaps the most famous left-handed individual was
Leonardo, who is not known to have had any love affairs."
Freud's main interest at that earlier time was to criticize Fliess's
idea of a connection between bilaterality and bisexuality.

Psychoanalysts refer to the combined efforts of inspiration
and elaboration that constitute the creative process, but have
not emphasized sufficiently the prolonged time interval that
may ensue before the two aspects of the creative efforts are
integrated and synthesized.[2] It remains an unanswered psychoanalytic problem as to what goes on in the psychic structure
during the prolonged pregnant interval between inspirational
conception and the elaborated delivery. What is of interest at
the moment is that criticism can be as creative as art itself
when it avoids, as Freud has suggested (and we have noted
earlier), an idealized identification with the artist or his work
and instead produces an inspirational response in the critic
which dwells within him and is subsequently elaborated by
him with the aid of his connoisseurship of the given art, the
particular artist, his collected works, and the specific work
under consideration. As to Freud's qualifications for being a
critic in the area of connoisseurship, Graf (1942) wrote, "Freud
was one of the most cultivated persons I have ever known. He

[2] A parallel to this sequence between creative inspiration and subsequent elaboration is to be found in Freud's contemporary, George
Bernard Shaw, also born in 1856. In 1899 Shaw had his first conscious
image (inspiration) for *Pygmalion*, which was written in 1912. Freud
wrote *Leonardo da Vinci* twelve years after his inspiration and Shaw
wrote *Pygmalion* some fifteen years after his inspiration. (For fuller details on the unconscious origins of Shaw's *Pygmalion* see Chapter 9.)

knew all the most important writings of poets. He knew the paintings of the great artists, which he studied in the museums and churches of Italy and Holland."

Although Freud's first major applied psychoanalytic, non-biographical, literary study was of Jensen's *Gradiva*, published in 1907, it was not Freud's first effort in the area of criticism. It will be remembered that, although not published until 1942, in 1904 Freud had written "Psychopathic Characters on Stage." Thus Freud's first full adventure in literary criticism was in drama. Here too we can trace the creative inspiration to what took place in earlier years and evolved a few years later. It is more than likely that the creative ferment for the final production of this short study occurred at least four years earlier during his preoccupation with the dramas of *Oedipus Rex* and *Hamlet*, which he commented on in his monumental study of *The Interpretation of Dreams*, published in 1900.

In this work Freud tells us much about the stuff that psycho-pathological dramas are made of.[3] Utilizing *Hamlet* as "the foremost modern drama of this kind" he tells us that the hero "is not psychopathic but becomes so only in the course of action we are going to witness." He informs us that the play-wright must create through the play's action the character of the hero; the psychopathy is not clinical psychopathy but rather an art-created psychopathy structured on what we have come to term the aesthetic ambiguity of the portrait. One of Freud's prerequisites for the psychological drama (1942, p. 463) is that the hero's "repressed desire is one of those that are similarly repressed in all of us, the repression of which belongs to an early stage of our individual development, while the situation of the play shatters precisely this repression. Because of these two features it is easy for us to recognize ourselves in the hero." Here Freud states what we now express in terms of ego psychology—that in the process of artistic creation and communication there is a mutual identification between the

[3] See chapters 10 and 12 on Freud 1942.

artist and audience, i.e., the artist while creating identifies with his audience and the audience subsequently identifies with the artist's communication.

In the same study, Freud discusses the prerequisite for the enjoyment of several forms of creative art. He distinguishes epic poetry, dance, drama, and particularly tragedy from one another. He emphasizes that drama delves into the deepest emotional possibilities and that one may characterize "drama by this very relation to suffering and misfortune, whether as in the play mere apprehension is aroused and then allayed or as in tragedy actual suffering is brought into being" (1942, p. 460). He states that drama "is supposed to manage to transform even the forebodings of doom into something enjoyable and it therefore depicts the embattled hero rather with a masochistic satisfaction in succumbing" (1942, p. 460).

Freud (1942, p. 464) does not fail to distinguish between artful and artless psychopathological drama.

> Possibly it is because of the disregarding of these three prerequisites that so many other psychopathic characters become as useless for the stage as for life itself. The sick neurotic is to us a man into whose conflict we can obtain no insight [empathy] when he presents it to us in the form of the finished product. Conversely, if we are familiar with this conflict, we forget that he is a sick man just as when he becomes familiar with it he himself ceases to be sick. It is thus the task of the dramatist to transport us into the same illness—a thing best accomplished if we follow him through its development.

In "Psychopathic Characters on Stage" Freud emerges as the first and a first-rate psychoanalytically oriented modern drama critic. Preliminary and quickly drafted as this study on drama was, it still serves as a vital standard for measuring whether a dramatist has created an artistic work.

This paper, written in 1904, was dedicated to Max Graf, at that time a young music critic. In 1942 Dr. Graf offered it for publication and wrote an accompanying article entitled, "Reminiscences of Professor Sigmund Freud." It would be worthwhile to report here the atmosphere and the design of these historical meetings between Freud and his disciples may yet again be repeated in order to achieve what modern connoisseurs, such as Trilling in literature, Edel in biography, Lesser in fiction, Langer in history, and Schapiro in art, tell us is our future direction—a psychoanalytically oriented criticism.

Graf (1942) reminisces that shortly after meeting Freud in 1900, and having expressed his interest in his theories, he was invited into the

circle of his [Freud's] first pupils, although I was not a physician but a writer, a music critic. . . . Gradually Freud gathered around a circle of interested and inspired pupils. One day he startled me by announcing that he would like to have a meeting in his house once a week; he wanted there not only a number of his pupils [Adler, Stekel, and Federn] but also personalities from other fields of intellectual endeavor. He mentioned to me Herman Bahr, the writer who was then the leader of modern artists in Vienna, who had a keen feeling for all new intellectual trends. Freud wanted to have his theories discussed from all possible points of view. He asked me whether I would be interested in such an undertaking. Thus I was for several years a member of this group of friends which met every Wednesday in Freud's house. The majority of this group was naturally made up of physicians who were familiar with the new Freudian psychology. There were a few writers, I who was a music critic and Lehar, the musical esthete from the Vienna State Academy of Music. I took over the task of investigating the psychology of great musicians and the process of creating music, utilizing psychoanalysis for this task. The gatherings followed a definite ritual. First one of the members would present a paper. The black coffee and cakes were served, cigars and cigarettes were on the table and consumed in great quantities. After a social quarter of an hour, the discussion would begin. Despite the fact that the contrast among the personalities of this circle of pupils was great, at that early period of Freudian investigation all of them were united in their respect for and inspiration with Freud (pp. 467, 470).

Dr. Graf's reminiscences of the atmosphere of Freud's Wednesday meetings could well serve as a model for the constituents of a seminar to promote the much needed psychoanalytically oriented critic of tomorrow. In the world's increasing design of collective living and working, it would not be surprising if future authoritative criticism might be the collective authorship of critic and psychoanalyst.

Inherent in the romantic era of art is the condition that the artist will continue to create works of art that will represent man's dreams and fantasies. Psychoanalytic supplementation to a critic's armamentarium is essential to the current cultural trend of art. In a cooperative effort, psychoanalysis and criticism may then evolve a more systematized psychology of creation and appreciation. The critic who has intuitive psychoanalytic insight, reinforced by a psychoanalytic education, will not only be in a better position to comprehend the artist's content and its relationship to the artist's personality and his life, but can also deepen our appreciation of art through his greater psychological insight and aesthetic connoisseurship.

14

The Crisis in Creative Acting:

The Stanislavski Method versus

Representational Acting

STANISLAVSKI'S NEW CONCEPT of the art of acting is an integral part of the historical alteration in all fields of arts and sciences, that is, a concept that places more importance upon the individual and less on nature. In the field of literature this is referred to as the romantic movement; art expresses man's inner emotions and ideas and is no longer the reflection of nature. Before Stanislavski, acting lagged behind its fellow arts and was mainly representational. In representational acting, living the part is merely preparatory to what is intended by the actor. His ambition is to perfect the part, then to memorize it and to reproduce it constantly. In Stanislavski's concept of creative acting, it is essential that the actor live the part every moment and every time he acts it.

Stanislavski does not totally discredit representational acting. The following excerpt expresses the nature of both art forms, the differences between them and their final aesthetic values. Beginning with representationalism, he writes:

This type of art is less profound than beautiful. It is more immediately effective than truly powerful; in it the form is more interesting than its content. It acts more on your sense of sound and
sight than on your soul. Consequently it is more likely to delight
than to move you. . . . Your astonishment rather than your faith
is aroused. . . . But delicate and deep human feelings are not subject to such technique. . . . Nevertheless, representing the part
since it follows our process in part must be acknowledged to be
creative art (1936, p. 22).

The writer, painter, sculptor, or composer, by the nature of
his art, leaves a true record of his talents in his creative works.
This is obviously not the case in the performing arts, if we
exclude cinema and recordings and their siblings, radio and
television. For an actor or director in theater to leave a true
representation of his actual creations becomes almost impossible. Legendary evaluations of the renowned are the natural
result in this field of endeavor. The absence of a permanent
record operates in two directions. In the field of valuation it
tends to exaggerate favorably the works of the artist.[1] Second,
in the realm of perpetuation, acting and directing tend to be
lost arts. That is, if they are not carried on by capable disciples
from one generation to another, their method and style are
likely to disappear. Examples of such traditional preservations
are to be found in fields of culturally inherited performing arts,
such as dancing, singing, as well as acting.

The measure of Stanislavski's creative genius as actor and
director confronts us with the above-mentioned difficulties
relative to the performing arts. In this respect, we can only
accept the statement of drama critics, highly recognized theatrical authorities, and audiences who saw his works and attested universally to his greatness. He was actively engaged in
his professional career for fifty years, the last forty years with
the Moscow Art Theatre which he cofounded and codirected

---

[1] It is similar to the state of mourning in which the lost object becomes
exaggeratedly loved after death.

with Nemirovich-Danchenko. In this organization he introduced the repertory system. He overcame the natural handicaps of his art form and through his writings left a significant and unique legacy in recorded form on the theories and technique of acting.[2]

We shall examine these theories and techniques, since their application deals predominantly with the utilization of psychological principles and mechanisms. His system has psychodynamic validity.[3]

A passage from Stanislavski's book, *An Actor Prepares,* gives us the true aims of his art form.

> Our experience has led to a firm belief that only one kind of art, soaked as it is in the living experience of human beings, can artistically reproduce the impalpable shadings and depths of life. Only such art can completely absorb the spectator and make him both understand and also inwardly experience the happenings on the stage, enriching his inner life and living impressions which will not fade with time (Stanislavski, 1936, p. 16).

Stanislavski conceives of creative acting as an art which communicates from the unconscious of the actor to the unconscious of the spectator. Knowing what Stanislavski demands from his actors, it is of interest to examine how he induces them to do this. Briefly, he wants the actor to identify as completely as possible with the created character. The actor must live the part and "fit his own human qualities to the life of this other person and thus create the inner life of a human spirit."

There is no question that the conscious identification with another, be it a real person or created character, elicits in the actor some of the characteristics of the "person" with whom he

---

[2] For fuller details see Chapter 6.

[3] Neither in his autobiography or in his books on technique does Stanislavski ever mention Freud or his works. However, art and science of our century have so many crossroads that Stanislavski's awareness of psychoanalysis seems extremely likely.

has identified. There is a parallel to the daily work of the analyst. In Freud's writings on technique, he suggests that the analyst listen to the analysand's associations with free-floating attention. In this process he partially identifies with his patient, and thus gains understanding of the patient's unconscious. At this point the artist and the analyst part company. The aim of the analyst is to lay bare unconscious wishes and fears. The aim of the actor is to express unconscious content in an artistic form.[4]

Fenichel (1946) takes up the question of identification in the personality of the potential actor. He suggests that actors often lack a distinctive personality, ego development, and are "rather a bundle of identification possibilities." Actors are correspondingly inhibited in their object relationships; and objects rather than relations are used for identification and are sources of narcissistic gratification.

I found this to be so in the case of a professional actor who came for analysis with complaints of feeling depersonalized and "not quite knowing who and what I am." In his earliest development he was rather severely restricted by his mother from putting stray objects (dirt, lollipops, toys) into his mouth, nor was he permitted to play with dirty objects (mud, dirt, and so forth). His subsequent attitude toward school learning was that he became part of the knowledge and would master it by creating from it an enactable role. It was totally foreign and incomprehensible to him to hear other people talk of "taking in" or digesting knowledge. The early relationship to animate and inanimate objects seemed to hinder the development of his ego's permanent borders and he constantly longed for new objects to identify with. Being in a state of

[4] Grotjahn (1957) states: "The work of the scientist is concerned with the transformation of objective truth into knowledge. The work of the analyst stands between the work of the artist and the scientist. Like the artist he is concerned with inner truth; like the scientist he limits himself to understanding and interpretation. Unlike the artist, he creates not by giving form but by giving insight and knowledge."

identification produced a state of temporary ego stability and, when he was acting dramatic roles, his feelings of depersonalization decreased.[5] This patient was an enthusiastic follower of the Stanislavski system.

Ego psychology of creative expression confirms one other major component in Stanislavski's theory and technique of creative acting. The actor should develop a controlled, responsive, and prepared vocal and physical apparatus. This requires extensive training of the actor's voice and body movements. The intensity of this preparation has given rise to an erroneous belief that the Stanislavski Method is a rigid system in which improvisation is not permitted. Stanislavski writes:

> In order to express a most delicate and largely subconscious life, it is necessary to have control of an unusually responsive, excellently prepared voice and physical apparatus. This apparatus must be ready instantly and exactly to reproduce most delicate and all but intangible feelings with great sensitiveness and directness. That is why an actor of our type is obliged to work so much more than others, both on his inner equipment which creates the life of the past, and also on his outer physical apparatus, which should reproduce the results of the creative work of his emotion with precision (1936, p. 15).

According to psychoanalytic ego psychology, the ego, in the state of artistic creativity, is well organized and integrated, and functions optimally in transforming unconscious derivatives into artistic forms. Partial regression has the limited purposes of permitting unconscious expression to enter consciousness. Kris has illustrated this in poetry, where stringencies are as essential as ambiguities to the total creative expression. Stanislavski's demands for well-developed vocal and physical apparatus would be in the service of having a well-integrated ego participate in the creative expression.

[5] In Chapter 1 the psychological development and the character of the actor are more fully explored.

Psychoanalysis has often stressed the relationship between acting and various types of exhibitionism. A familiar experience is that of the actor—the "ham," for instance—who is predominantly interested in showing himself to the audiences. In this case, the performance is a form of sexualized exhibitionism. In Stanislavski's concept of creative acting, such performances would come under the heading of exploitation of the given art form. In his system, the actor exhibits and utilizes the body to express "delicate and deep human feelings." Psychoanalysis would consider this as a thoroughgoing sublimation of exhibitionism (in both aim and object); it would also evaluate this form of exhibitionistic body functioning as an autonomous function of the ego. His specific theories and technique of acting are outgrowths and extensions of his specific type of resolution in childhood of exhibitionistic and aggressive conflicts via acting and directing.

In Stanislavski's method of acting, no actual performance can avoid containing some representational aspects along with the major creative expressions. "Side by side, we see moments of living a part, representing the part, mechanical acting and exploitation. That is why it is necessary for actors to recognize the boundaries of art" Stanislavski, 1936, p. 30). Analysis would contend that any instinctual drive, such as the exhibitionistic drive, is partly enacted sexually and partly sublimated. Again it is a matter of degree whether a given exhibitionistic act is neurotic, perverted, or sublimated.

It has been mentioned in the earlier psychobiographical chapter that Stanislavski left us a rare legacy in his three books, *My Life in Art, An Actor Prepares,* and *Building a Character.*[6] Perhaps the most glowing tribute to his legacy is a worldwide group of disciples and followers—creators in their own right— who perpetuate Stanislavski's system in the theater, dramatic

[6] See Chapter 6. Masters of the performing arts have rarely recorded in writing the theories and concepts utilized in the development of their arts.

schools, and experimental workshops. In England, the United States, and Israel there are the most enthusiastic students and practitioners of his system. The teachings and the traditions of Stanislavski are still preserved and revered in the Soviet theater of today.

The Stanislavski Method has often been misused by dramatic directors and teachers for the purposes of so-called "clinical" self-analysis and "clinical" analysis of their pupils. This coincidental abuse of Stanislavski's psychologically valid theories of acting does not detract from their usefulness as a plausible means of promoting creative artistic and unconscious expression in its proper application. These clinical abuses of the Stanislavski Method would be expected to occur more often in the United States and England where so many other abusive practices of psychoanalysis flourish.

It is of interest that Stanislavski's theories of acting, developed in a culture so alien to and uninformed about modern psychoanalysis, harmonize so well with Freudian concepts (such as identification and sublimation of exhibitionism) and contain a thoroughgoing awareness of the individual's unconscious psychic life. It is more curious that Stanislavki's concepts of art have not only been honored but remain uncensored in the Soviet Union, which has often taken to task those artistic leaders who deviate toward an acknowledgment of man's unconscious drives which naturally rebel against his personal and communal morality. In official Soviet thinking, man's tendencies toward self-expression, self-indulgence, and self-interest are only attributable to the evils of capitalism and the deprivations of colonialism. There is no consideration either of man's innate unsublimated instinctual strivings or of his inborn narcissism.

It remains an enigmatic paradox that the Stanislavski Method of acting, sponsored by the Soviet Union, is in the vanguard of modern art, whereas drama, literature, and painting in the Soviet Union lag behind in a decadent form of representational art in the guise of social realism. Whether it is accidental or intentional, Soviet censorship seems to be tolerant of an art of acting that reflects man's unconscious emotional life. But it remains intolerant of forms of literature and drama which mirror man's unconscious ideas and drives so often in conflict with his social and moral ideals and milieu.

15

The Crisis in
Creative Playwrighting:

Author versus Analyst—

Art versus Portraiture

AMERICAN DRAMA HAS BEEN afflicted with a brand of realism which is as aesthetically inferior as the social realism of the Soviet theater. Our playwrights have an affinity toward plays of biographical realism based on the lives of the living and the recently dead. Equally flagrant is the prevailing trend toward "clinical" and "psychiatric" realism.

AUTHOR VERSUS ANALYST

For more than a decade we have been besieged by a plethora of plays whose characters are portrayed as clinical case studies of neurosis, psychosis, or perversion and whose plots develop the solution to, or the dissolution of, the hero's mental illness by expected therapeutic agents, ranging from psychiatrists to social workers, psychoanalysis to shock treatment, and finally from prescribed doses of maternal to sexual love. Far too often one finds himself witnessing at the theater reconstructed scenes of a psychiatrist's practice. During the intermission time of any of our current dramas of psychiatric realism the lobby is customarily filled with playgoers transformed by what they have witnessed into standing study groups of case history discussants.

Whether deftly or ineptly done, the subject of the mentally ill has become a predominant preoccupation of the playwright and his public. But matters are much the same at home on our television and radio sets, let alone the local movie house. An overwhelming number of their scripts are concerned with case histories of the mentally ill in which the central character or characters will be loved and understood, sympathized with or treated by competent and kindly psychiatrists or psychiatrically oriented family doctors, relatives, lovers, or friends, as the case may be. Their motivations will be explained and their childhood traumas will be uncovered.

A few examples of such dramas witnessed in the 1950's and 1960's are *The Bad Seed, The Shrike, A Clearing in the Woods, Tea and Sympathy, Cue for Passion, A Loss of Roses,* and *Natural Affection.* As yet this is not the absolute diet of our theater but the danger is imminent.

Does the public want a documented case history with accompanying therapy on the stage? Must the playwright provide us with a diagnosis and a prescription? Does the dramatist have to be a psychoanalyst as well as a creator? Or do we want a portrayal of man's psychic sufferings from his universal unconscious conflicts in aesthetically communicated forms? All this does not mean that psychopathological characters do not belong in the theater. Psychological drama is as traditional as social, religious, or historical drama.

However, psychological drama fails as art when the characters are too clinically drawn and when their unconscious motivations are given overspecific labels, such as incestuous love, parental death wishes, homosexuality, and the like. Such dramatizations, even when they are occasionally valid, only reach the intellect of the audience. The communication between the stage characters and the audience remains sterile.

Occasionally, dramatists and more often screen writers have consulted psychiatrists and psychologists to assist them in achieving authenticity for their psychological plays and movies. The results have been uniformly disappointing. Rarely does a truly creative psychological work ever emerge from such joint efforts. Curiously enough, dramas or movies whose subject matter seems to beg for psychiatric consultation succeed admirably without it. The recent British films *The Mark* and *The Loneliness of the Long Distance Runner* are good examples. The utilization of authenticated psychological concepts and techniques only clutter an intended creative work with literal data which will bog it down with mundane realism.

On the American scene of modern drama two dramatists who have created outstanding psychopathological characters that are artful and meaningful on the stage are Eugene O'Neill and Tennessee Williams. The heroine of *A Streetcar Named Desire* has already been cited as a case in point.[1] Blanche DuBois is a canvas full of psychopathological portrayals. Is she neurotic, psychotic, prostitute, or nymphomaniac? Blanche remains an unlabeled clinical entity, but to the unconscious of her audience she communicates a life of deprivation of parental care and love, homeless living, and a need to be rescued. Psychoanalysis confirms that prostitution and nymphomania are steeped in such early infantile deprivations. Williams knows this solely as an artist, as it should be, and communicates this by poetic revelations. Blanche never states bluntly that she never had a mother's nurturing love.

In this play Williams avoids the trap of psychiatric clichés. Beginning with *Summer and Smoke* and continuing in later plays, such as *Sweet Bird of Youth, Garden District, The Night*

[1] See Chapter 10.

of the Iguana, and *The Milk Train Doesn't Stop Here Anymore,* his "neurotic" heroines seem to be written in the current trend of more conscious diagnostic depiction, unlike his plays of the 1940's.

Like Blanche DuBois, Arthur Laurents' heroine in *A Clearing in the Woods* is a neurotic woman. Laurents devised the skillful technique of revealing her character by the use of three earlier age versions of his heroine (young woman, adolescent, and child) that appear and live on stage simultaneously with her present version. These younger identities serve the function of revealing the heroine to herself and secondarily to the audience. Accurate as the operative psychodynamic structure may or may not be, we are asked to witness passively and rationally a well-documented unfolding of a psychotherapeutic process of self-understanding. Despite the technical artfulness and the intelligent dialogue, the full potential of creative theater has not been realized; the audience has only witnessed a cleverly and sensibly dramatized clinical case.

Committed as we now are to illustrate by comparison, we might then view the widower father of Ephraim Cabot in O'Neill's *Desire under the Elms* side by side with the widower in Paddy Chayefsky's *Middle of the Night.* Chayefsky has produced a realistic picture of a widower father who finds himself more vigorous and biologically active than he thought he was. His hero (like Laurents' heroine) struggles through a well-dramatized and well-documented psychotherapeutic process on stage in which he justifies his intended actions to himself and his relatives and lastly to his passive and rational audience.

O'Neill creates for us in Ephraim Cabot a vigorous widower in his seventies who brings a third wife into his home of three sons, fully grown but unmarried men. Ephraim, sculptured in muscle and might, needs no explanation for his new marriage. His justification is communicated to the audience by the permanent imprint of O'Neill's powerful creation. O'Neill confronts us with a timeless and universal portrait of a father's biological and sexual kingdom which he refuses to surrender to his sons. We do not have to look about us to find Ephraim Cabot; he resides within us; he is man's universal unconscious. Such a creation is more than representational art.

However, the 1960's has a hopeful air with the emergence of some promising playwrights. Among them we find Edward Albee, who can mold original psychopathological characters and create unborrowed psychological dramas such as *The Zoo Story* and *Who's Afraid of Virginia Woolf?* What is refreshingly revolutionary is his ability to create more than one major psychopathological character in a single play. Unlike Williams, his plays are not restricted to any given geographical culture. Liberated from past conventions, his plays succeed in encompassing a multiplicity of significant psychological characters who interact with each other in vibrant currents which revitalize our psychological and social drama without reference to a library or literature of clinical case histories.

To put it bluntly, there can be no real marriage between the psychologist and the dramatist. A direct union of the two (unlike the union between psychoanalysis and criticism) results in a malformed hybrid creation which is neither scientific nor aesthetic. It is therefore essential that communication between the author and the analyst should remain exchangeable but never bcome interchangeable.

A LIVELY THEATER OF LIVES:
ART VERSUS PORTRAITURE

In the past decade the American theater has also been infested with earthbound dramas of the lives of contemporaries. These dramatizations of lives of our times are not automatically useless for the stage. The critical question is whether or not such plays add to the stature of the American theater. The answer is a definite "no." The inferiority of biographical dramas, such as *Sunrise at Campobello* (F.D.R.'s life during his struggle with polio), *Compulsion* (the psychopathological lives of Leopold and Loeb), *Disenchanted* (the alcoholic and literary deterioration of F. Scott Fitzgerald), is attributable to the limitation created by the very choice of such themes. The playwright is restricted to realistic and accurate data and cannot create situations or ideas at the risk of being or feeling accused of nonauthentic representation. He has the misconception that creative drama can be served via an artistic representational portraiture of famous lives that have been filled with dramatic and tragic content. This makes for a one-dimensional conscious portrayal in contrast to a more dynamic and aesthetic communication between the audience and author in which the latter can use his native tools of fantasy and reality.

Sunrise at Campobello is a well-documented dramatization of a period in the life of Franklin Delano Roosevelt. The play opens in mid-summer of 1921, at the time he was stricken with infantile paralysis, and ends in the early summer of 1924, when he recovered sufficiently to stand on his feet long enough to deliver the nominating oration for Alfred E. Smith.

Intended as a symbolic portrayal of a heroic figure, the play mainly tells a vivid medical and psychological tale of a healthy-minded man's desperate struggle to recover his physical powers so that he can continue to live and work. Do not look here for an aesthetically re-created image of a great American who may some day deserve the dramatic portrayal of a legendary hero. At best you will find a well-constructed, thoroughgoing facsimile of the living man to which you can easily bring your own stirring memories of his endearing personality and great achievements. It is then the audience and not the author who re-creates the image of the four-time president.

Writing on the subject of characters on the stage in 1904, Sigmund Freud (1942, pp. 460–461) stated:

All varieties of suffering are the theme of drama which promises to create out of them pleasure for the spectator. . . . When the spectator puts himself in the place of the sufferer from physical illness, he finds nothing within himself of enjoyment or of psychological give and take. . . . He who is ill has but one desire: to get well, to get over his condition; the doctor must come with the medicine; . . . *the play of fantasy must cease.* . . .

It might be argued that the Greek and Shakespearean classics were more often than not historical biographical dramas—dramas of lives. The heroes of these dramas, however, were depicted as legendary figures and thus the ingredient of fantasied creation was inherent.

The dramatic adaptation of a work of art such as *Look Homeward, Angel* added no new dimension to the stature of the novel. At best it was a task in which the original artistic achievement was maintained. Nevertheless, it restricted the multiple messages of a fine work of art to the single interpretation of its current arrangement. It is noteworthy that *The Diary of Anne Frank, Look Homeward, Angel,* and *Long Day's Journey into Night*—three biographical dramas about contemporaries—won the coveted Pulitzer Prize in consecutive years.

I am aware that I differ with many drama critics when I contend that the success of O'Neill's *Long Day's Journey into Night* was ensured by the sensational and confessional exposé of the author's family. O'Neill's personal tragedy of tuberculosis is overshadowed by the revelation of his mother's narcotic addiction and his father's and brother's alcoholism. We might further raise the question: Had the fact of his mother's addiction been widely known prior to the appearance of the play, would the play still have appeared to be as moving and meaningful?

O'Neill created his autobiographical play out of a unique set of circumstances. Aware of his literary limitations, but driven by personal emotional needs to write his life story, O'Neill was restricted to the use of the drama medium and was unable to utilize the more appropriate vehicle of prose biography. He was the master American playwright whose works readily influenced trends in our theater. It is regrettable that his request for a twenty-five year posthumous interval before the appearance of his autobiographical play was not heeded. The current popularity of plays on contemporary lives might have been lessened.

There is little doubt that the "This Is Your Life" infestation in the legitimate theater also comes from the latter's intimacies with television and movies. In its constant and daily need for new material, the video drama of necessity has to tap all available resources. Long ago it hit upon the fruitful formula of the dramatization of lives. Such dramatizations often enhance the educational effectiveness of the presentation but do nothing to advance creative drama. Large sections of the American theater audience are willing to accept this brand of aesthetic ersatz.

An indirect contribution to the American malady of a "Theater of Lives" stems from a misunderstanding and abuse of psychoanalytic and psychiatric knowledge on the part of writers. Earlier it was noted that our playwrights were writing psychiatric case histories in lieu of created characters in inner conflict. The current dramas of contemporary lives often partake of the case history type of orientation and rarely attain the stature of creative biographical drama. Thus our combined malady of clinical and biographical realism fits well into what Robert Brustein (1964), the drama critic of *The New Republic*, called "peep-hole realism" in describing the autobiographical play *Marathon '33*. The dramatizations of the marathon dance addiction of the 1930's and of current jazz and drug addiction (*The Connection*) are hailed as experiments in a new form of living theater. Intended to be vital living experiences in theater for audiences, they mainly achieve the excitement of sideshow realism by offering a full view of our freakish patterns and pastimes.

In contrast to this we have seen an array of European biographical plays that challenges our supremacy. These plays present original themes and often original portrayals. They are adventurous in nature and spirit even when not altogether dramatically successful. Such French plays as *Caligula* and *Becket* by Camus and Anouilh, respectively, and British plays such as *A Man for All Seasons* (the life of Sir Thomas More) and *Luther* by Robert Bolt and John Osborne are provocative biographical dramas. They strive for fresh insights and new perspectives on the lives of historical figures. Europe rarely produces plays based on the lives of contemporaries. If they are to be written, they will be written by Americans. The plays *Anastasia* and *The Diary of Anne Frank,* both dealing with the lives of Europeans, were written by Americans. Dramas about the lives of the Irish poet Dylan Thomas (not unlike *Disenchanted,* the F. Scott Fitzgerald tale of alcoholic and marital deterioration) and the Soviet leader Joseph Stalin have been recently added to our "lively" American theater of lives. We are actively creating a repertoire of reportage.

Some years ago, Kenneth Tynan, the visiting British drama critic, wrote in a *New Yorker* review:

Whether or not it denotes a waning of invention I am uncertain, but the American theatre seems to be expending a large part of its energy on the life stories (or episodes therefrom) of people still living or fairly recently dead. *The Diary of Anne Frank* and *Sunrise at Campobello* exemplify what I mean; so, among shows that are still running, do *Gypsy* and *The Gang's All Here,* and we are promised, later in the season, entertainments based on the careers of Fiorello LaGuardia, Harry Golden, the singing Trapp Family, and Laurette Taylor. To lean so heavily on latter-day biography is not, I submit, an activity that one immediately associates with a healthy creative theatre. This reflection is prompted by William Gibson's *The Miracle Worker,* at the Playhouse, which deals with the childhood of Helen Keller . . . (1959, p. 132).

Mr. Tynan, currently the literary manager of the recently organized British National Theatre, offers some excellent unofficial advice for the cultural ills of the American theater.

Is it then a moment of crisis in American culture in which psychological curiosity about our own lives and our contemporaries' has overshadowed the aesthetic and creative search for the inner nature of contemporary man? Certainly the science of psychology has intended no such rivalry with the arts.

The scientist creates knowledge from objective truths; the psychoanalyst creates knowledge from inner truth; the artist creates aesthetic forms which express both objective and inner truths. Psychoanalysis, delving into the same unconscious area as art, may have innocently and unintentionally lured the artist away from his own aesthetic language. The American dramatist should avoid writing his characters from the lively stories of contemporaries or from the case histories of the mentally ill. He must retain the conviction that his inherent talent to create and communicate will return him to his artistic abode.

16

Psychoanalysis and Theater:

Past, Present, and Present–Future

THE PAST AND THE PRESENT

Prior to the classical era of Greek civilization, no separation existed between audience and stage, nor was there any distinction between actor and audience. Everyone enacted and celebrated the rituals and festivals derived from traditional myths. During the late classical Greek period not only were distinctions established but the dramatist appeared as a creator of original variations on the traditional myths. Subsequently, acting and dramatic writing became distinctive careers to which people with given qualities and capacities were attracted. The respective abilities of the actor and dramatist were recognized and appreciated by the community and probably experienced by the chosen artists as a special and honorific relationship to society and the divine.

Through the ensuing centuries, acting and dramatic styles have been transformed under various influences of concepts of arts, as from classical to romantic, and of changes in socioeconomic conditions. The development of drama is interwoven with the appearance of various religions in the course of civilization. Greek mythological dramas about legendary heroes are studded with religious concepts as represented by the various gods. Thus the Aeschylus trilogy based on the lives of the members of The House of Atreus is as much a religious drama as it is a mythological and historical one. Varying religious concepts of gods, God, Son of God, and the godlessness of atheism shape the dramas in which they are expounded. A play based on Greek religious mythology is inherently different in its style and design from one based on a Biblical or atheistic concept.

The earliest known Egyptian play, the *Abydos Passion Play*, dating back to the second and perhaps the third millennium before Christ, celebrates the death and resurrection of Osiris, a deified hero, corn-god, patron of fertility, and lord of life and death. The earliest Syrian and Babylonian Passion dramas revolved around Lord Tammuz (Adonis), god of the waters and the crop. Each year the god died; each year he returned only to die again. Historians of the drama tell us that the primitive playwright was a priest who taught man the first uses of prayer and rites which harness nature, providence, or God to the service of mankind. Psychoanalytically viewed, the use of religious content in dramatic themes inevitably leads to psychological drama, since religion represents the indispensable role of conscience and morality inherent in man's psychic structure, without which no conflict is ever fully portrayed or resolved.

In spite of the variety of influences that have effected apparent differences in the style and form of various plays, the essence of dramatic themes remains basically unchanged. Each civilization, including our modern one, offers contributions of dramas based on the original myths. New dramas can readily be reduced to the original tales. In this sense the historical development of drama had great significance for the development of psychoanalysis.

In the early days of psychoanalysis, when the quantity of

clinical material was as yet insufficient to validate hypotheses, the study of works of art seemed useful to reinforce the clinical evidence. The important problem was to show the universality and ubiquity of fundamental themes in our mythological and literary heritage, and to demonstrate that these themes were still to be found in the fantasy life of contemporary man. Thus ageless art was called on to rescue the newborn psychoanalytic science.

As psychoanalysis developed it paid back its debt of gratitude to art. Psychoanalysis has established that in Western literature the themes of incestuous impulses, guilt, and aggression have predominated from the time of ancient Greek civilization to our contemporary era. Later, psychoanalysis established the importance of the relationship of the infant and young child to the mother in the preoedipal period. These formulations deepened the understanding of universal literary themes. Thus Oedipus and Hamlet were originally viewed by Freud (1937) and Jones (1923) solely from the aspect of rivalry between father and son. Subsequently they were viewed from the additional vantage of the son's unfulfilled longing for, and revengeful wishes against, a mother who had abandoned her infant (Jones, 1948).

Through the years, psychoanalysis expanded its contributions to art when it could repeatedly demonstrate the intimate continuity between the personal life of the artist and his creative works. Psychoanalytic research then established a relationship between the process of creative imagination and the nature of thought processes observed in clinical study.

With sixty years of psychoanalysis behind us, we are able to go beyond demonstrating the recurrent unconscious wishes in literary themes. Applying our expanding knowledge of ego psychology, we now can gain insight into the significance of each different thematic variation based on a common unconscious core. These differences correspond to different defense organizations of the author's ego around a universal unconscious fantasy. This holds equally true for myths. In the dramatist's theme (and in man's legendary myths) a universally shared unconscious wish has been "externalized and artistically attired in correspondence with needs from various levels of psychic integration of the individual" (Arlow, 1961). Besides these alterations in the artist's psychic structure, socio-economic changes and scientific discoveries exert a modifying influence on literary themes and modes of expression. A variety of ancient and modern plays, commonly based on the Orestes–Electra legend, will be presently examined to substantiate these formulations.

Through the centuries, the dramas based on the House of Agamemnon legend depict various solutions of man's timeless conflicts, reflecting the thinking of the given times and the given dramatist. In old Athenian days, man's moral structure was externalized and realized in the structure of the Furies. In the ancient plays, Aeschylus and Euripides called on the Furies to resolve the moral conflicts of Orestes and Electra.

Aeschylus dealt with the entire story from the first sin of the ancestor to the final release of Orestes from his burden of guilt. Euripides was concerned only with the return of Orestes and the punishment of the murderers. Orestes' act, by Euripides' account, was both inevitable and sinful and could not have been the will of any good power. Aeschylus' ability to assuage Orestes' guilt and Euripides' final condemnation of Orestes' deed are indications of the varying severity of the religiously influenced superegos of the two dramatists.

Sophocles, drawing on the same legend, did not utilize the Furies and passed no judgment. He neither approved nor condemned; rather, he portrayed the psychological make-up of Electra and Orestes. As a dramatist, Sophocles' superego did not stand in his way; hence we are confronted with the views of an apparently enlightened man. Biographical accounts of Sophocles' life support such assumptions about his psychological make-up. From the memoirs of an anonymous scholar who lived two hundred years after Sophocles' death, one gathers "a picture of a childhood spent under the best of influences of a prosperous and enlightened home, a youth educated in a harmonious physical and intellectual discipline—a manhood devoted to the service of the state in art and public affairs, and an old age regarded with affectionate respect" (Watling, 1957). Sophocles' development was fitting for a man of his times. He was born when Athens was in the infancy of its newly created democracy, taking its first steps with its equipment of popular government.

In a current version, Sartre in *The Flies* searches for an existentialist solution to the Orestes–Electra dilemma. Eugene O'Neill's *Mourning Becomes Electra* and Jack Richardson's *The Prodigal* show two different modern psychologically oriented solutions to the ancient legendary conflict. While both plays deal with the workings of man's conscience (the superego), each play remains individually representative of the changes that have taken place from the 1930's to the 1960's. O'Neill's play shows his full awareness as an artist of the process of the guilt-ridden conscience of man;[1] a study of O'Neill's personal life reveals that he suffered from a severe superego and unresolved oedipal conflicts not unlike those of the Orestes–Electra legend.[2] *The Prodigal* attempts a solution for a subsequent generation, educated and guided by the knowing parents of the thirties, to produce a progeny who can avert the pangs of an excessively strict conscience and realize themselves in a more rational resolution of these unconscious conflicts.

The transition from the Furies to man's superego is characteristic of the general alteration in art from classicism to romanticism. The transition from the exaltation of the conscious intellect to the recognition of the ego as man's exclusive executive agency again reflects the change from classicism to

[1] See Chapter 12.
[2] See Chapter 8.

romanticism. Classicism nurtured the concept of man's central position in the universe and his divine origin in nature. Classicism reflected on nature and the external nature of man's world and was overshadowed by romanticism, which emphasized the inner world of man.

The art of acting has been affected by the general historical change in art. The romantic influence is discerned in Stanislavski's new concept of acting. Representational acting gave way to a dynamic concept of living the part every moment it is played and each time it is played. These changes in dramatic acting have modified and augmented the audience's aesthetic response to drama. Modern drama demands of its creators—writers, directors, and actors—an artistic communication of inner truths. The audience can now respond to such artistic expression with a more complete unconscious aesthetic reaction. In our advancing romantic era, all ears have become attuned and accustomed to an aesthetic communication which concerns the inner life of man.

The change from classicism to romanticism has brought into prominence the type of dramatist who, as Kris (1952) puts it, "borders on pathology and conquers it in his work." A study of the lives of Strindberg, O'Neill, and Shaw, as well as many others, underscores this thought that modern dramatists who are close to pathology find their place more readily in the romantic era of literature than they might have in the classical one.[3]

Today we find instances in which other art forms use psychoanalytic insights in content and form as well as a part of the given medium. As Ernst Kris has pointed out, "creative artists of our day are wont to use free association as a training ground for creative thinking or as an independent mode of ex-

[3] Other psychoanalytic writers, including Hartmann (1944) and Kris (1949), have pointed out similar phenomena in the structure of political situations, which attract certain personalities as the main participants in a given historical period.

pression and some among the surrealists have assigned to their work the function of documenting the process of creation itself, thus making explicit what previously had been implicit" (Kris, 1952). To whatever degree this has occurred in the plastic arts, it is even more pronounced in the dramatic arts.

Dramatists in the romantic idiom are better able to paint and put into words man's dreams and fantasies than their classical ancestors. Today's dramatist's preoccupation with self is predictable and acceptable. His artistic achievement in part depends on his capacity to dissociate himself from the reality of his actual experience and from the personal aspects of the daydreams with which he has lived.

Thus modern drama and psychoanalysis are allies in man's current cultural advances. Led by dramatists and actors who are mindful of inner truth, modern drama contributes to psychological insights. The modern dramatist, like the modern psychologist, explores the inner nature of man. At one moment the artist might arrive at the insight before the scientist, or vice versa. But in the long run their works complement and supplement each other. They are time-bound together in an era of discovering the nature of inner phenomena.

THE PRESENT–FUTURE

While we have traced the past and present relations between psychoanalysis and drama, as yet no reference has been made to the avant-garde theater of today (and perhaps tomorrow)— the "Theater of the Absurd." Has the knowledge and growth of psychoanalysis contributed to the development of this new form of theater with its marked departure from the traditional classical and romantic play? Can psychoanalysis contribute to the understanding and appreciation of the Theater of the Absurd as it can to modern drama?

Perhaps we are too closely enmeshed in the circumstance of

its birth and infancy to account for its existence, its future growth, and final significance. We can only be certain that it is a reactive expression to our current world.

The Theater of the Absurd is in part an outgrowth of the existentialist theater and philosophy wherein man's condition is viewed as senseless, devoid of purpose or ideals, and in essence is absurd. Contrasted to the "antiliterary" playwrights of the Theater of the Absurd, existentialist dramatists, such as Sartre and Camus, communicate the meaninglessness of man's situation in highly skilled conventional literary style within the context of the established schools of logic and reason.

The Theater of the Absurd writer who subscribes to existentialism does not argue the case of man's absurd position; rather he portrays life as absurd in his drama. This type of avant-garde dramatist utilizes a new literary form of absurdity to coincide with his acceptance of the existentialist viewpoint. Hence the Theater of the Absurd drama is characterized by its intentional abandonment of reality in plot and character. It also de-emphasizes conventional logical communication within the dialogue and disavows conventional literary style.

In the more successful avant-garde dramas this new literary form seems to be an aesthetic outgrowth of the existentialist communication. In the too frequent dramatic failure of the Theater of the Absurd the *nouveau mode* of presentation seems to be only a technical device that merely propagandizes and advertises the existentialist viewpoint, but does not communicate it. We are as yet unable to determine whether or not it is an evolutionary development or a revolutionary departure.

Will the Theater of the Absurd be the established literature of the future? Does it represent a short-lived anarchy against a more orderly intellectual and aesthetic world? Is it a sound original departure appropriate to our cultural development? The answer to these questions lies in its future development and should be left to the literary critics who must commit themselves to a prognosis regarding the survival or demise of the Theater of the Absurd. Literary historians of the future may write about this form of theater as a relevant force in the history of civilization, or they may ignore its existence as a picayune and minor aberration of our times.

If the Theater of the Absurd is intended to be an art form rather than a technical device, one supposes that the avant-garde dramatist is searching for a deeper communication to the audience than could be achieved via a more logically embellished communication. To be in tune with the Theater of the Absurd, we, the audience, must approach its language with an immediate regression identical with the author's departure from logical and reality-oriented thought processes. The author's communication and own responses are more totally in the realm of the preconscious and unconscious world. Some of these dramatic efforts seem to have fulfilled their ambitions. Plays such as Beckett's *Waiting for Godot* and Genet's plays, *The Blacks* and *The Balcony*, are examples.

Dispensing with conscious elaboration is destined to enigmatic effects and results. There is the constant danger that the dramatist has not momentarily suspended a world of vital reality from which it is an unspoken yet related point of departure but has ignored reality entirely. Such a play offers only an exercise in the language of unconscious ideas and feelings using or abusing dialogue and acts as the only familiar vestiges of the theater. One cannot then conclude that the dramatist of such an unsuccessful avant-garde play is necessarily an unrealistic, absurd man and that the author of a prosaic traditional play suffers from a too sober or rational personality. The art forms of reality and unreality are not synonymous with the mental state of the authors who employ them. As a case in point, Martin Esslin in his authoritative book on the Theater of the Absurd offers a brief sketch of Samuel Beckett, the leading avant-garde dramatist, as "the most balanced and serene of men" (Esslin, 1961).

If a psychoanalyst attempts to assay the psychic state of an avant-garde dramatist during the creative phase, he might best describe it as an intentional suspension of reality in the service of the dramatist's ego. His subsequent regression toward preconscious and unconscious sources are then elaborated in aesthetic language which aims at inner responses that are contiguous with a broad ambiguous spectrum of relevant aspects of reality. The spectrum may range from man's manners and customs to his religion, his politics, and his philosophies. The dialogue often consists of an integrated scale of preconscious and unconscious responses to an unidentified reality. Artistry is achieved when the dramatist succeeds in creating through his dialogue images and feelings that are consistently and emphatically evocable from his audience.

The Theater of the Absurd puts the onus on the audience to ferret out and decode the artist's communication and reassemble its meaning in the world of reality. When the aesthetic message is a vital one, the task of finding its continuity with reality is less difficult for the audience. There is a general agreement as to whether it serves as a comment on human nature, religion, or other aspects of current society.

In Beckett's *Waiting for Godot* the audience never fails to understand that the unseen created character of Godot is an anthropomorphic allusion to philosophical query of eternity, death, fate, God, the millennium, and the infinite. The play succeeds in portraying the soul-searching core within each man which explores the meaning of his existence on earth. The main visible characters, Vladimir and Estragon, represent individualized and humanized allusions to man's intellect and body. Vladimir constantly expresses the importance of postponement of bodily gratification while Estragon impatiently desires to and then does gratify his bodily needs of hunger and urination.[4] The dialogue between Vladimir and Estragon is the fusion and diffusion of man's dual nature—his psyche and his body, his executive functions and his instincts, his ego and his id. Dualism is again woven into the drama's theme through the additional created characters of Pazzo and Lucky, who represent the problems of mastery and slavery in the living world. It is not difficult to relate Pazzo and Lucky to ancient lords and slaves, kings and subjects, bosses and workers, and master and subjugated races. Beckett succeeds in creating a dynamic quadrille of characters which animates man's duality in his inner nature and outer life.

What is important to evaluate is whether the avant-garde elaboration is an optimal approach to such a vital and fundamental theme. Literary critics are in accord that *Waiting for Godot* is a highly creative dramatic achievement in a truly contemporary medium. If the Theater of the Absurd continues to produce dramas of this caliber it may hopefully strive for its niche in the permanent collection of dramatic literature.

Offhand, one would think it difficult to correlate the life of the avant-garde playwright to any of his plays, which seem so remote from reality. While such a correlation is not a *sine qua non* for creativity, the question arises regarding the quality of a work of art in which the artist's personal involvement may be missing.[5] As yet, there has been no serious investigation of this matter by critics or biographer or psychobiographer to establish the validity of the impersonal nature of avant-garde

[4] They call each other Gogo and Didi. Was it a clang association to the sounds of the universally known words—ego and id—that unconsciously determined for Beckett (literary disciple and heir of James Joyce) the appropriate choice of the nicknames Gogo and Didi (ego and id) for his created characters?

[5] It has already been mentioned that the dramatist who can transcend his personal theme may have a greater creative talent (see Chapter 2). The assessment of the avant-garde dramatist's creative capacity from such criteria becomes complicated. We are never certain as to whether the author has momentarily departed from or completely ignored his reality.

theater.[6] Usually, the personal stamp of the writer can more readily be discerned from the characteristic designs and quality of his abstract dialogue than from the nature of his plots or his character types.

Can psychoanalysis shed any light for us on the development of the avant-garde theater? Sociologically viewed, the Theater of the Absurd reflects the widespread state of negation toward conformity engendered by the catastrophes of the world wars of our century, the idolatry of mechanization in our society, and the impending threat of global annihilation. Have our social, political, and scientific experiments been so disappointing as solutions for man's salvation that this generation has taken refuge in discovering the truth within itself? Do its members hope that a global brotherhood will be achieved when mankind offers solutions of coexistence that recognize that the psychic and emotional innards of all men are also equal? Do they feel that such inner searches offer more promising answers than the various political ideological programs which have as yet failed to overcome the inequalities within their ranks and among their respective domains?

Has this generation noted that the stable contributions and advances of our century have been in the romantic era of art and psychoanalysis, which have symbiotically emerged and in which the inner life of man has been deemed as most valuable? Are the cultural and artistic leaders of this new generation trying to further this trend as they dig deeper into man's inner life for an answer to the existentialist's philosophy? The contributions of psychoanalysis to these various aspects of life are also being assimilated by this new generation. Such attempts at assimilation are evident in the increasing literature on existentialist psychoanalysis.

[6] Esslin, in the same biographical sketch of Beckett (1961), refers to his "period of Wanderjahre. . . . It is surely no coincidence that so many of Beckett's later characters are wanderers and tramps, and that all are lonely."

The avant-garde theater is an expression of this new direction in the world of drama. We should not be surprised to find the dramatist in the avant-garde movement of world leadership. The psychology of the artist, and especially the dramatist, throughout history, has been characterized by his rebellious nature toward the conventions of the world. What remains to be seen is whether or not the avant-garde drama will serve in its present form the advancement of theater arts as it serves the needs for common understanding.

The Theater of the Absurd drama succeeds in communicating when it conveys to the audience the concise range of realities which the writer finds to be absurd and from the recognition of which his drama makes its departure. Too often, the avant-garde dramatist does not convince us of his personal affirmation of the absurdity of man's situation. We are often caught in the dilemma as to whether the author had previously arrived at an existentialist position or only shares a similar unconventionality from another set of causes.

The unconventional dramatist's abandonment of reality may represent a personal brand of social or psychological contrariness. Such sociopsychological deviations may be seen in such contemporary English dramatists as John Osborne, Arnold Wesker, and Harold Pinter. These writers emerged in the midst of their country's mild social revolution initiated by a welfare state. Their themes and styles range in unconventionality from Osborne's angry young man drama, *Look Back in Anger* to Pinter's Theater of the Absurd drama, *The Dumbwaiter*. In spite of their diversity in dramatic form, they have in common an expression of groping for an identity in a world in which man, regardless of his social origins, cannot locate a site in which he can feel the reality of his existence. Ultimately, this new generation of English dramatists is wittingly or unwittingly approximating and partaking of the French orientation of existentialism. In cases of purely personal psychological unconventionality, the author may only offer us an exhibitionistic display of his virtuosity in negativism or regressive irrationality. As a point of interest, Alfred Jarry, often considered the nineteenth-century father of the Theater of the Absurd, was so motivated in his play *Ubu Roi* and in his personal life.[7] In the current scene, we too readily attribute artistic intent and ability to anyone and everyone who expresses his unconscious in any given art medium.

A concomitant outgrowth of our psychoanalytically oriented culture has been an excessive adoration of man's unconscious. Whereas the science of psychoanalysis emphasizes the role of the unconscious as sowing the seeds of our cultural produce, the more careless enthusiasts of psychoanalysis often mistake the roots for the fruits. From such an orientation we also tend to view our entire population as potentially creative artists. The effort of the child (and even the monkey) who finger-paints, dances, or play-acts spontaneously is often seriously displayed as equivalent to the work of creative expressionistic artists. Unschooled and untalented painters and writers also claim recognition as the peers of creative expressionistic artists simply on the basis that they have access to their unconscious imagery. There is the true story told by a well-known painter who was asked by the parents of a five-year-old boy to attest to the artistic genius of their son. After viewing the little boy's art work, he responded to the parents as follows, "Your child may be a genius, but paint he can't."

It is characteristic of our times to overestimate the value of any artistic efforts that emphasize unconscious content. There is as much blind and blundering faith in our awe of the unconscious as there was in the Dark and Middle Ages regarding the awe of God.

Hopefully, the discoveries of psychoanalysis will be mean-

---

[7] Jarry justified his Theater of the Absurd on the basis that recounting comprehensible things only serves the purpose of dulling the mind and falsifying memory, whereas the absurd exercises the mind and puts memory to work.

ingfully incorporated into the lives of our entire citizenry. Then the teachings of psychoanalysis will be properly respected and appropriately applied, rather than exaggeratedly exalted and indiscriminately evoked.

What effect such an integration will have on the theater and art of the future is a matter of conjecture. One can imagine that the best contributions of the avant-garde theater will be fused with the best of modern and classical theater into a single harmonious art form.

References

Chapter 1

Ekstein, R., & Friedman, S. W. The function of acting out, play action, and play acting in the psychotherapeutic process. *J. Amer. psychoanal. Assn.*, 1957, 5, 581–629.

Fenichel, O. On acting. *Psychoanal. Quart.*, 1946, 15, 144–160.

Greenacre, Phyllis. Woman as artist. *Psychoanal. Quart.*, 1960, 29, 208–227.

Hárnik, J. The various developments undergone by narcissism in men and women. *Int. J. Psychoanal.*, 1924, 5, 66–83.

Kris, E. Approaches to art. In E. Kris, *Psychoanalytic explorations in art.* New York: International Univer. Press, 1952.

Chapter 2

Clark, B. H. *Eugene O'Neill: the man and his plays.* New York: Dover, 1947. Copyright 1927, 1947 by Barrett H. Clark; published by Dover Publications, Inc., New York 14, N.Y., at $1.35; excerpts reprinted by permission of the publisher.

Dent, A. (Ed.) *Bernard Shaw and Mrs. Campbell: their correspondence.* New York: Knopf, 1952.

Ellman, R. *James Joyce.* New York: Oxford, 1959.

Gelb, A., & Gelb, Barbara. *O'Neill.* New York: Harper, 1962.

Glover, E. The concept of dissociation. In E. Glover, *Studies in psychoanalysis.* Vol. 1. *On the early development of mind.* New York: International Univer. Press, 1956. Pp. 307–323.

Greenacre, Phyllis. The childhood of the artist. In *The psychoanalytic study of the child.* Vol. 12. New York: International Univer. Press, 1957. Pp. 47–72.

Greenacre, Phyllis. Play in relation to creative imagination. In *The psychoanalytic study of the child.* Vol. 14. New York: International Univer. Press, 1959. Pp. 61–80.

Kris, E. Approaches to art. In E. Kris, *Psychoanalytic explorations in art.* New York: International Univer. Press, 1952. Pp. 13–63. (a)

Kris, E. On preconscious mental processes. In E. Kris, *Psychoanalytic explorations in art.* New York: International Univer. Press, 1952. Pp. 303–320. (b)

Magarshack, D. *Chekhov: a life.* New York: Grove, 1952.

Moses, M. J. *Henrik Ibsen: the man and his plays.* New York: Mitchell Kennerly, 1908.

Weissman, P. *Mourning becomes Electra* and *the prodigal. Mod. Drama,* 1960, **3,** 257–259.

CHAPTER 3

Craig, E. G. *Index to the story of my days.* New York: Viking, 1957.

Ewen, D. *Leonard Bernstein.* New York: Bantam, 1961.

Freud, S. Analysis of a phobia in a five-year-old boy (1909). In *Collected Papers of* . . . . Vol. 3. New York: Basic Books, 1959. Pp. 149–289.

Greenacre, Phyllis. The childhood of the artist. In *The psychoanalytic study of the child.* Vol. 12. New York: International Univer. Press, 1957. Pp. 47–72.

Greenacre, Phyllis. Woman as artist. *Psychoanal. Quart.,* 1960, **29,** 208–227.

Stanislavski, K. *My life in art.* New York: Theatre Arts, 1924.

Walter, B. *Theme and variations: an autobiography.* J. A. Galston (Trans.) New York: Knopf, 1946.

CHAPTER 4

Bentley, E. *Bernard Shaw.* New York: New Directions, 1957.

Beres, D. The contribution of psychoanalysis to the biography of the artist. *Int. J. Psychoanal.,* 1959, **40,** 26–37.

Eliot, T. S. *The music of poets: the third W. P. Ker memorial lecture.* Glasgow: Jackson, 1942.

Freud, S. Leonardo da Vinci and a memory of his childhood (1910). *Standard edition.* Vol. 11. London: Hogarth, 1957. Pp. 59–137.

Greenacre, Phyllis. The childhood of the artist. In *The psychoanalytic study of the child.* Vol. 12. New York: International Univer. Press, 1957. Pp. 47–72.

Kris, E. Approaches to art. In E. Kris, *Psychoanalytic explorations in art.* New York: International Univer. Press, 1952. Pp. 13–63.

Miller, A. In *The New York Times,* February 17, 1965, p. 36, col. 4.

Schneider, D. *The psychoanalyst and the artist* (1950). New York: International Univer. Press, 1954.

CHAPTER 5

Beres, D. The contribution of psychoanalysis to the biography of the artist. *Int. J. Psychoanal.,* 1959, **40,** 26–37.

Schapiro, M. Leonardo and Freud: an art historical study. *J. Hist. Ideas,* 1956, **17,** 147–178.

CHAPTER 6

Beres, D. The contribution of psychoanalysis to the biography of the artist. *Int. J. Psychoanal.,* 1959, **40,** 26–37.

Gorchakov, N. M. *Stanislavsky directs.* New York: Funk & Wagnall, 1954.

Greenacre, Phyllis. The childhood of the artist. In *The psychoanalytic study of the child.* Vol. 12. New York: International Univer. Press, 1957. Pp. 47–72.

Magarshack, D. *Stanislavski: a life.* New York: Chanticleer, 1951.

Stanislavski, K. *My life in art.* New York: Theatre Arts, 1924. Copyright 1924 by Little, Brown, & Company, renewed 1952 by Elizabeth Reynolds Hapgood; excerpts reprinted by permission of Theatre Art Books, New York.

Stanislavski, K. *An actor prepares.* New York: Theatre Arts, 1936. Copyright 1936 by Theatre Arts, Inc., 1948 by Elizabeth R. Hapgood for the Stanislavski estate; excerpts reprinted by permission of Theatre Arts Books, New York.

Stanislavski, K. *Building a character.* New York: Theatre Arts, 1949.

CHAPTER 7

Bishop, J. *The day Lincoln was shot.* New York: Harper, 1955.

Clarke, Asia B. *The unlocked book.* Eleanor Farjeon (Ed.). New York: Putnam's, 1938. Copyright 1938 by G. P. Putnam's Sons; excerpts reprinted by permission of G. P. Putnam's Sons.

Jacobson, Edith. Contribution to the metapsychology of psychotic identifications. *J. Amer. psychoanal. Assn.,* 1954, 2, 239–262.

Knight, R. P. The relation of latent homosexuality to the mechanisms of paranoid delusions. *Bull. Menninger Clin.,* 1940, 5, 149–160.

Lehrman, P. Some unconscious determinants of homicide. *Psychiat. Quart.,* 1939, 134, 605–622.

Nunberg, H. Homosexuality, magic and aggression. *Int. J. Psychoanal.,* 1938, 19, 1–16.

Ruggles, Eleanor. *Prince of players—Edwin Booth.* New York: Norton, 1953.

Stärcke, A. The reversal of the libido sign in delusions of persecution. *Int. J. Psychoanal.,* 1920, 1, 231–235.

Van Ophuijsen, J. H. W. On the origins of the feeling of persecution. *Int. J. Psychoanal.,* 1920, 1, 235–240.

Weissman, P. Ego and superego in obsessional character and neurosis. *Psychoanal. Quart.,* 1954, 23, 529–543.

Wilson, G. W. John Wilkes Booth, father murderer. *Amer. Imago,* 1940, 1 (No. 3), 49–60.

CHAPTER 8

Beres, D. The contribution of psychoanalysis to the biography of the artist. *Int. J. Psychol.,* 1959, 40, 26–37.

Clark, B. H. *Eugene O'Neill: the man and his plays.* New York: Dover, 1947. Copyright 1927, 1947 by Barrett H. Clark; published by Dover Publications, Inc., New York 14, N.Y., at $1.35; excerpts reprinted by permission of the publisher.

Engel, E. A. *The haunted heroes of Eugene O'Neill.* Cambridge: Harvard, 1953.

Glover, E. The concept of dissociation (1943). In E. Glover, *Studies in psychoanalysis.* Vol. 1. *On the early development of the mind.* New York: International Univer. Press, 1956. Pp. 307–323.

Greenacre, Phyllis. The childhood of the artist. In *The psychoanalytic study of the child.* Vol. 12. New York: International Univer. Press, 1957. Pp. 47–72.

Jacobson, Edith. Contribution to the metapsychology of psychotic identifications. *J. Amer. psychoanal. Assn.,* 1954, 2, 239–262.

Kris, E. The personal myth: a problem in psychoanalytic technique. *J. Amer. psychoanal. Assn.,* 1956, 4, 653–681.

O'Neill, E. *Long day's journey into night.* New Haven: Yale, 1956. Copyright 1955 by Carlotta Monterey O'Neill; excerpt reprinted by permission of Carlotta Monterey O'Neill and Yale University Press.

O'Neill, E. *Plays of* . . . . New York: Random House, 1941. 3 vols. *Desire under the Elms* is copyright 1924, 1952 by Eugene O'Neill. Published in England in *All God's Chillun Got Wings;* London: Jonathan Cape, 1925.

Peck, M. W. A psychiatrist views the drama. *Psychoanal. Rev.,* 1935, 22, 306–313.

Wittels, F. Psychoanalysis and literature. In S. Lorand (Ed.), *Psychoanalysis today.* New York: International Univer. Press, 1944. Pp. 371–380.

CHAPTER 9

Bentley, E. *Bernard Shaw.* New York: New Directions, 1957. Copyright 1947, © 1957 by New Directions; excerpts reprinted by permission of the publishers, New Directions.

Campbell, Mrs. P. *My life and some letters.* New York: Dodd, Mead, 1922.

Dent, A. (Ed.) *Bernard Shaw and Mrs. Campbell: their correspondence.* New York: Knopf, 1952.

Erikson, E. H. The problem of ego identity. *J. Amer. psychoanal. Assn.,* 1956, 4.

Ervine, S. *Bernard Shaw, his life, work and friends.* New York: Morrow, 1956.

Freud, S. Formulations regarding the two principles in mental functioning (1911). In *Collected Papers. . . .* Vol. 4. New York: Basic Books, 1959. Pp. 13–21.

Giovacchini, P. Shaw's *Major Barbara:* a study of communication. Paper read at Amer. Psychoanal. Assn., Chicago, 1957.

Greenacre, Phyllis. The childhood of the artist. In *The psychoanalytic study of the child.* Vol. 12. New York: International Univer. Press, 1957. Pp. 47–72.

Henderson, A. *George Bernard Shaw: man of the century.* New York: Appleton-Century-Crofts, 1956.

Pearson, H. *GBS: a full length portrait.* New York: Harper, 1942.

Shaw, G. B. *Selected plays.* New York: Dodd, Mead, 1948. 4 vols. The excerpt from *Pygmalion* is reprinted by permission of the Public Trustee and The Society of Authors.

Shaw, G. B. *Shaw on music.* New York: Doubleday, 1956.

Stein, M. The marriage bond. *Psychoanal. Quart.,* 1956, 25.

Terry, Ellen. *Ellen Terry and Bernard Shaw, a correspondence.* New York: Putnam, 1931.

CHAPTER 10

Abraham, K. Manifestations of the female castration complex. In K. Abraham, *Selected papers.* London: Hogarth, 1927.

Agoston, T. Some psychological aspects of prostitution; the pseudo-personality. *Int. J. Psychoanal.,* 1948, 26, 62–67.

Atkinson, B. Drama section. *The New York Sunday Times,* Dec. 2, 1956, p. 1.

Beres, D. The contribution of psychoanalysis to the biography of the artist. *Int. J. Psychoanal.,* 1959, 40, 26–37.

Deutsch, Helene. Feminine masochism. In *The psychology of women.* New York: Grune & Stratton, 1948. Pp. 239–278.

Empsom, W. *The seven types of ambiguity.* New York: Harcourt, 1931.

Freud, S. Psychopathic characters on the stage (1904). *Psychoanal. Quart.,* 1942, 2 (4), 456–476.

Graf, M. Reminiscences of Prof. Sigmund Freud. *Psychoanal. Quart.,* 1942, 2 (4), 465–476.

Kris, E. Prince Hal's conflicts. In E. Kris, *Psychoanalytic explorations in art.* New York: International Univer. Press, 1952.

Kris, E., & Kaplan, A. Aesthetic ambiguity. In E. Kris, *Psychoanalytic explorations in art.* New York: International Univer. Press, 1952.

Williams, T. *Twenty-seven wagons full of cotton and other plays.* New York: New Directions, 1946. *This Property Is Condemned* is copyright 1945, 1953 by Tennessee Williams; excerpts reprinted by permission of the publishers, New Directions.

Williams, T. *A Streetcar named desire.* New York: New Directions, 1947. Copyright 1947 by Tennessee Williams; all rights reserved; excerpts reprinted by permission of the publishers, New Directions.

Chapter 11

Breuer, J., & Freud, S. *Studies in hysteria* (1895). New York: Nervous & Mental Disease, 1947.

Eckermann, P. *Conversations of Goethe with Eckermann.* (Everyman's ed.) New York: Dutton, 1930.

Freud, S. *The interpretation of dreams* (1900). New York: Macmillan, 1937.

Freud, S. Female sexuality (1931). *Standard edition.* Vol. 21. London: Hogarth, 1961. Pp. 223–243.

Kanzer, M. The "passing of the Oedipus complex" in Greek drama. *Int. J. Psychoanal.,* 1948, 29, 131–134.

Kanzer, M. Oedipus trilogy. *Psychoanal. Quart.,* 1950, 19, 561–572.

Seidenburg, R., & Papathomapoulos, E. Daughters who tend their fathers: a literary survey. In *The psychoanalytic study of society.* Vol. 2. New York: International Univer. Press, 1962. Pp. 135–160.

Watling, E. F. (Trans.). *Sophocles: the Theban plays*. Harmondsworth Middlesex: Penguin, 1957.

Weissman, P. Psychosexual development in a case of neurotic virginity and old maidenhood. *Int. J. Psychoanal.*, 1964, **45**, 110–
   120.

CHAPTER 12

Beres, D. The contribution of psychoanalysis to biography of the
   artist. *Int. J. Psychoanal.*, 1959, **40**, 26–37.

Clark, B. H. *Eugene O'Neill: the man and his plays*. New York:
   Dover, 1947. Copyright 1927, 1947 by Barrett H. Clark; published by Dover Publications, Inc., New York 14, N.Y., at
   $1.35; excerpts reprinted by permission of the publisher.

Freud, S. Psychopathic characters on the stage (1904). *Psychoanal.
   Quart.*, 1942, **9**, 459–464.

Sievers, W. D. *Freud on Broadway*. New York: Hermitage, 1955.

CHAPTER 13

Edel, L. *Literary biography: the Alexander lectures*. Toronto: Univer. of Toronto, 1957.

Freud and the Arts. *London Times lit. supp.*, May 4, 1956.

Freud, S. Psychopathic characters on the stage (1904). *Psychoanal.
   Quart.*, 1942, **9**, 459–464.

Freud, S. Leonardo da Vinci and a memory of his childhood (1910).
   Standard edition. Vol. 11. London: Hogarth, 1957. Pp. 59–137.

Graf, M. Reminiscences of Professor Sigmund Freud. *Psychoanal.
   Quart.*, 1942, **9**, 465–476.

Jones, E. *Hamlet and Oedipus*. London: Gollancz, 1949.

Langer, W. The next assignment. *Amer. Hist. Rev.*, 1958, **43**, 283–
   304.

Lesser, S. *Fiction and the unconscious*. Boston: Beacon, 1957.

Schapiro, M. Leonardo and Freud: an art historical study. *J. Hist.
   Ideas*, 1956, **17**, 147–178.

Trilling, L. Freud and literature. In L. Trilling, *The liberal imagination*. New York: Viking, 1950. Pp. 34–57.

CHAPTER 14

Fenichel, O. On acting. *Psychoanal. Quart.*, 1946, 15, 144–160.

Grotjahn, M. *Beyond laughter.* New York: Blakiston, 1957.

Stanislavski, K. *An actor prepares.* New York: Theatre Arts, 1936. Copyright 1936 by Theatre Arts, Inc., 1948 by Elizabeth R. Hapgood for the Stanislavski estate; excerpts reprinted by permission of Theatre Arts Books, New York.

CHAPTER 15

Brustein, R. Drama review. *New Repub.*, Jan. 11, 1964.

Freud, S. Psychopathic characters on the stage (1904). *Psychoanal. Quart.*, 1942, 9, 459–464.

Tynan, K. Drama review. *New Yorker,* Oct. 31, 1959. © 1959 The New Yorker Magazine, Inc.

CHAPTER 16

Arlow, J. Ego psychology and the study of mythology. *J. Amer. psychoanal. Assn.*, 1961, 9, 371–393.

Esslin, M. *The theatre of the absurd.* (Anchor ed.) New York: Doubleday, 1961.

Freud, S. *The interpretation of dreams* (1900). New York: Macmillan, 1937.

Hartmann, H. Psychoanalysis and sociology. In S. Lorand (Ed.), *Psychoanalysis today.* New York: International Univer. Press, 1944.

Jones, E. A psychoanalytic study of Hamlet. In E. Jones, *Essays in applied psychoanalysis.* London: Hogarth, 1923.

Jones, E. The death of Hamlet's father. *Int. J. Psychoanal.*, 1948, 29, 174–176.

Kris, E. Roots of hostility and prejudice. In E. Kris, *The family in a democratic society.* New York: Columbia, 1949.

Kris, E. Approaches to art. In E. Kris, *Psychoanalytic explorations in art.* New York: International Univer. Press, 1952.

Watling, E. F. (Trans.) Introduction to *Sophocles: the Theban plays.* Harmondsworth Middlesex: Penguin, 1957.

Acknowledgments

Several of the foregoing chapters were published in preliminary form in journals and other books. Thanks are due the following publishers for gracious permission to revise those essays for this book.

Journal of the American Psychoanalytic Association (International Universities Press)
Journal of the Hillside Hospital
Modern Drama
Psychoanalysis and the Social Sciences, Warren Muensterburger and Sidney Axelrod, eds. (International Universities Press)
Psychoanalytic Quarterly
The Psychoanalytic Study of the Child, Ruth Eissler *et al.,* eds. (International Universities Press)
The Psychoanalytic Study of Society, Muensterburger and Axelrod, eds. (International Universities Press)

Index

267